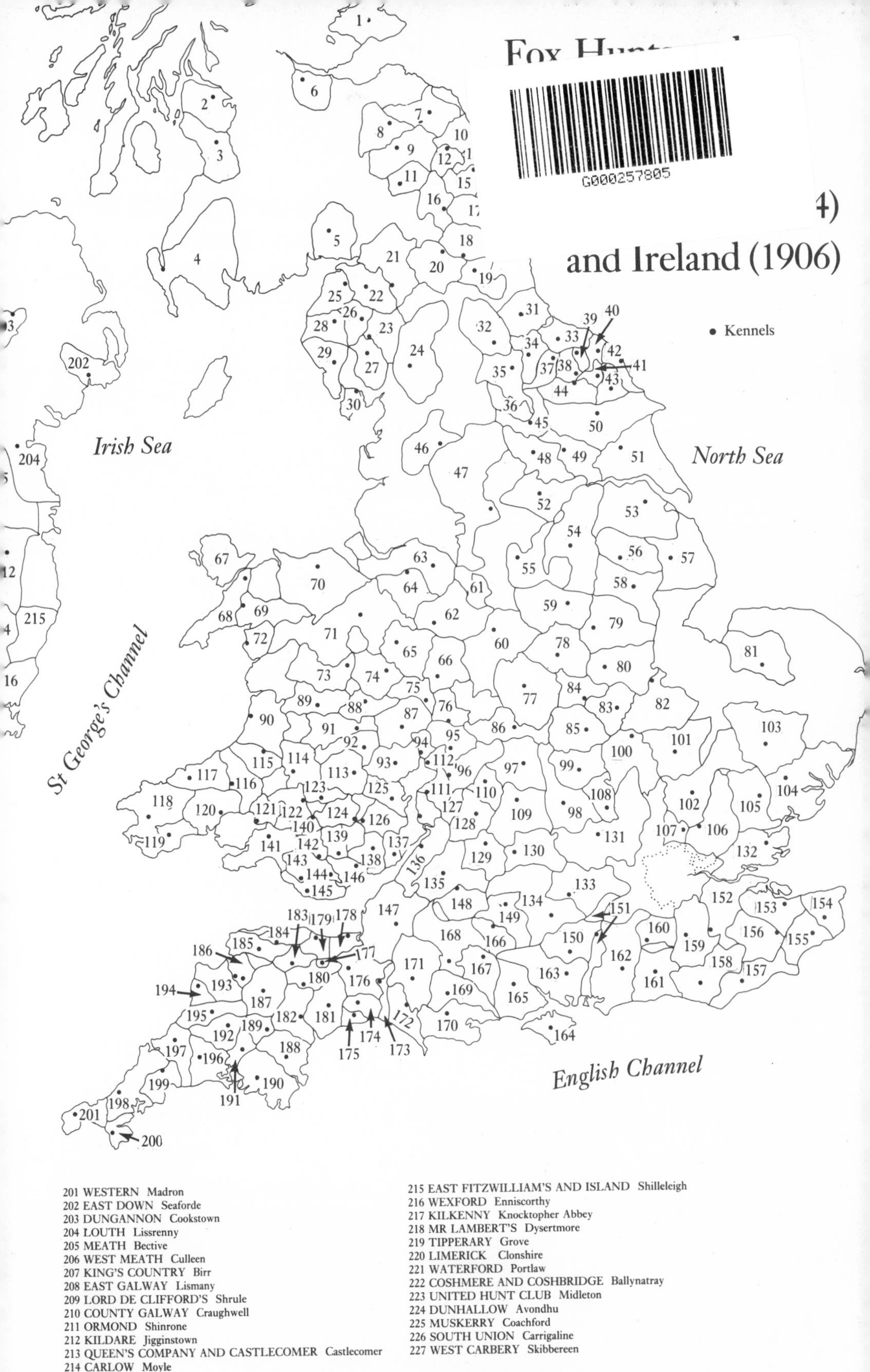

and Ireland (1906)
Kennels
Irish Sea
North Sea
St George's Channel
English Channel
201 WESTERN Madron
202 EAST DOWN Seaforde
203 DUNGANNON Cookstown
204 LOUTH Lissrenny
205 MEATH Bective
206 WEST MEATH Culleen
207 KING'S COUNTRY Birr
208 EAST GALWAY Lismany
209 LORD DE CLIFFORD'S Shrule
210 COUNTY GALWAY Craughwell
211 ORMOND Shinrone
212 KILDARE Jigginstown
213 QUEEN'S COMPANY AND CASTLECOMER Castlecomer
214 CARLOW Moyle
215 EAST FITZWILLIAM'S AND ISLAND Shilleleigh
216 WEXFORD Enniscorthy
217 KILKENNY Knocktopher Abbey
218 MR LAMBERT'S Dysertmore
219 TIPPERARY Grove
220 LIMERICK Clonshire
221 WATERFORD Portlaw
222 COSHMERE AND COSHBRIDGE Ballynatray
223 UNITED HUNT CLUB Midleton
224 DUNHALLOW Avondhu
225 MUSKERRY Coachford
226 SOUTH UNION Carrigaline
227 WEST CARBERY Skibbereen
Compiled from Hunt map published by Hampton Editions Ltd

FOX HUNTING

By the same author

THE LETTERS OF EDWIN LUTYENS
(co-editor, with Clayre Percy)

JANE RIDLEY

FOX HUNTING

COLLINS
London · 1990

William Collins Sons & Co. Ltd
London · Glasgow · Sydney · Auckland
Toronto · Johannesburg

First published 1990

BRITISH LIBRARY CATALOGUING IN PUBLICATION DATA

Ridley, Jane
Fox hunting.
1. England. Foxes. Hunting, history
I. Title
799.25974442

ISBN 0-00-217949-0

Photoset in Linotron Janson by
Rowland Phototypesetting Ltd
Bury St Edmunds, Suffolk
Printed and bound in Great Britain by
T. J. Press (Padstow) Ltd, Padstow, Cornwall

For Clayre and Stephen

Contents

Illustrations

Figures

Acknowledgements

I want to thank the following for supplying information: Brigadier Lyndon Bolton; British Field Sports Society; Michael Harrison; Dr Tony Hayter; League Against Cruel Sports; Mrs Paddy Leng; Miss Elizabeth Rowell; Colonel and Mrs John Scott; Mrs Elaine Robson Scott. The London Library's Higginson Collection has been indispensable.

Illustrations have been kindly supplied by Dr John Clarke; R. Clapperton, Photographer, Selkirk; Miss Sylvia Hayles; Viscount Ridley; and the Radio Times Hulton Picture Library (nos 29, 30). Anstruther Thomson family scrapbooks were generously lent by the Hon. Mrs Weir; and also by the Hon. Moyra Campbell and the Hon. Fiona Campbell. I am grateful to the executors of the tenth Duke of Northumberland for illustrations from the Records of the Park House Club; and to the Hon. Mrs Pease for Portman family photographs.

Introduction

'The English country gentleman
galloping after a fox – the unspeakable in
full pursuit of the uneatable.'

Oscar Wilde, 1893

Fox hunting isn't strictly necessary. The Duke of Northumberland had a fox's head devilled in the 1790s after a very severe hunt and ate most of it; but this piece of bravado was sufficiently exceptional to go down in the annals of sporting history.[1] Most foxes aren't hunted for food.

In the middle ages foxes were unceremoniously killed as vermin. The wood or covert where the fox lived was surrounded by people with all kinds of dogs, and the fox was dug or bolted out of its daytime earth or hole. The fox was then coursed or chased by dogs. Sometimes it was caught in nets set round the wood.[2] Tudor statutes empowered church wardens to pay bounties for dead foxes.

Country gentlemen who kept hounds in the seventeenth century usually hunted hares. If a fox got up they hunted it above ground. Nicholas Assheton, a Lancashire squire, certainly wasn't particular about what (or when) he hunted:

> June 24th 1617. To Worstow Brook. Tryed for a foxe: found nothing. Towler lay at a rabbit, and wee stayed and wrought and took him. Home to Downham to a foot race.
>
> June 25th 1617. I hounded and killed a bitch foxe.

> After that to Salthill. There wee had a bowson [badger].
> Wee wrought him out and killed him.[3]

Specialized fox hunting began after the Restoration of Charles II in 1660. Hounds were bred and trained to hunt foxes and nothing else (the technical term is 'entered to fox'). The fox was hunted above ground. Its earths were stopped or blocked at night, preventing it from going to ground when it returned from its nocturnal foraging expedition. The object was both to get rid of a verminous pest, and to have an enjoyable hunt.

In 1698 Thomas Boothby, a Leicestershire squire, started hunting foxes over what was later to become the famous Quorn country. The inscription on his horn claims, 'With this horn he hunted the first pack of foxhounds then in England fifty-five years.'[4]

In fact, England's oldest fox hunt is probably the Bilsdale, in the Yorkshire Dales. It was founded by the wicked second Duke of Buckingham. He lived openly with the Countess of Shrewsbury after killing her husband in a duel. Exiled from the court of Charles II in the 1670s, and 'worn to a thread with whoring', he died of a chill caught hunting in 1687. Lord Arundell of Wardour, Catholic privy seal to James II, kept a famous pack of foxhounds which he hunted in Hampshire and Wiltshire between 1670 and 1694.

The Duke of Monmouth was another fox hunter. He owned a pack of foxhounds at Charlton, near Goodwood. He joked that when he became king he would keep his court at Charlton. The master of Monmouth's hounds, Mr Roper, was forced to go into exile abroad after Monmouth's rebellion in 1685. He was restored to favour three years later, and William III witnessed a fox hunt at Charlton.[5]

Under the Stuart kings, hunting was idealized as a courtly, noble sport, an antidote to the vice and indolence of cities. It made you get up early, it was good for your health. Nicholas Cox, who wrote a treatise on hunting in 1674, contrasted the healthy, country pleasures of hunting with the 'besotting Sensualities and wicked Debaucheries' of the city, where nature was inverted, day turned into night, and the only recreation was 'Wine, Women and a Bawdy Play'.

Too much hunting, however, was thought to make men brutish. If we do nothing but hunt, warned Cox, we go wild, 'haunting the Woods till we resemble the Beasts which are Citizens of them'. Men who talked only to dogs became addicted to slaughter, which is 'wholly dishonourable, being a servile employment'. Gentlemen did other things besides hunt. Hunting was a recreation fit for kings, princes and nobles, wearied by the excess and luxury of the city. It mustn't become a lifetime's occupation.[6]

Stuart fox hunting was still quite similar to the royal sport of stag hunting. Reliable old hounds or 'tufters' hunted for the fox in cover. If they found, the rest of the pack was uncoupled, or released, to join in the chase. 'Let such as you cast off at first, be old Staunch-Hounds, which are sure,' wrote Nicholas Cox. 'If you hear such a Hound call on merrily, you may cast off some other to him; and when they run it on the full cry, cast off the rest.' The heroes of a famous hunt with the Duke of Buckingham's Bilsdale were the hounds:

Then in Wreckledale Scrags
We threw off our dogs
In a place where his lying was likely;
But the like was ne'er seen
Since a huntsman I have been
Never hounds found a fox more quickly.

There was Dido and Spanker,
And Younker was there
And Ruler that ne'er looks behind him;
There was Rose and Bonnylass
Who were always in the chase:
These were part of our hounds that did find him.

Mr Tybbals cries away
'Hark away! Hark away!'
With that our foot huntsman did hear him;
Tom Mossman cries 'Godsounds,
Uncouple all your hounds
Or else we shall never come nigh him.'[7]

The language used by fox hunters probably reflects the courtly, stag-hunting origins of the sport. *Tally-ho*, a stag-hunting cry, was imported from France probably in the seventeenth century. Henry IV of France sent huntsmen to the court of James I to teach the latest French techniques of stag hunting. (Hunting at the English court under Elizabeth had degenerated into coursing deer within the park palings, the old virgin occasionally taking pot shots at driven stags with a crossbow.) The new French techniques were later transferred to fox hunting. *Taiaut*, the huntsman's cry when the stag had gone away, was anglicized as 'tally-ho'.[8]

The huntsman's *Whoo-whoop* at the death of the fox is borrowed from stag hunting. The dead stag was broken up as the fox is today.

Stag hunting was still the sport of nobles in the first half of the eighteenth century. The Duke of Beaufort's hounds hunted stags from Badminton until 1770, when they switched to foxes. The Belvoir in Rutland was founded in 1730 to hunt stags. It was taken over by the Manners family (the Dukes of Rutland) in about 1750, switching to hunting foxes in 1762.

The Brocklesby in Lincolnshire, family pack of the Pelhams (the Earls of Yarborough), was an exception. Founded in 1713, it consisted of sixteen couple of foxhounds.[9] In Sussex the Charlton foxhounds flourished under the patronage of the Duke of Richmond.

Queen Anne was a rather keen stag hunter. Too fat to ride, she tore after the Royal Buckhounds in Windsor Forest at breakneck speed, driving a specially built high-wheeled curricle – to the dismay of her courtiers who were supposed to keep up. After her death in 1714 royal hunting degenerated. Neither George I nor George II much liked hunting.[10] In 1728 the Royal Buckhounds took to hunting the carted stag: a tame deer was taken to the meet in a cart, released in front of the hounds and collected again at the end of the hunt.

Meanwhile, Whig propagandists caricatured the country gentry as uneducated bumpkins who did nothing but hunt foxes. In the *Spectator* of 1711 Addison and Steele created Sir Roger de Coverley, a Tory booby squire, notorious for 'his remarkable enmity towards Foxes'. Henry Fielding created Squire Western in *Tom Jones* (1749). Coarse, unread, untravelled and Tory, Western goes to bed too drunk to see, and gets up to hunt before it's light.

The Whig caricature stuck. Country gentleman equals Tory equals fox hunting equals stupid is an association of ideas which still persists. It's a stereotype, imprinted into historians' subconscious by Macaulay's sketch of the gentry in his *History of England*, which is itself based on Fielding.

Fox hunting, which had started as the sport of nobles at the courts of Charles II and James II, was seen in the eighteenth century as the sport of Tory country gentlemen. As the Whigs monopolized office at Court after 1715, Toryism retreated to the country, and so did the sport of fox hunting. Many eighteenth-century fox hunters wore the green coats of the country party.

Of course, some Whigs hunted. Britain's first prime minister, Sir Robert Walpole, architect of the Whig ascendancy who grew rich on the pickings of office, was an ardent hare hunter. He entertained huge hunting parties in Norfolk. He was said always to write to his huntsman before he dealt with state papers.

Great Whig aristocrats founded packs of foxhounds. John, first Earl Spencer, founded the Pytchley hunt in about 1750. It remained the Spencer family pack until 1894. The Fitzwilliam or Milton Hunt in Northamptonshire was founded in 1769 by Earl Fitzwilliam. Fitzwilliam was nephew and heir to another vastly rich Whig, the Marquess of Rockingham, patron of Edmund Burke; in 1782 when Fitzwilliam succeeded to Rockingham's Yorkshire estates he set up a second hunt at Wentworth.[11] The fox itself is called Charlie after another (non-hunting) Whig, Charles James Fox.

Fox hunting could be awfully slow. You started at daybreak. Squire Draper, who founded what later became the Holderness Hunt in Yorkshire in 1726, always breakfasted at four a.m. in the hunting season. So did the womanizing Squire Forester, who hunted in Shropshire with his mistress Miss Phoebe Higgs. His hunting guests arrived booted and spurred the day before the meet, sat down to dinner at four o'clock, and didn't leave the table until after hunting breakfast (red beef and eggs beaten up in brandy) at four the following morning.[12]

At daybreak you drew – 'beat the Bushes etc after the Fox', as Nicholas Cox described it – for the drag or scent left by the fox at night. Then you hunted slowly up to the full-bellied fox, which was walked to death. On 26 January 1739 the Charlton Hunt had a record ten-hour hunt, starting at 7.45 a.m., and covering twenty-four miles – so it wasn't exactly fast. The Duke of Richmond rode a horse called Slug. When Slug slowed, he changed to Saucy Face.[13]

The stag-hunting technique of drawing for the quarry with a few old hounds was dropped, and fox hunters dispensed with the foot huntsman or harbourer who used to cast off the rest of the pack once the quarry was found. After about 1700 huntsmen acquired a new assistant, the whipper-in, often but strictly incorrectly shortened to whip. ('Whippers-in' don't appear in the House of Commons until after 1770.)

Squire Draper's daughter Diana whipped in to him. She died, to the amazement of all, with 'whole bones in her bed'. The Duke of Richmond employed a whipper-in at the Charlton Hunt in the 1720s. Instructions written out in 1746 by Lord Tankerville, who managed Richmond's hunting for him, show the whipper-in playing a subordinate role: he keeps the hounds together, but he mustn't speak to them or crack his whip.[14]

By 1781, when Peter Beckford wrote his classic *Thoughts on Hunting*, the whipper-in played a far more active role. He had become a second huntsman, rather than the huntsman's mate. His job was (and is) to stand outside the covert and view the fox away, or spot the fox leaving covert, let it get well away and then *halloa* – let out a piercing shriek – which is the signal for the huntsman to bring the hounds up and lay them on after the fox. During the hunt, the whip helps the huntsman, if possible anticipating the fox's movements. It's here that the whip needs genius. Great whips have an instinctive knowledge of what the fox will do, galloping miles ahead to an open earth. They ride to the fox not to hounds.

The second whipper-in rode behind the huntsman and kept the hounds together. This was a far less demanding job and 'any boy that can halloo, and make a whip smack, may answer the purpose'.[15]

Squire Forester's whipper-in, Tom Moody, was famous:

> No hound ever open'd with Tom near a wood,
> But he'd challenge the tone, and could tell if t'were good;
> And all with attention would eagerly mark,
> When he cheered up the pack, hark! to Rockwood, hark! hark!
> Hie! wind up! and cross him! Now, Rattler, boy! hark!

At his funeral in 1796 the coffin was carried by six earth-stoppers, followed by his old horse and four old hounds; after the burial three view-halloos were given over the grave.[16]

The huntsman's role also changed. If foxhounds are left to themselves, they're unlikely to kill their fox. The huntsman's art – and it is an art – consists in knowing when and how to help the hounds during the hunt. Developments in this art after 1750 transformed fox hunting.

The most obvious moment for the huntsman to intervene is when the hounds come to a check – when they stop running because the scent gives out or they overrun the line. When hounds check they throw up. This, said Jorrocks the Cockney sportsman created by Surtees, 'doesn't mean womitin' mind, but standin' starin' with their 'eads up, instead of keepin' them down, tryin' for the scent'. The huntsman helps them to find the line again by making a cast: 'That's to say,' (Jorrocks again), 'trots his 'ounds in a circle round where they threw up.'[17]

The Victorians came to regard casting as a branch of science. Thomas Smith, a nineteenth-century Master, developed the 'all round my hat' cast, based on the principle of first holding the hounds the way you don't think the fox has gone. Casting is more intuition than science. Thomas Smith's knowledge of the fox's movements was almost uncanny. He boasted that as Master of the Hambledon in Hampshire, the worst-scenting country in England, he killed ninety foxes in ninety days. 'If I were a fox,' said a fellow Master, 'I would sooner have a pack of hounds behind me than Tom Smith with a stick in his hand.'[18]

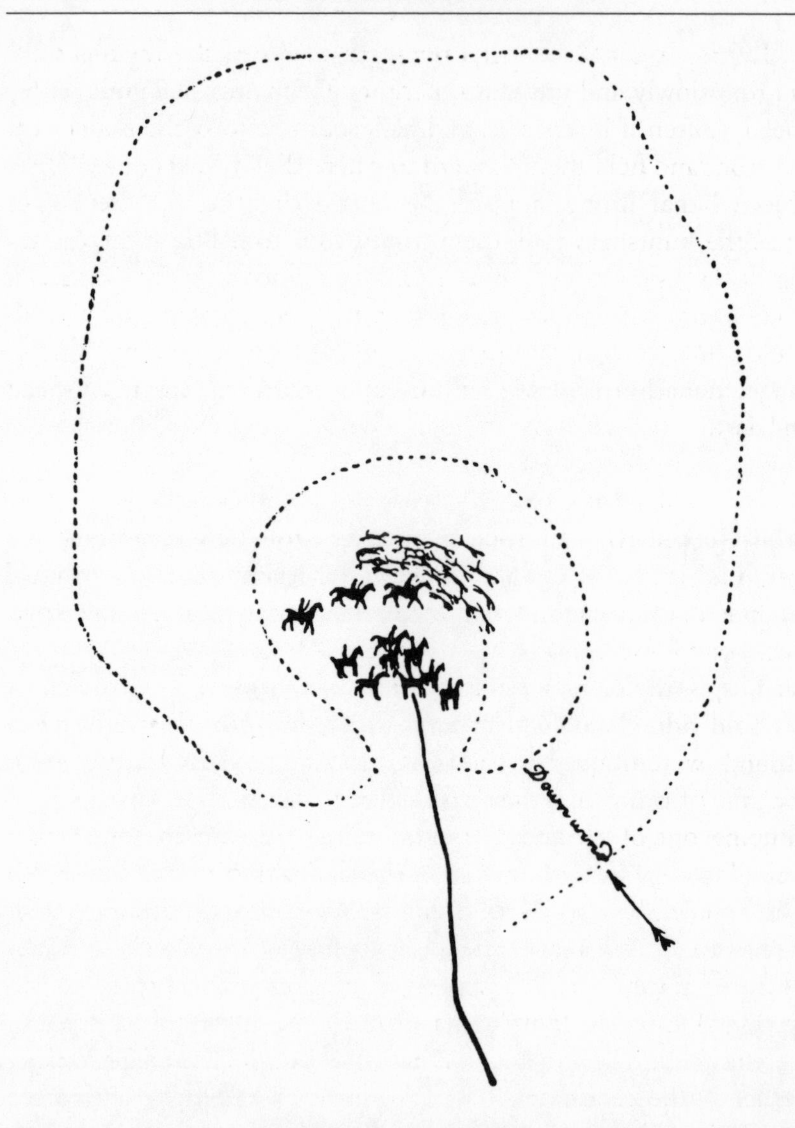

Diagram by Thomas Smith illustrating his 'all round my hat' cast, 1838. The hounds are first cast up wind, though the fox is most likely to have run down wind.

Lifting was another vital innovation. When the hounds were hunting slowly and the huntsman thought the fox had gone on far ahead – often if it was seen and halloaed – he took the hounds off the scent and held them forward to where the fox had gone. Purists objected that lifting stopped the hounds hunting for themselves since the huntsman took them from halloa to halloa, often changing foxes as he went. But lifting had one great advantage: it made hunting much faster. If the earths were stopped, the hounds could be kept running for miles on end. Fox hunting was no longer a matter of slowly hunting up a cold drag. It was all speed and dash.

Poor George III, who rode at nineteen stone, loved hunting, but feared leaping. 'A King and the father of a family,' said he, 'should not ride bold.' Trundling along behind the carted stag – the Royal Buckhounds were in the habit of making frequent stops for him to catch up – the King survived unhurt.[19]

Bold riding was for fox hunters. By the 1780s Masters of Fox Hounds were frequently complaining about people who hunted for the sake of riding and didn't care about hounds. The 'flying leap' – jumping out of a canter or gallop rather than from a standstill – was allegedly invented by a hard-riding Shropshire gentleman, Mr Childe of Kinlet, the Flying Childe, in about 1780. It could seriously threaten the huntsman's art.

After about 1750 fox hunters rode cross-bred horses, the offspring of English draught mares and Thoroughbred sires. They were faster and lighter than the native work breeds used for hunting earlier in the century.[20]

The specialized foxhound is said to descend from two older types of hound: the Southern hound and the Northern beagle. The Southern hound contained genes from four different types of French staghounds, including the royal White hound and the black St Hubert's hound. Big and slow, it was famed for its scenting powers. The small Northern beagle or Gazehound, which was indigenous to the north of England, was remarkable less for nose than speed.[21]

William Somerville, a Warwickshire squire and author of 'The Chase', a hunting poem of 1735, praised the result.

> In thee alone, fair land of liberty!
> Is bred the perfect hound, in scent and speed
> As yet unrivall'd, while in other climes
> Their virtue fails, a weak degen'rate race.

Like breeders of racehorses, aristocratic hound breeders were often obsessed with pedigree. Foxhounds in aristocratic kennels were pure-bred, like Thoroughbred racehorses, and were bred from parent stock of the same type, with great attention to family trees.

The earliest surviving hound books were kept by Mr Orlebar of Hinwick Hall in the 1700s. Most kennels today contain descendants of two of Mr Orlebar's hounds: Shifter 1719 and Tipler 1717. In 1722 Mr Orlebar gave fifteen couple of hounds to the Duke of Grafton, who hunted at Croydon and in Suffolk. Grafton was a cousin of the Duke of Richmond (hound marriages closely mirror aristocratic family alliances), and the genes of Shifter and Tipler got into Richmond's Charlton kennel. The Charlton hounds were eventually given to George IV, and had to be destroyed in 1821 when they went mad like George III.

Richmond gave a hound called Ringwood 1741 to Mr Pelham of Brocklesby. The Brocklesby Hound Books, which start in 1746, show Ringwood siring sixteen litters in 1746–8. When the Brocklesby became what's called a 'governing kennel', supplying sires for most kennels in England, Ringwood – and through him Shifter and Tipler – was strongly represented.[22]

Lord Bathurst proved in the 1930s that all well-bred foxhounds are descended from five hounds bred between 1748 and 1830: Lord Yarborough's Drunkard 1748, John Warde's Anthony 1781, Hugo Meynell's Stormer 1791, Lord Darlington's Benedict 1812 and Lord Scarborough's Saladin *c.* 1830.

Fox hunting was getting more elaborate. Hare hunting, by contrast, could be done when you felt like it, as a ride after breakfast to get up an appetite for dinner. It was slow and quiet. The enjoyment lay in watching hounds work for themselves, following the hare's every step as it doubled and looped through flocks of sheep and over greasy fallows. Hare coursing was even more informal. In Norfolk in the 1780s Parson Woodforde – always on the look out for good things to eat – went out coursing on foot at a moment's notice whenever anyone spotted a hare. He paid hare-finders a shilling per hare.[23]

John Byng, a hare-hunting enthusiast who kept diaries in the 1780s and 1790s, thought fox hunting was getting far too fancy. Hare hunting, he said, was like 'ground fishing in a good perch hole . . . Fly fishers are the fox hunters who overrate their own performances, and undervalue the simple, and more certain, pastime of the (beagling) ground anglers.'

You couldn't take foxhounds out just when you felt like it. Hunting was becoming a social event, an institution with elaborate rituals and a culture and a language of its own. Gentlemen assumed that only gentlemen were capable of appreciating the art of hunting hounds. The hunt servant, thought John Byng, 'may ride, and halloo, and murder, but is totally ignorant of the refinement and true pleasure'.[24]

Hunt countries or territories varied enormously in size. At the end of the eighteenth century the fifth Earl of Berkeley hunted a country stretching 120 miles from Berkeley Castle to Berkeley Square. He used to make a stately progress between his kennels at Cranford, Middlesex, at Gerrards Cross, Buckinghamshire, and at Nettlehead [sic] in Oxfordshire, as well as Berkeley Castle. His hunt servants wore yellow tawny livery. Hunt servants with the Old Berkeley Hunt, which was formed out of the fifth Earl's country round Aylesbury in 1801, still wear yellow coats today.[25]

At the other extreme were squires who kept harriers to hunt on their own relatively modest property. If they hunted foxes they got permission to hunt on their neighbours' land. In Devonshire half the resident gentry and most of the farmers kept hounds of some sort in the 1820s: one Devon squire boasted of having hunted with seventy-two local packs.[26] In Hampshire there were so many packs of foxhounds that you could set out for a day's hunting not knowing with what pack you would hunt; if you stood on the nearest hill you would be pretty sure to hear a pack of hounds to fall in with.

Five packs of foxhounds and ten packs of harriers hunted within ten miles of Newbury in 1780. By 1820 there was just one pack of foxhounds. William Cobbett, who had hunted hares on foot as a boy near Farnham, deplored the change. He blamed it on the 'hellish' paper money and wartime inflation, which he thought had bankrupted the old resident gentry.[27]

Irish squireens' packs of harriers (which often in fact hunted foxes) survived side-by-side with the 'official' packs of the Anglo-Irish throughout the nineteenth century. In England, by contrast, informal gentry packs tended to merge to form bigger, more formal countries. Hunting here mirrored and reinforced the cohesion of rural society. An unwritten law of fox hunting grew up, condemning invasions of another hunt's territory as ungentlemanlike poaching.

The size of countries was dictated by hunting techniques. Early-morning hunting was very effective at mopping up foxes. At daybreak, it's easy for hounds to find the drag left by the fox overnight; the fox is tired and full-bellied, and least able to run away from the hounds. Long, slow hunts are relatively economical on foxes. After killing your early-morning fox, you went home for an afternoon's drinking rather than try for another fox.

After about 1780, faster hunting made possible mid-morning meets. By eleven a.m. the fox runs faster. More foxes are missed by the hounds. The overnight drag has gone, and foxes are lying out in odd places. You're likely to get through more foxes, trying for a second fox after a morning hunt. Drawing for afternoon foxes is very wasteful. Coverts are disturbed and rendered useless for weeks; if a fox is found it has to be given up when the light goes. The Rev. J. Austen-Leigh, nephew of Jane Austen who wrote a history of the Vine Hunt in Hampshire, reckoned that new techniques required twice as much country and three times as many foxes.[28]

Pressure on fox supplies was increased by a longer hunting season. The eighteenth-century fox-hunting season was very short,

1 Cockney sportsmen. 'The Epping Easter Stag Hunt', 1795.

2 'A Fox-Hunting Breakfast', 1798

3 'The Meet at Blagdon' by J. W. Snow, 1836. Sir Matthew White Ridley, Master of the Northumberland Hounds, is second from right. Third from right is his huntsman, J. Boag, possibly the model for Surtees's James Pigg.

4 John Warde, hard-riding Master of the Bicester, 1778-97

5 Lord Alvanley, Meltonian and wit, 1822

6 Earth-stopping was a serious business (1798)

lasting from 25 December to 25 March. Putting the start of the season back to November meant more foxes were needed.

In parts of the country there was a shortage of foxes. Hugo Meynell, Master of the Quorn, was forced to take his hounds out of Leicestershire in 1794 to allow stocks to build up. The Duke of Beaufort was seriously short of foxes in the Badminton country, prompting him to take his hounds to north Gloucestershire, where he hunted the country which became known as the Heythrop. (Heythrop hunt servants still wear green Beaufort livery, though the sixth Duke gave up the country in 1835.)

Some foxes were robbed from neighbouring countries. Sir Roger de Coverley was allegedly up to this trick back in 1711, secretly sending away for foxes 'which he used to turn loose about the country by night, that he might the better signalize himself in their destruction the next day'.

Robbing was considered unsporting. Letting foxes out of a bag (bag foxes) in front of the hounds was, on the other hand, perfectly proper.

George Templer, who hunted from Stover in South Devon in about 1820, kept sixty tame foxes which he pursued with dwarf foxhounds. If there was no wild fox to be found, a tame fox was turned out and, when it showed signs of exhaustion, grabbed by the tail before the hounds could get it.[29]

The trouble about bag foxes was that they were thought to spoil the hounds. They smelled so strong and they were so stiff and weak after being tied up in a bag that they discouraged the hounds from hunting the real thing.

Beckford recommended rearing foxes in captivity and releasing them, like pheasant poults. London game dealers supplied foxes, known as Leadenhallers. John Mytton spent £1,500 on pheasants and foxes from a London dealer in about 1820.

In the open grass countries of the Midlands, where the habitat is unfavourable to foxes, hunts planted coverts and constructed artificial earths. The area of gorse in Lincolnshire doubled between 1800 and 1850. Earth-stoppers monitored fox litters, guarding them

Bagged foxes from Leadenhall Market, 1896
Notorious Covert Owner: 'There he goes, my Lord! Isn't he a beauty?'
Noble Master: 'H'm – yes. A fine fox. But why didn't you tell your keeper to pick the straw out of his brush?'

at night from fox thieves. And Mr Corbet, a wily Warwickshire MFH, paid thieves forty shillings a year to abstain from stealing his fox cubs.[30]

The long-term solution to the fox shortage was preservation. This wasn't easy to achieve. For obvious reasons, farmers saw foxes as pests. Foxes are notorious predators of hens, geese and ducks. A fox who gets into a hen roost will kill as many terrified, flapping birds as he can. Foxes also kill lambs. This is far less common, and it's hard to be sure whether a lamb was already dead before the fox took it, but farmers have long seen foxes as a real threat to lambs.[31]

A farmer complained to the *Sporting Magazine* in 1793: 'The laws of the country hold out a reward to be paid by the churchwardens of every parish for the destruction of a rapacious, noxious animal; and the sportsmen, on the other hand, have formed a resolution to discharge or distress every tenant who shall have the audacity to "interrupt gentlemen's diversion" by destroying a litter of fox's cubs.'[32]

Fox hunting depended on persuading farmers to preserve foxes against their better judgement. Fox hunting was (and is) underpinned by farmers' support; without them it couldn't exist.

Landlord pressure on farmers took many forms. The 1793 *Sporting Magazine* quoted a Leicestershire landowner who offered to renew the leases of farmers friendly to foxes on moderate terms, threatening non-renewal for tenants who destroyed foxes. This was very similar to the pressure put on tenants to vote for their landlord's candidate in nineteenth-century county elections.

The owners of land didn't always get their own way. In the 1820s fox shooting was still a popular sport in Devon, where the Rev. Jack Russell, breeder of the eponymous fox terrier, kept hounds. When a fox was sighted, the church bells rang and a crowd of men with guns turned up at the fox's earth. Russell and his hounds once ran into a crowd of fox shooters. 'Who are you, sir,' an angry young farmer asked Russell, 'to come here and spoil our sport? You have no business here.' 'As much as you have,' replied Russell. 'The owner has given me leave to hunt over this estate, and I mean doing so whenever I please. So get a horse, come out with me, and I'll show you some fine sport, if you'll give up shooting foxes.'[33]

This was a bit like converting the heathen or rescuing fallen women. Shooting foxes was a sin, condemned by Parson Russell. From about the 1820s men who killed foxes by other means than hunting were branded as vulpicides. It was a very effective taboo.

In the novels of Surtees, published in the 1840s and 1850s, the worst cads and villains shoot foxes. Marmaduke Muleygrubs in *Handley Cross* is a parvenu staymaker who apes the gentry and lives in a fake castle; he betrays himself by shooting his foxes and ordering a bag fox for the meet. No real gentleman would ever commit vulpicide.

Unlike the polecat and the marten, which became extinct in lowland Britain between 1850 and 1915, the fox prospered. The fate of polecats and martens has been blamed on intensive game-keepering after 1850. The fox's survival, on the other hand, may have been due to the vulpicide taboo. Keepers were instructed by their employers to provide foxes for the hunt.[34]

Hunt records for the second half of the nineteenth century show a marked upward trend in the number of foxes killed or run to ground per day out. The upward curve probably reflects increasing fox numbers, since hunting techniques didn't become more efficient after 1870.

Gamekeepers didn't like preserving foxes. 'Huntsmen seem to think,' a gamekeeper complained in 1902, 'that after the preserver has spent thousands of pounds in making game coverts, and hundreds annually preserving game, these coverts are to be kept for the sole enjoyment of the MFH and his followers.' Nevertheless, most keepers obeyed their employers and left foxes alone. 'Gamekeepers,' said Reginald Herbert, Master of the Monmouthshire 1886–1903, 'carry out what they know or guess to be the vices or wishes of their employer. If the employer insists on foxes as well as pheasants, he will get them.'[35]

CHAPTER ONE

The Noble Sport

'Fox hunting is now become the amusement of gentlemen; nor need any gentleman be ashamed of it.'

PETER BECKFORD, 1781

Hugo Meynell started to hunt foxhounds from Quorn Hall in Leicestershire in 1753. By the time he gave up in 1800, he was recognized as the inventor of the Meynellian Science: new-style fast fox hunting.

Meynell didn't transform fox hunting singlehanded, as his admirers claimed. He was chiefly notable as a hound breeder. His hounds at Quorn were descended from the pack formed by Lord Arundell of Wardour in the 1670s. Using the latest techniques of in-and-in breeding (from brother and sister) developed by Robert Bakewell with his New Leicester sheep at nearby Dishley Hall, Meynell bred a pack capable of keeping up with a fast-running fox at midday.

At first, he hunted over unfenced ridge and furrow. The country was undrained and boggy. Leicestershire was transformed by late-eighteenth-century enclosures. Hedges and roads were laid out in grids of straight lines. Too heavy to plough, the clay land was laid down to permanent pasture for fattening beef cattle. Graziers made young thorn hedges bullock-proof by digging ditches on one side and running a stout oak rail (an oxer) along the other.

The result was a strongly fenced grass country which carried a screaming scent. Meynell's Leicestershire Quorn became the prime hunting country of England.

Meynell didn't own an acre of land in Leicestershire, and he hunted everywhere by courtesy. To the graziers he was 'uniformly civil, and even polite'. He had to be. Leicestershire's open country supported few indigenous foxes, but in Meynell's time they were strictly preserved by the farmers. In the 1790s he killed between fifty-four and ninety-two foxes a year, hunting three days a week.

Meynell disliked new hunting techniques. He never cast his hounds if he could help it, and he disliked lifting. Though he wasn't particularly interested in riding, his hounds attracted more and more hard riders. Meynell complained that since Childe of Kinlet brought the flying leap to Leicestershire in 1780 he hadn't had a moment's peace. The Billesdon-Coplow Run in 1800, his last season, was twenty-eight miles in two hours fifteen minutes. The Duke of Richmond's record 1739 hunt had been twenty-four miles in ten hours. The pace was hotting up.

Meynell disciplined his field of riders with sarcasm rather than curses. When someone rode over the scent and then insisted he was right, Meynell bowed and smiled: 'You may be perfectly right, sir, and I quite wrong, but there is gross ignorance on *one* side or the other.'

He never had more than four subscribers to his hounds. One was 'Prince' Boothby, his brother-in-law, grandson of Thomas Boothby who had started hunting the Quorn country in 1677. A rich man, Meynell was a friend of Dr Johnson, and just as comfortable at London parties as he was at Quorn. His contacts with society probably contributed as much to his success as his skill as a sportsman. He made fox hunting *à la mode*.[1]

Another rich fox-hunting pioneer, Mr Corbet, hunted the whole of Warwickshire at his own expense from 1791 to 1811. Corbet made Warwickshire into a leading grass country by means of a large fortune and 'a truly gentlemanlike demeanour'. He was always polite in the field. 'Pray, Sir, hold hard, you will spoil your own sport.' He muttered as he galloped past someone who'd trodden on a hound: 'Killed the best hound in my pack, *that's all*!' He was very much aware that he hunted by consent. Every Sunday morning he paid farmers' wives for hens killed by foxes, and he advertised his meets three weeks in advance in the papers. He was very lucky: he hunted Warwickshire at a time when wartime prosperity meant farmers had plenty of money.[2]

Like George III, Mr Corbet never jumped, but waited for the fences to be knocked down for him. John Warde, who hunted what later became the Bicester from 1778 to 1797, when he took the Pytchley, was a harder rider. Hunting diaries found among his papers show his hounds often giving a 'charming burst' or fast hunt. Warde's record day with the Pytchley in 1802 (the Marston Wood Hunt) was a circle of thirty-five to forty miles in four and a quarter hours.[3]

Down in Dorset, Peter Beckford kept hounds and wrote his elegant exposition of the art of hunting. Beckford was a cultivated Enlightenment dandy, living on a West Indian fortune. He toured France and Italy, calling on Rousseau and Voltaire. He was said to 'bag a fox in Greek, find a hare in Latin, inspect his kennels in Italian, and direct the economy of his stables in exquisite French'. Much of what he wrote on technique still holds good today. But his book had a wider purpose. As well as writing a practical manual, he set out to elevate and idealize fox hunting.

Attacking the early-eighteenth-century view of hunting as the sport of boors like Roger de Coverley and Squire Western, Beckford declared that hunting was the art of civilized gentlemen. Citing Virgil, Horace and Pliny, Beckford commended country life as a haven of classical values. Hunting was 'the soul of a country life; it gives health to the body and content to the mind, and is one of the few pleasures we can enjoy in society, without prejudice either to ourselves or our friends'.[4]

Beckford's ideal can be glimpsed in the early-eighteenth-century paintings of John Wootton: the huntsman, stiff and stately, his hair dressed and powdered, stands in a classical landscape, surrounded by urns and ruins. In fact, the virtues Beckford claimed for hunting – health, morality, social intercourse – had formed part of a seventeenth-century sporting ideal, glorifying the hunting Stuart kings; and that ideal itself was drawn from much earlier medieval and Classical sources.[5]

When John Byng visited the Duke of Bedford's splendid new hunt kennels at Woburn in 1794, there was a hound kitchen with coppers and boilers, separate apartments for the bitches 'during their accouchements', and abundant supplies of coal, straw and milk. Next door were 'those miserable hovels erected for the sons of Adam; who . . . regret they are not born foxhounds'. An aristocracy which splurged so much on housing its dogs, altogether neglecting its cottagers, deserved a French Revolution, he thought.[6]

Hunting went on fast and furious throughout the Revolutionary and Napoleonic Wars. Wellington's officers came out wearing regimental scarlet coats. Fox-hunting gentlemen, who before 1800 had worn a variety of colours, adopted a scarlet uniform. Instant traditions were invented to give the new uniform legitimacy. (Much the same was done for the Scottish kilt, which was invented at roughly the same time.) Scarlet, some suggested, was the colour of royal huntsmen, commemorating hunting's royal origins; in places, it had also been the Tory colour.

Swells called the scarlet coat pink, allegedly after Mr Pink, the tailor. This was only briefly the correct term. Lord Willoughby de Broke, who was blooded in the 1870s and a stickler for correctness, thought you should never say pink; red was correct, though scarlet was permissible. Writing in 1980 the Duke of Beaufort agreed.[7]

The gentleman's scarlet coat was usually single-breasted cutaway, with a single button. (Hunt servants wore scarlet frock coats: when the hounds belonged to the Master they wore six buttons in the tail of the coat to denote livery.) Scarlet went with top boots – black with tops – which replaced the long black Wellington boot, bent over the knee. The colour of the leather top varied with different hunts, and fashion changed from pink – cleaned with champagne and apricot jam – to dark mahogany.

Fashion in breeches changed too, from tight-cut white leather to 'roomy breeches of broadish striped cord, not exactly white, but what will scour to white'. Gentlemen wore hats and the hunt servants caps, for 'a gentleman in a cutaway coat and a cap looks as a courtier would in a round hat'. The tie – stock is a modern term, condemned by Willoughby de Broke and the Duke of Beaufort – should be blue birds' eye spots. Only a 'snob' wore a black tie with top boots.[8]

When the fashion-conscious George IV hunted with the Royal Buckhounds as Prince of Wales, he laughed at his father's slow horses and homely clothes. As King after 1820 he ordered a dozen skin-tight corduroy breeches though he was too heavy to ride, and made the Royal Buckhounds go much faster. 'I hope you will get them so fast,' he said to his new huntsman in 1822, 'that they will run away from everybody.'[9]

1810 to 1830 was a 'golden age' in Leicestershire. The town of Melton Mowbray came into its own. It was within hacking distance of meets of what later became known as the shire packs: the Quorn, Cottesmore, Belvoir and Pytchley. You could hunt six days a week from Melton. Meltonians like Lords Forester, Wilton and Alvanley kept twelve hunters or more, and as many as three hundred hunters were stabled in the town in the season.

This was the heyday of the great gentlemen huntsmen: Thomas Assheton Smith, Master of the Quorn 1806–17, George Osbaldeston, twice Master of the Quorn between 1817 and 1827, and Master of the Pytchley 1827–34, and John Musters, Master of the Pytchley 1821–7.

In the 1850s the sporting journalist H. H. Dixon, 'the Druid', drove round Leicestershire in a gig with Dick Christian, the Meltonian rough-rider, then nearly eighty. Assheton Smith, Dick Christian told the Druid, 'was always for being away as quick as possible . . . He'd get away with three or four couple of hounds; then they'd come to a check and the run was spoiled.' Osbaldeston was if anything worse. He was 'the oddest man you ever saw at a covert-side. He would talk for an hour; then he would half-draw, and talk again, and often blow his horn when there was no manner of occasion'.[10] Hence the rhyme:

> Who is the trumpeter blowing his horn?
> That is the trumpeter coming from Quorn,
> The very worst huntsman that ever was born.

Musters was a better huntsman, but even he had faults. According to Osbaldeston, he was so jealous of his reputation for killing more foxes than anyone else that when he lost a fox he faked marking to ground, training his hounds to bay at the first hole they came to. Once he was caught out by a 'rustic', who looked into the hole and pronounced it empty. 'How should you know, you clod-hopper?' demanded Musters. 'This 'ere 'ole is as chock full o' cobwebs as it can 'old,' rejoined the rustic. Exit Musters, red-faced.[11]

It's unfair to judge Osbaldeston or Assheton Smith by the purist standards of, say, Beckford. What the Osbaldeston-Assheton Smith generation were really remarkable for was *pace*.

As Master of the Quorn, you had to go fast to survive. Three hundred galloping horsemen thundered at your back. In front loomed black bullfinches – high unplashed thorn hedges jumped through rather than over – and terrifying oxers with a four-foot rail two yards beyond the hedge. Double oxers (rails in front and behind the hedge) were even worse.

Crack riders negotiated these appalling obstacles leaning well back in the saddle, legs stuck out straight in front, 'hailing a cab' with the right hand. Hounds were a bore. 'I'm the worst fellow in England to remember hounds' names,' confessed Dick Christian. 'I never took no notice of them; no matter to me what they were, as long as they went fast enough.'[12]

Assheton Smith was probably the boldest rider of his day. 'I'll be with my hounds,' he declared, and literally hurled himself 'at places which *he knew* no horse could leap over, but his object was to get one way or other into the field with his hounds'.

His horses were schooled to ride for a fall, and he was a pastmaster at falling. He never let go of the reins, so lost no time catching his horse. At the meet he vaulted from his hack to his hunter without dismounting. Stories multiplied of the horrendous obstacles he'd jumped – one of the worst, witnessed by Dick Christian, was 'a ravine twelve foot perpendickler, blame me if it ain't, and twenty-one across'. He once came upon Captain John White, a Quorn thruster, who was stuck in a bullfinch at the only place it could be jumped. 'Get on,' said Smith. 'I cannot. I'm fast,' said White. 'D—n it, if you are in such a hurry, why don't you ride at me and charge me?' Smith duly did, sending White and his horse into the next field, and away they went as if nothing had happened.[13]

Riding hell-for-leather like this was very demanding on horseflesh. In Leicestershire, the cross-bred hunter – offspring of a draught mare and a Thoroughbred horse – was superseded by a pure or seven-eighths Thoroughbred. 'I have never heard of any great thing done,' said Dick Christian, 'but it was done by a Thoroughbred horse.' Horse prices shot up. In Warwickshire hunters fetched two to five hundred guineas. In Leicestershire they cost up to eight hundred guineas.

Horses often weren't fit enough to survive. The practice of bleeding tired horses didn't help. Thirteen horses died after a run with the Warwickshire. 'I never saw such a sight,' recalled a witness, 'as the stableyard at Dunchurch, buckets of blood on all sides.'[14]

Taking a second horse which you changed on to at about one o'clock saved horseflesh. Lord Sefton, Master of the Quorn 1800–2, who weighed twenty stone, got through three horses a day. Clipping horses improved condition, though not everyone approved as it was thought to encourage lazy grooming.[15]

Nimrod, alias Charles James Apperley, chronicled and publicized the 'steeple-chasing mania' of the 1820s. Nimrod's hunting tours first appeared in the *Sporting Magazine* in 1822. The magazine's circulation trebled. Equipped by his editor with five hunters and a hack, Nimrod toured the country, allegedly receiving the record-breaking payment of twenty pounds per page.[16]

Nimrod was a hard-riding sportsman who had hunted in Leicestershire beyond his means. When his rich wife left him, he took to journalism. Writing from inside the sporting world, he excelled at conveying the style and dash of the new hunting:

> A report is flying about that one of the field is badly hurt, and something is heard of a collar-bone being broken, others say it is a leg; but the pace is *too good* to inquire. A cracking of rails is now heard, and one gentleman's horse is to be seen resting, nearly balanced, across one of them, his rider being on his back in the

> ditch, which is on the landing side. 'Who is he?' says Lord Brudenell to Jack Stevens. 'Can't tell, my Lord; but I thought it was a queerish place when I came o'er it before him.' It is evidently a case of peril, but the pace is *too good* to afford help.[17]

Fast, masculine and rich – this is the Quorn in Osbaldeston's time. 'A man with five hunters and a hack,' said Nimrod, 'makes a very respectable appearance in the Provincials, but he has no business in Leicestershire.'

Very few resident Leicestershire gentlemen came out with the Quorn in the 1820s. The field was made up of 'strangers' from outside the country, the pace set by the 'crack riders' Nimrod delighted to name. The members of the Melton Old Club, which had only four best bedrooms, made up a social and equestrian elite: Lords Alvanley and Brudenell, Captain Maxse, Mr Moore, Val Maher and Sir James Musgrave.

Beating up the lower classes was a Meltonian hobby. Osbaldeston and his whips charged the Northampton shoemakers when they invaded the course at the Pytchley hunt races. Assheton Smith stood as a Tory for the radical borough of Nottingham in 1818. He was met by placards saying 'No fox-hunting MP', and shouted down. He got the crowd on his side by offering to fight any man who came forward. During the 1831 Reform riots Captain John White read the Riot Act to a Derbyshire mob. 'By God! If you don't clear off, and I order my men to charge, I'll cut you down as if you were so many bloody Frenchmen.' The mob went home immediately.[18]

Meltonians dined in hunt uniform (red with a white lining) and, according to Nimrod, never talked hunting at dinner (this is hard to believe). The Meltonian, wrote Nimrod, was conspicuous in the field from 'the exact Stultz-like cut of his coat' – Stultz of Clifford Street was *the* London tailor – 'his superlatively well-cleaned leather breeches and boots, and the generally apparent high breeding of the man'. In short, the Meltonian was 'the very *beau-ideal* of his *caste*'.

Splattering his copy with lords and gentlemen, Nimrod introduced the outsider to a glamorous world of galloping bloods and dandies. Henry Alken, working in the 1820s, illustrated much of Nimrod and copiously caricatured Leicestershire hunting. Remarkable for their movement, his light-hearted etchings had the same popular appeal as Nimrod's journalism.

Hunting for Nimrod was as much social climbing as killing foxes. 'A winter in Leicestershire,' he wrote, 'has ever been found to be, to those who are entitled to it, the *passe partout* that leads to the best society in the world.'

In the *Sporting Magazine* Nimrod laid down rules for jumping six-yard-wide brooks and putting a blown horse at stiff timber – the greatest trial of nerve, he thought, next to being shot at. He revelled in stories of gruesome falls. Mr Stanhope went out with the Atherstone one Monday with his arm in a sling, having had a fall on Friday. He fell at a brook and was knocked out, and when Nimrod rode past he seemed as dead as if he'd been shot at Waterloo. Refusing to see a doctor, Mr Stanhope insisted on hunting with the Quorn on Thursday, when he rode at some impossibly high rails and got another tremendous fall. The doctor found two broken ribs and a beaten-in breastbone. Mr Stanhope, commented Nimrod, 'is not a bad sort of man to breed from'.[19]

Jack Mytton, Master of the Albrighton in Shropshire 1817–21, jumped nine yards over a brook in cold blood on the way home from hunting. Nimrod's *Life of Mytton* lovingly chronicles his pranks: shooting wildfowl in snow in his nightshirt, riding his horse across the Severn though he couldn't swim, setting fire to his nightshirt to cure his hiccups.

Mytton was a drunkard and a wastrel. (When told he shouldn't sell his estate because it had been in his family for five hundred years, he replied: 'The devil has it! Then it is high time it should go out of it!') But he wasn't a clodhopping squire. He wore silk stockings and paper-thin boots which gave him wet feet all winter, and even when drunk he could quote his Latin authors.[20]

Another Master of Hounds admired by Nimrod was Lord Darlington of Raby, later Marquis and then Duke of Cleveland. He hunted the vast Raby country in Yorkshire and Durham from 1787 to 1840.

Lord Darlington took his hunting very seriously. He hunted his own hounds four days a week, and fed them whenever he could. Each year he published a large folio volume of diaries, the *Operations of the Raby Pack*. His second wife, the adventuress daughter of a market gardener, and his daughters by his first wife – Ladies Arabella, Laura and Augusta Vane – hunted three days a fortnight; they wore scarlet habits, rode Thoroughbred horses and jumped everything. At Raby, where Nimrod stayed with him, Lord Cleveland, as he then was, lived in princely state. The stud groom came in after dinner to receive lengthy instructions for the next day's hunting.

'Is Moses sound?'
'Yes, my Lord.'
'I shall ride him. Also Bergami.'
'Yes, my Lord.'
'Dick, Swing.'
'Yes, my Lord.'
'Will, Salopian.'
'Yes, my Lord.'
'Lady Cleveland, Raby.'
'Yes, my Lord.'
'Edward, The Parson.'
'Yes, my Lord.'
'Lady Arabella, the Duchess.'
'Yes, my Lord.'
'George, Obadiah.'
'Yes, my Lord.'
'That's all!'
'Yes, my Lord.'

Out hunting, Lord Darlington wore an old-fashioned straight-cut scarlet coat, with a gold fox embroidered on the collar, a leather belt and a tall hat. 'I was riding Wizard,' he wrote after a good hunt in 1821, 'who carried me with his accustomed ease, elegance and superiority . . . he went with his head up and proud of his place, like a monarch clothed in coronation robes.'

Lord Darlington was a fox hunter of the old school. He thought more of hounds than horses. He scorned Leicestershire, noting after a fast hunt in 1824 that 'many a dandy Meltonian would have called out for his Mamma's milk to have supported his horse and himself before we reached Thornton Hall whin'. He succeeded in refusing permission to the first Stockton and Darlington railway in 1820 because it went through a favourite covert.[21]

Lord Darlington adopted an eighteenth-century outlook in encouraging his wife and daughters to hunt. Nimrod encountered very few women who actually rode to hounds on his tours; he raised an eyebrow that the Ladies Vane jumped fences and still retained their femininity.

Before 1800 hunting ladies were few, but accepted. Lady Salisbury was Master of the Hatfield Hunt 1775–1819. She was a notoriously hard rider, wearing a sky-blue habit. In old age she was so blind that she went out on a leading rein. When she came to a fence her groom shouted, 'Damn you, my lady, jump!'[22]

By Nimrod's time sexual roles were far more polarized. Ladies were expected to stay demurely at home. By making hunting sound so dangerous and brutal, Nimrod helped mark it out as exclusive male territory. Riding for a fall at a blind, hairy bullfinch was not sport for the weaker sex. During the French Wars of 1793–1815 hunting was promoted as training for war. The scarlet coat was a military uniform. Women had no place in a hunting field which was an army at play. Ladies were banned from the Old Club at Melton. When the courtesan Harriette Wilson ran her lover to ground at Melton and dined at the club, wretched, dirty prostitutes tapped at the windows and the men who weren't too sleepy sneaked out of the room.[23]

Nimrod portrayed hunting as the sport of an aristocratic caste. So did F. P. Delmé Radcliffe, Master of the Hertfordshire Hunt 1835–9. The 'noble science' for Delmé Radcliffe was essentially a matter of breeding – of hounds, horses and men. His slogan was, 'blood will tell'. 'It will be found,' he wrote, 'in *ninety-nine cases out of a hundred*, where the harmony of any society is disturbed by an obnoxious individual, that he is a cock-tail; a low, underbred fellow;

one, in short, who never could have had a grandfather.'[24]

Like Leicestershire hunting, *battue* shooting – driving partridges and pheasants out of coverts over standing guns – was the sport of a closed caste. Imported from the Continent in the 1790s, it peaked in the 1820s. The exclusiveness of the *battue* was underlined by legislation strengthening the Game Laws, which since 1671 had confined the killing of game to the owners of land. In 1803 the death penalty was introduced for poachers guilty of armed resistance to arrest, and in 1817 night poaching was made punishable by transportation.

Radicals like Cobbett attacked the new Game Laws as class legislation, intended solely to benefit the landed classes. The gentry responded by insisting that the Game Laws alone ensured a resident gentry. The French Revolution, they said, was the consequence of a debased nobility deserting their estates for the corrupt attractions of the metropolis. England was unique – stable politically because the gentry, lusting for blood, stayed on their estates, infatuated with field sports.

According to this theory, the only reasons gentlemen lived in the country were fox hunting and shooting, together with what the radical critic Egerton Brydges described as 'the collateral pleasures of committing suspected poachers, or peppering the legs of real ones'. It followed, wrote Brydges, that 'foxes, partridges and pheasants (we wish we could add *peasants* also, – for as these are allowed to be shot *ad libitum*, by any gentleman duly qualified, under the name of poachers, it seems a ridiculous oversight not to have declared them *game* at once) . . . are the main pillars of our free constitution'.[25]

Pheasants and Game Laws certainly divided gentlemen and peasants. Foxes, which weren't protected by Game Laws, arguably brought classes together. Hunting was at the same time the most exclusive and the most democratic of sports.

CHAPTER TWO

Open To All

Select is the circle in which I am moving,
Yet open and free the admission to all,
Still, still more select is that company proving,
Weeded out by the funker and thinned by the
 fall!
Yet here all are equal – no class legislation,
No privilege hinders, no family pride –
In the 'image of war' show the pluck of the
 nation,
Ride, ancient patrician! democracy ride!

W. BROMLEY DAVENPORT,
The Dream of an Old Meltonian, *c.* 1865

In 1843 a novel called *Handley Cross* was published anonymously. The first edition of 750 copies sold badly. But *Handley Cross* has since become a classic, immortalized by its hero, Mr Jorrocks.

The author was Robert Smith Surtees, a little-known sporting journalist. He had replaced Nimrod as hunting correspondent at the *Sporting Magazine* in 1830, where his lacklustre copy failed to fill the gap left by Nimrod. Surtees departed in 1831 to found and edit a rival publication, the *New Sporting Magazine*. In 1838 he inherited his father's estate at Hamsterley Hall, Durham, where he lived the life of a Tory country gentleman. He failed to get into Parliament, kept his own hounds – they had to be destroyed when they started eating sheep – and hunted with Lord Elcho. But he couldn't stop writing. Standing at a short-legged desk set on a table, he wrote all day without stopping for meals. He poured out a flood of words, creating what Kipling described as 'a heavy-eating, hard-drinking hell of horse-copers, swindlers, match-making mothers, economically dependent virgins selling themselves blushingly for cash and lands: Jews, tradesmen, and an ill-considered spawn of Dickens-and-horsedung characters'.[1]

'What's the meaning of Jorrocks?' asked Surtees's friend, Captain Freeman, Master of the Southwold. 'I don't understand that Jorrocks.' He might well ask. Jorrocks the Cockney grocer, dropping his *h*s and rolling around in his saddle, seemed hardly at home in the noble sport.

Jorrocks was one of the City merchants who rode out early on winter mornings to Croydon, the Melton of the South, to hunt with the Surrey. His hunting – all trot, trot, bump, bump – is constantly contrasted with Nimrod's neck or nothing.

In *Handley Cross* Nimrod appears in person, as the celebrated hunting correspondent, Pomponius Ego. Mr Jorrocks has by now taken a pack of hounds in the spa town of Handley Cross, and he invites Pomponius down for the day. It is of course a disaster. Pomponius doesn't realize that James Pigg the huntsman is hunting an aniseed drag; but Jorrocks is sadly disappointed by Nimrod's snobbish report of the day's sport.

Jorrocks is the antithesis of Nimrod's *beau-ideal* of a Meltonian. He gets off at the jumps and pulls his horse over, shouting, 'Come hup! I say, you hugly beast!' He rides home after a fall with a muddy coat, and a townswoman calls out: 'He's always on his back, that old feller.' 'Not 'alf so often as you are, old gal!' replies Jorrocks. He is proud of his trade as a tea merchant, boasting of being 'a Post Hoffice Directory not a Peerage man'.

Social climbing, or what he called tuft hunting, brought out the worse in Surtees. He wrote reams of under-edited satire on matchmaking mammas and scheming virgins. Nimrod's snobbishness was an irresistible target for him. Surtees, who was an indifferent horseman, may also have been jealous of Nimrod's reputation for bold riding.

Handley Cross is larded with quotes from Beckford, which Jorrocks thinks the 'werry best book wot ever was written'. In his 'Sporting Lectures' Jorrocks restates the purist ideal of hunting as a matter more of hounds than riding. This is associated with honest, straightforward, masculine Englishness: Jorrocks's nightly two pints of port, his vast joints of beef (food for Surtees had great social significance) and his plain-speaking contempt for social climbers.

The Cockney sportsman was a well-established type. In about 1700 D'Urfey pilloried the City merchants who hunted deer in the outskirts of London, their spurs upside down:

> A creature bounceth from the bush which made them all
> to laugh,
> My Lord he cried, 'A hare! a hare!' but it proved an Essex
> calf.

Gillray cartoons of the 1790s made the same joke, mocking the 'cit' or Cockney sportsman for his ignorance of country sport. Surtees took the 'cit' stereotype and turned it round. Though a Cockney, Jorrocks knows far more about sport than most countrymen, and certainly more than the perfumed, ringleted dandies who hunted from Melton.

Cockney sportsmen like Jorrocks could hunt, even though they didn't own an acre of land, because hunting was open to all. Shooting, by contrast, was a class-based sport, even after the repeal of the property qualification for killing game in 1831. 'Do away a little with the *exclusive* character of shooting,' Queen Victoria begged 'Bertie', Prince of Wales. 'With hunting (much as I dislike it on account of the danger) this is the case, and that is what makes it so popular.'[2]

Since Hugo Meynell's time, when hunting became an organized social event, commentators had stressed its *social* benefits. 'The Field,' wrote John Hawkes, an admirer of Meynell's, in 1808, 'is a most agreeable Coffee-house, and there is more real society to be met with there than in any other situation in life. It links all classes together, from the Peer to the Peasant. It is the English man's peculiar privilege.'[3]

Sometimes it was argued that hunting actually dissolved class barriers. Hunting, said Nimrod, is 'a sort of Saturnalian amusement'. Rank and privilege are set aside, and the boldest rider takes precedence for the day. 'A butcher's boy upon a pony may throw the dirt in the face of the first Duke in the kingdom.'[4] Alken drove the point home with his 'Sporting Anecdotes' of 1833, a series of prints depicting the hunting butcher, the sweep, the miller and the tailor. Much was made of the story of the chimney sweep who hunted with the Duke of Beaufort in about 1830.

The argument about equality originated in Leicestershire in the 1820s, at a time when hunting there was in fact becoming more exclusive. In Leicestershire, smarmed a sporting encyclopaedia of 1840, 'there is less fear than in most other fox-hunting localities, that the feelings of the high-bred sportsman should be annoyed by the interruption of farmers, the brusqueries of the vulgar'. Businessmen from Leicester and Nottingham who came out with the Quorn in black coats were ostracized in the 1840s. The pauper in receipt of outdoor relief who hunted with the Pytchley in about 1840 was soon stopped by the guardians and his horse Ratepayer was sent to the kennels.[5]

Harry Hieover – the sporting journalist Charles Bindley – enthused in 1853 about the freemasonry which united hunting men. Leicestershire, he had to admit, wasn't quite the same. If a farmer came out with the Quorn, he would be politely received, so long as he didn't give himself airs, and no one would so much as mention a plough in his presence. 'But *one* attempt at equality his fate is sealed; aristocracy will often welcome a man of another grade as being with them, but he must not attempt to be one *of* them.'[6]

Hunting society in the 1840s and 1850s was analysed pretty accurately by Surtees. He agreed that it was open to all. Hunting, he wrote in 1848, 'reverberates through the whole of our social system . . . the joy that a good run inspires in the breast of the peer descends through all classes, even to the humble pedestrian who witnesses either the find or the finish'.

But the fact that all classes were involved didn't mean that hunting was a 'leveller of rank'. Heaven forbid. Surtees was a Tory, obsessed by class: he was fascinated by things like clothes and food, or even by how servants touched their hats, because they told so much about social distinctions. For him the point about hunting was that it underpinned the class structure, rather than dissolving it. 'The hunting field is a place where deference is voluntarily paid to station, because it is in the hunting field that station never demands it.'[7]

The theory of hunting as open to all was always qualified in practice by the cost. Costs rose steadily as hunting became more elaborate. In 1826 Colonel John Cook estimated the cost of hunting two days a week at £1,170 p.a., rising to £1,625 for three days and £1,935 for four days. In 1821 Sir Bellingham Graham was given £4,000 to hunt the Quorn. In the 1840s Robert Vyner, a Warwickshire MFH, calculated that each fox cost £50 to kill in a first-class shire pack killing a hundred foxes – £5,000 a year. The Heythrop cost £1,489 in 1848–9. By the 1860s a four-day-a-week provincial country was reckoned to cost about £2,500.[8]

Inflated by fashion, hound prices soared. Ralph Lambton's Durham pack were sold for a record price of 3,000 guineas in 1838 to Lord Suffield of the Quorn. Trained to hunt for themselves, they were a disaster in Leicestershire and Suffield sold them back to the north, to Mr Robertson of Ladykirk, Master of the Berwickshire, for £1,000 in 1840. Ten of Osbaldeston's hounds were sold at Tattersall's for 1,360 guineas. The coal-rich Sir Matthew White Ridley, Master of the Northumberland Hunt, bought a pack of hounds from Lord Scarbrough in 1837. He had his family painted with his hounds in front of his house.[9] Expensive hounds were rich men's playthings, investments in social prestige.

Only the very rich could afford to keep their own private packs, paying all expenses themselves. At Badminton the Duke of Beaufort was 'a prince in his own neighbourhood'. The hunt was an 'open-air club', free to all and carried on entirely at the Duke's expense. Five thousand people turned up to a lawn meet at Badminton in 1863;

a thousand sat down to breakfast, and luncheon was provided for four or five hundred of the upper class.[10]

Surtees, who hated grandees, disliked private aristocratic packs belonging to great lords. He thought magnate masters were overbearing and autocratic. Because they paid for everything themselves they treated the hunt like a private fief. Lord Scamperdale in *Mr Sponge's Sporting Tour* (1853) spends £2,500 on his hounds and behaves like a tyrant in the field, doing all he can to prevent the visiting Mr Sponge from hunting with him.

> 'You perpendicular-looking Puseyite pig-jobber! By Jove! you think because I'm a lord, and can't swear or use coarse language, that you may do what you like – but I'll take my hounds home, sir – yes, sir, I'll take my hounds home, sir.' So saying, his lordship roared HOME to Frostyface [the huntsman]; adding, in an undertone to the first whip, 'bid him go to Furzing-field gorse'.

This kind of thing went on in real life too. Sir Richard Sutton, Master of the Quorn 1847–55, was rich enough to dispense with the subscription. When someone came up and told him where to draw, he replied: 'Gentlemen, I have only one hobby: it costs me £10,000 a year and *I go where I like*.'[11]

Rich masters often hunted vast countries. Lord Elcho, with whom Surtees hunted, had a huge country on the Borders, divided today between the Berwickshire, North Northumberland, Percy and Morpeth hunts. James Farquharson, 'the Meynell of the West', inherited his grandfather's vast East India fortune, and hunted the whole of Dorset at his own expense for more than fifty years from 1806.

Vast hunting countries weren't always popular, as Farquharson discovered in Dorset. The squires grumbled that they didn't get enough hunting; because Farquharson couldn't get round his country, there was no incentive to preserve foxes for him, and the hunting got worse. In 1857 Mr Digby of Sherborne Castle organized a requisition of landowners, requesting Farquharson to turn certain coverts over to the Blackmore Vale. Farquharson replied that splitting the country was contrary to 'the rights and laws of fox hunting'. Digby's response was to warn Farquharson not to draw his coverts. Farquharson gave in and resigned.[12]

Farquharson was supported throughout by the farmers, who 'adored' him; his enemies were the gentry. What the gentry wanted was *control* over their hunting; but they could only control the hunt if they contributed to its costs.

One device giving greater gentry control was the hunt club. Country gentlemen around 1800 had a mania for clubs. Dining clubs sprang up in county towns, each with its own rules, forfeits, blackballs and colourful dress uniform. The Jedforest Club, founded by Lord Ancram in 1810, dined four times a year in the Spread Eagle Inn at Jedburgh wearing coats of forest green with gilt buttons; the club had no direct connection with the Jedforest Hunt, which was only founded in 1884.[13]

Some clubs were very informal. In Hexhamshire the Park House Club was formed by William Crawhall in 1829. Crawhall was agent to Mr Beaumont of Allenheads, and the club consisted of twelve friends and relations who stayed with him at Park House each autumn for 'slaughter'. Each member was asked to bring a contribution – a fat sheep and six pots of currant jelly, say, or three dozen bottles of port, or six dozen cigars and a round of beef – and they 'sported' for a week, shooting grouse and partridges on the moor and hunting with a pack of harriers which came along too.[14]

John Corbet, Master of the Warwickshire, formed a hunt club which met at the White Lion Inn in Stratford-on-Avon. Members subscribed five pounds for earth-stopping and dined every other Thursday throughout the season, wearing a scarlet coat with a black velvet collar, which became the distinctive collar of the Warwickshire Hunt. Corbet bred a famous hound called Trojan, and after dinner the Black Collars drank to the blood of the Trojans.[15]

Nimrod, who never hunted in Hampshire when he could help it, enjoyed dining with the Hampshire Hunt Club. Wearing blue coats and gilt buttons inscribed 'H.H.' with Prince of Wales feathers (George IV hunted with the H.H. as Prince of Wales in the 1790s), the club combined elegance with the jollity and good fellowship he thought proper to fox hunters of the present day.[16]

The H.H. Club owned the hounds. So did the Oakley Club. When Lord Tavistock gave up as Master of the Oakley in 1829 he sold the hounds out of the country, and the club was furious. A row broke out between the club, led by its secretary Samuel Whitbread, and the Duke of Bedford, supported by the landowners. Bedford appointed Grantley Berkeley Master without consulting the club; Whitbread threatened to withdraw the club's subscription of a thousand pounds, but eventually knuckled under when Berkeley threatened to fight a duel with him.[17]

In big countries with poor transport like Lord Elcho's or Lord Darlington's, the hounds moved between different kennels, and the gentry formed clubs which met when the hounds came to their part of the country. The squires around Bedale formed a dining club (1816) which met when Lord Darlington brought his hounds to the Bedale country. Darlington dined at the club every Thursday – much to the amazement of Nimrod, who couldn't imagine why a lord should condescend to dine in an inn. The club dealt with hunt business such as poultry claims, and when Darlington gave up the Bedale side in 1832 the club formed the nucleus for the Bedale Hunt.[18]

The Sedgefield Club was the headquarters of Ralph Lambton's Durham Hunt. Lambton, who was Surtees's hero, received a subscription of eight hundred pounds, and paid for the rest himself, hunting four or five days a week. When Nimrod stayed at the club in 1826, he found Lambton himself and a party of sixteen members, wearing undress uniform of scarlet coat and white buttons. Big coal fires blazed, and they dined at seven, which Nimrod thought rather too late for men going hunting next morning. It was a very jolly evening, demonstrating to Nimrod 'the solid advantages of fox hunting. The whole party seemed to possess but one soul . . . and the bottle went round *best pace* to a very late hour.'[19]

Hunt clubs like this certainly promoted jollity among the squires. But they were exclusively masculine, and gentlemen went there to get away from their wives. The rules of the Tarporley Hunt Club,

7 Hunting and Classical values. Peter Beckford by Pompeo Battoni, 1765.

8 Lord Henry Bentinck MFH, dressed like a Methodist preacher

9 Nimrod, dandy and journalist, by Maclise

10 H. H. Dixon, 'The Druid', on the road in search of copy

11 Nimrod's Leicestershire, drawn by Alken. Steeple-chasing mania, 'Hailing a cab' with the right hand.

12 'Come 'hup! I say, you hugly beast!' Jorrocks by Leech.

which hunted with the Cheshire Hunt, provided for a spinster Lady Patroness to be nominated and toasted at each club meeting. When a member married he gave the other club members a pair of buckskin breeches each (or two pairs if he married a second time).[20]

Clubs were pretty socially exclusive too. You couldn't buy your way in. Members were elected, and undesirables were blackballed.

Yorkshire, described by Nimrod as the most sporting part of His Majesty's dominions, was hunted by a total of thirteen packs of foxhounds, all of which were linked to the York Union Hunt Club. This, thought Robert Vyner (who was a crashing snob), was 'one of the most aristocratic societies in England, and none were admitted but those whose character would bear the strictest investigation on all points'.[21]

The subscription pack evolved out of the hunt club. The social and financial functions of the club were divorced, and a hunt committee formed, which raised subscriptions, held meetings and negotiated with the Master. By 1850 subscription packs were the norm, increasing from twenty-four in 1810 to a hundred in 1854.

Hunt clubs survived, but their role became purely social. Club members dined together and sponsored hunt balls. Hunt balls like those Surtees so enjoyed describing – drinking gooseberry champagne and dancing the Ask Mamma polka – were partly sponsored by the hunt club, and partly paid for by a tax on tickets.[22]

Robert Vyner hated subscription packs, complaining of 'the ignorance and conceit of many committee-men – who are too often elected on account of the length of their purses, from the vulgar and rich parvenus of the neighbourhood'. Subscription packs were less exclusive than hunt clubs. Anyone could subscribe, and the new rich who couldn't get into the club could buy themselves on to the committee. Anthony Trollope, who spoke for the urban fox hunter, was in favour of the subscription pack precisely because it was open to outsiders. 'Men now prefer,' he wrote, 'to hunt with subscription packs, in doing which they can pay their own proportion of the expenditure, and feel that they follow their amusement without other debt to the Master of their hunt than that which is always due to zeal and success in high position.'[23]

Most subscription packs were in fact gentry-dominated. The MFH was a figure of consequence in the county, often likened to the county member, his popularity measured in foxes not votes. 'Talk of a MP!' said Jorrocks. 'Vot's an MP compared to an MFH!' Lord Willoughby de Broke gave a table of precedence for mid-century Warwickshire, a kind of hunting Barsetshire:

The Lord-Lieutenant
The Master of the Foxhounds
The Agricultural Landlords
The Bishop
The Chairman of the Quarter Sessions
The Colonel of the Yeomanry
The Member of Parliament
The Dean
The Archdeacons
The Justices of the Peace
The lesser Clergy
The larger Farmers.[24]

Hunting became more formalized, evolving its own unwritten code of 'law' or custom. Hunts had no legal right to hunt over anyone's land. In 1809 the Earl of Essex brought an action for trespass against his brother, the Hon. and Rev. William Capel, Master of the Old Berkeley. Lord Ellenborough ruled that foxes were hunted for pleasure, not to kill vermin, and 'these pleasures are to be taken only when there is the consent of those who are likely to be injured by them'.[25]

Landowners were legally entitled to bar the hunt from drawing their coverts or crossing their land. But this didn't mean, said fox hunters, that landowners could kick out their local hunt and invite another hunt to draw their coverts instead. Allowing every landowner to nominate a pack of foxhounds to hunt his land would be a recipe for anarchy.

Hunt boundaries were largely decided by precedent. Hunting law laid down that 'when once the bounds of a hunting country were defined, no other Master of hounds could hunt a cover within those limits, without the leave of the Master in possession'.[26] An

MFH who drew coverts in another Master's country without the Master's permission was in the wrong, even if the landowner invited him.

Enforcement of hunting law was a problem. Like the vulpicide taboo, it depended largely on public opinion. Grantley Berkeley, who loved getting out his pistols – he fought a duel with a hostile reviewer – thought hunting law could only be effectively enforced if it was treated as a code of honour, sanctioned by the duel.

In 1838 a row broke out between George Wyndham, later Lord Leconfield, and his brother General Henry Wyndham. Illegitimate sons of Lord Egremont, both brothers were Masters of Hounds, hunting in Sussex. When George inherited Petworth in 1837 he brought his hounds from Chichester and started to hunt the country around Petworth, which had previously been hunted by Henry. The two packs clashed. A furious correspondence between the brothers ensued. The county was agog, and the gentry split into George and Henry camps. Three peers who were MFHs were asked to arbitrate. Henry argued that George was acting contrary to the laws of fox hunting. If George won, 'the title to every fox-hunting country in England would be shaken'. After some hesitation, the peers endorsed Henry's position. But George owned the land, and he took his revenge. He turned vulpicide, and killed all the foxes. Henry gave up and retired to Cockermouth, and George formed what became the Leconfield Hunt.[27]

In 1841 at a meeting of MFHs at Grillon's Club, Lord Hawke, Master of the Badsworth, proposed forming a club which all Masters of Foxhounds were to be asked to join. This came to nothing. Not until 1856, when a row blew up in Cheshire, did the MFHs form a committee to act as a tribunal, meeting at Boodle's Club.[28]

'You should endeavour to gain the good will of the farmers,' Colonel John Cook advised the potential MFH. 'If any respectable body of persons suffer from hunting, it is them.' A good show of farmers was the sign of a successful Master. Nimrod noted with approval, for instance, that as many as a hundred farmers came out with Sir

Thomas Mostyn, grand old man of the Bicester (1800–29).[29]

In the palmy days of agriculture, sixty or seventy scarlet-coated tenant farmers hunted with the Brocklesby in Lincolnshire. Asked where he got them, Lord Yarborough replied, 'Get them? I don't get them; I breed them.' Prosperous Lincolnshire farmers went hunting to make their home-bred horses, later selling them on to the shires. Yarborough always paid generously for hunt damage. He once sent for a tenant whose wheat field had been trampled and apparently ruined by the hunt. The tenant refused compensation, insisting that the trampled field had yielded a better crop than ever before.[30]

Stories like this were quoted by Colonel Cook to show that riding over wheat benefited the farmer by increasing his yield. Jorrocks knew better. Trying to convince a farmer of the advantage of squashed wheat, said he, was like arguing that 'a drove of hoxen would improve the prospects of a flower-garden by passin' a night in frolicsome diwersion'. 'Ware wheat! was the least the hunt could do.[31]

Outside Lincolnshire, very few farmers wore scarlet. Rough-riding graziers with the Quorn came out in long blue coats with gilt buttons. In the 1840s a hunting farmer typically wore a drab coat with flap pockets, cords, gaiters and double-soled boots. A gentleman farmer (who didn't own his land) wore a green cutaway with white cords and top boots.

Surtees thought that hunting farmers were a good index of agricultural prosperity. It depended very much where you were. Leicestershire graziers or farmers from Norfolk or Northumberland holding land at two or three thousand pounds a year could afford to keep hunters. They were a class apart from the slovenly, dawdling Durham smallholders Surtees so despaired of – men who couldn't afford to pay for next year's seeds, let alone afford a hunter.[32]

The poorer the farmers, the more hostile they were to hunting. Grantley Berkeley hunted carted stags near Harrow in the 1820s. The miserable farmers on the wet, undrained Harrow vale did all they could to stop Berkeley and the two hundred Londoners who came out with him. They fought riders, caught their horses and

Farmers against hunting. John Leech, 1850.

made them pay to get them back. They served notices not to trespass and extorted large sums for damage under threat of going to law. In the end hunting over Harrow vale became so expensive that Berkeley gave up.[33]

It was often argued that farmers profited from the sale of hay and oats or horses to fox hunters. But the men who took the biggest cut from hunting centres like Leamington, Coldstream or Melton weren't farmers but middlemen: grain merchants and professional horse dealers, flash confidence tricksters and sharks like Soapey Sponge who throng the pages of Surtees's novels.

Hunting tenant farmers met the gentry on terms of deference rather than equality. Allowing the hunt to draw his covert gave the farmer what Harry Hieover called the 'power to oblige', which in turn conveyed 'a justifiable feeling of independence'. 'In moving his hat to his superior he does it to show his sense of their different grades, and feels certain of the compliment being properly acknowledged: it is not the servile and forced obedience of the serf or slave, but the voluntary act of the man who knows he is liked and respected.'[34]

John Peel was a very different kind of farmer. He was a Cumberland yeoman or 'statesman', owning his own land and hunting his own hounds over today's Blencathra country from 1798 to his death in 1854. His hounds cost him four hundred pounds a year; he sold off his land bit by bit to pay for them.

Wearing a coat of 'hoddengray', home-spun Cumberland wool, down to his knees, Peel met at daybreak like a seventeenth-century fox hunter:

> D'ye ken John Peel with his coat so grey?
> D'ye ken John Peel at the break of the day? . . .
>
> From the drag to the chase, from the chase to the view,
> From the view to the death in the morning.

Sometimes on foot, sometimes riding a pony, Peel hunted both fox and hare. The afternoon was spent drinking; after a good hunt Peel sometimes drank for two days on end.[35]

Old-fashioned early-morning hunting persisted in the Yorkshire Dales, where the hounds were often trencher-fed – boarded out with individual members of the hunt, rather than living as a pack in kennels. The Bilsdale, which claimed descent from the Duke of Buckingham's hunt, functioned as a kind of primitive democracy of dalesmen. It was trencher-fed for two hundred years; it didn't have a paid huntsman, and the dalesmen who kept hounds all 'assisted' in hunting the pack.[36]

The neighbouring Cleveland Hunt was also trencher-fed. It was founded in 1817, and John Andrew, the first Master, combined hunting the hounds with a career as a smuggler (he spent two years in prison). As well as farmers, members of the hunt ranged from publicans and farriers through solicitors and a doctor from the town of Guisborough to the gentry Vansittart family.[37]

The cost of hunting the Cleveland in 1839–40 was £90 18*s*. 8*d*. The Wensleydale, another trencher-fed Dale pack, was even cheaper to run: total costs over the period 1863–70 were £153 6*s*. 6*d*., an average of £19 per year. The Master, Mr John Chapman (1833–74), was like Peel, an independent yeoman farmer. He disliked being called 'Squire', which he thought belonged to the tail of our aristocracy. He hunted three days a week, killing eighty hares and eleven foxes in a good season.[38]

At least a hundred and twenty-five packs of hounds, most of them harriers which also hunted foxes, existed in Wales between 1830 and 1885.[39] The handful of gentry packs, notably Sir Watkin Williams-Wynn's Wynnstay, wore pink coats, hunted smooth-haired hounds and met at eleven a.m. In the wild hill country, ignored by the Victorian sporting press, hunting techniques were more like John Peel's.

Nimrod's grandson, Captain Newton Wynne Apperley, hunted in the 1860s and 1870s in Cardiganshire with the Gogerddan, family pack of the Pryses, who had kept hounds since at least 1600. Apperley's hunting diary tells of getting up at two a.m. to get on to the hill by daylight to find the fox's drag. The hounds were often called out by farmers whose sheep had been killed. Mountain hunting was hard work. On 28 January 1870 Apperley went out at six a.m. on foot in a hard frost, ran a fox to ground and dug from 3.30 p.m. to 7.30, the last hour and a half by candlelight. The farmers insisted on going on until the fox was killed, as it was a sheep-killer. They knew it was the right fox because the dead sheep were marked with a broken tooth, which this fox had.

Some of the Gogerddan hounds were rough-coated Welsh hounds. Thought to descend from the Old Southern hound, which was crossed with the Northern beagle to breed the modern English foxhound, Welsh hounds were often obstinate and bad-tempered but they were persistent hunters. They needed to be independent; as Apperley's hunting mentor, Colonel Pryse, remarked: 'When the wild animal, for wild he is in this country, is killed, the merit is solely due to the hounds, as no huntsman can assist them to any great extent.'[40]

In the 1860s K. V. Horlock, MFH and journalist who wrote under the name of 'Scrutator', deplored the bad old days when 'few manufacturing towns were without a subscription pack kept up by a club of clerks and apprentices, to the great loss of their own time, injury of the surrounding country, and general demoralization of the neighbourhood'.[41] Town packs like this had often been trencher-fed. The tradesmen of Crawley in Sussex kept a foot pack of 'drowsy blue-mottled southern harriers' which was collected on hunting days by a man in hobnailed boots blowing a horn through the town.[42] The Tanatside originated in the early eighteenth century as the town pack of Oswestry. After 1795, when the Mayor, the Rev. T. R. Lloyd, became Master, it was known as the Oswestry Corporation Hunt, though it wasn't paid for by the rates.[43]

Most town packs disappeared after about 1800, failing to adjust to the new hunting. What was desirable and morally improving for the upper classes was thought bad for clerks and apprentices. Popular sports like the Stamford bull running were banned, while the noble sport of fox hunting was actively promoted. At the same time fox hunting was defended on the grounds that it was open to all.

CHAPTER THREE

Black Coats and Scarlet Women

'If you go on like this, my bloody arse
will be as red as a beef-steak.'

Skittles to her pilot with the Quorn, *c.* 1860

Thomas Assheton Smith, MFH, died at the age of eighty-two in 1858. An anonymous letter appeared in *The Times*, criticizing the dead Master for squandering his talents and encouraging others by his example to do the same. Is man's existence as a moral agent, asked the letter writer, completely satisfied by success in the field?

After hunting the Quorn (1806–16) and the Lincolnshire Burton (1816–24), Assheton Smith had returned home to Hampshire, where he created the Tedworth Hunt in densely wooded country. Felling woods and making rides, he carved a respectable country out of unhuntable woodland. Assheton Smith had an income of fifty thousand pounds a year from his slate quarries on Snowdon, which he managed himself; he also designed steam yachts, and built himself a glass-roofed winter garden six years before the Crystal Palace.

At the Tedworth Assheton Smith ruled with a rod of iron. He never tried to make himself agreeable. He hardly drank, but ate vastly. Before hunting he bolted a vast breakfast of hashed mutton. Hunting for him was a religion and a vulpicide was worse than a murderer. He terrified the ladies at breakfast one morning by dropping the newspaper with an exclamation of horror. 'What has happened?' they asked, fearing a European calamity. 'Happened?'

he groaned. 'Why, by Jove! a dog fox has been burned to death in a barn!'

Assheton Smith became a legend in his lifetime. In 1840 he took his hounds to Leicestershire and two thousand horsemen turned up at the meet. 'Is it not to him,' asked his biographer, neatly turning round the charges against his hero, 'that we owe in great measure the high tone and character of the chase, and that fox hunting has

Assheton Smith's hall table at Tedworth House

continued, in spite of our refinement and civilization, the powerful element in our social system?'[1]

The heroes of mid-century fox hunting differ strikingly from the Osbaldestons and Jack Myttons of the generation before. Pugilism, wit and 'coarseness' are decidedly out. The new men are eminent Victorians, earnest, sober and hard-working.

Lord Henry Bentinck, Master of the Burton 1842–62, was a workaholic. His passion was hound breeding. Lord Henry wasn't interested in hounds' looks but in their performance. This he measured by staying out hunting late in the afternoon until dark and, mounted on his third horse, galloping to the head of his hounds to see which were leading. He then rode home forty miles or so to Welbeck and wrote notes on the hounds; after dinner he interviewed his huntsman and told him what casts he ought to have made when he went wrong.

Lord Henry hunted six days a week. In winter he only saw

Welbeck by daylight on Sundays. Then he played catch-ball with the young hands, to see what sort of action they had. 'Lord a' mercy,' recalled his whip, 'how I cussed that ball.' Lord Henry drank little else but water and never swore. Except when hunting, he always dressed in black with a white tie. He was sometimes mistaken for a Methodist preacher. This was misleading. Jack Anstruther Thomson, a fellow Master and no slouch, once remarked, 'Six days a week is too much for any man.' 'When the church is abolished,' replied Lord Henry, 'there will be no obstacle to hunting seven.'

Lord Henry greatly admired William Goodall, huntsman at the Belvoir 1841–59. After Goodall's death, Lord Henry wrote a treatise on Goodall's Practice. Goodall was a purist. He treated his hounds like women, never bullying, deceiving or neglecting them. He never interfered with his hounds 'until they had done trying for themselves and felt the want of him.' Goodall killed about eighty foxes each season in the 1840s, and sometimes over a hundred in the 1850s.[2] He was successful partly because he lived with his hounds and knew them far better than a gentleman could. In the shires the Victorians came to insist on professional huntsmen.

Anthony Trollope, the novelist, denounced Surtees's novels for their coarseness, which he thought gave hunting a bad name. Books about hunting, said Trollope (he had Surtees in mind), too often describe 'a set of loud, ignorant men, who are always hallooing "Yoicks", and who are generally exercising the keenest of their intellects in cheating each other out of a ten-pound note in some matter of horseflesh'.[3] Surtees's satire was too cynical. Victorians wanted their morals served neat: they bought preachers of sermons like Trollope, or the moralizing novels of George Whyte-Melville.

Son of a Master of the Fife Hounds, Whyte-Melville was a gentleman of leisure, an ex-officer who hunted with the Pytchley and took up writing as a hobby. In his best-selling *Market Harborough* (1861), Mr Sawyer, a country gentleman with muscular calves, visits the shires, where he meets swells like the elegant and languid

Honourable Crasher and learns that what passes for sport at home in 'the old country' is nothing beside a 'quick thing' on a Thoroughbred in the shires. For Whyte-Melville there was all the difference in the world between the provinces and the shires.

Whyte-Melville's novels have been described as 'one long campaign against drinking and gambling'. Whyte-Melville himself was almost too nice to be true: people suspected him of humbug until they learned that he gave all his royalties to charity – and he received advances of fifteen hundred pounds on most of the twenty-eight novels he published between 1853 and 1878.[4]

A quiet, sympathetic horseman, Whyte-Melville was always impeccably turned out. He hated getting muddy out hunting, and he loathed falling. His *Riding Recollections* (1875) describes a very different style of riding to hounds from the steeplechasing mania celebrated by Nimrod. For Whyte-Melville what mattered was crossing a country – if possible taking your own line rather than following a leader or 'pilot' – without falling yourself or harming your horse. He even wrote a chapter on 'The Abuse of the Spur'. Hunters, he thought, should be Thoroughbred, and schooled to a double bridle, which became standard hunting gear.

The man who distressed or killed his horse came to be seen as a fool, not a hero. 'To ride your horse fairly, to get to the end of many runs with few falls, and to finish a season with a soundish stud' was now the aim of hunting men.[5]

Whyte-Melville was a national figure, well known outside the sporting world. He was killed in 1878 out hunting with the Beaufort, when his horse stumbled and fell in a ploughed field. In the House of Lords that night someone leaned over and whispered to Disraeli, then Prime Minister: 'Poor Whyte-Melville has been killed!' 'Dear, dear,' said Disraeli, fitting his glass into his eye. 'Pray, how did *that* happen?' 'Killed in the hunting-field!' 'How very dramatic!' the Prime Minister solemnly replied.[6]

Fourteen years before Whyte-Melville had persuaded an old friend, Jack Anstruther Thomson, to take the Pytchley. Anstruther Thomson, ex-Master of the Atherstone, was then at home hunting the Fife, where he had gone to repair his finances. No saint – he got through most of his family money, regularly deserting his wife and many children for the hunting season – Anstruther Thomson had boundless, extrovert charm. At 6′ 2 ½″ high and weighing sixteen stone, he crashed through rather than over Pytchley hedges, wearing boots like leather thigh waders, and plunged into rather than over brooks hoping to touch bottom, ‘a sight to watch rather than a

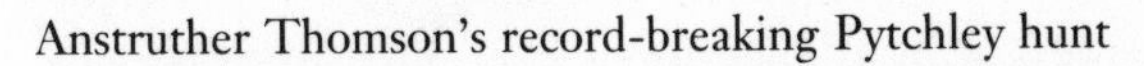
Anstruther Thomson's record-breaking Pytchley hunt

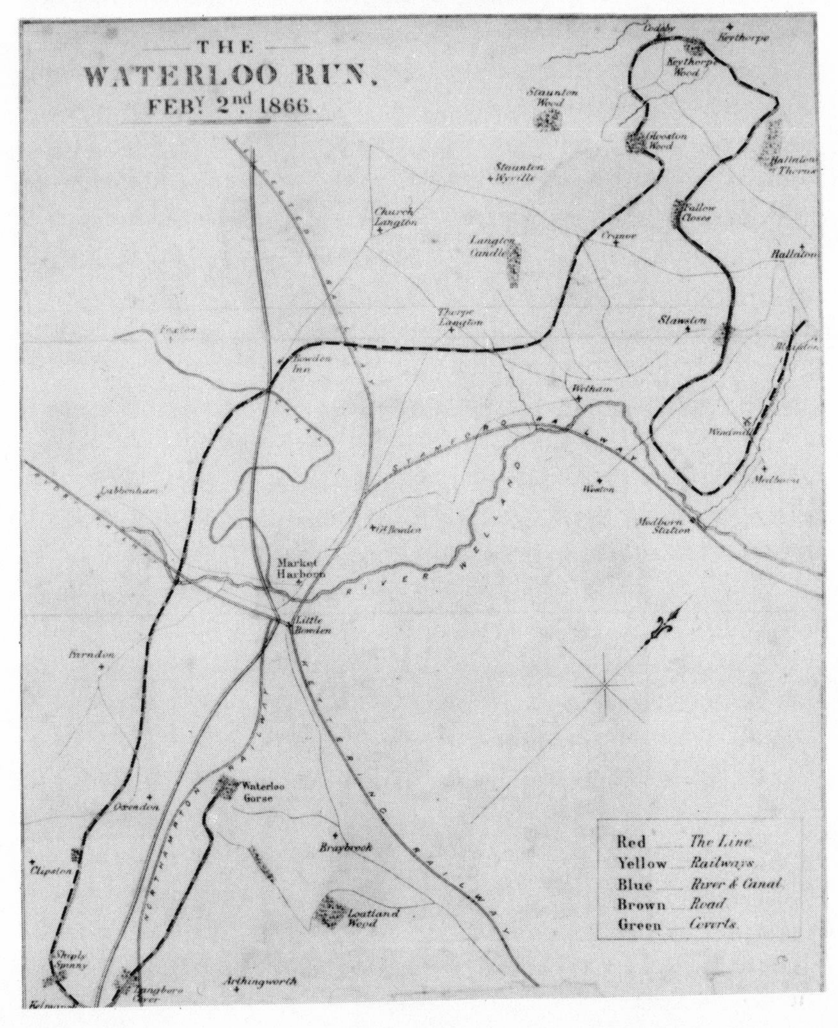

tempting example to follow'. Yet he was kind to his horses, never losing his temper.

Anstruther Thomson broke all Pytchley records with his Waterloo Run of 2 February 1866. Hounds ran eighteen miles in one hour fifty minutes without a check, crossing only three ploughed fields. Neither of his whips were up when hounds checked, and Anstruther Thomson kept his hounds on the line single-handed for another hour and three-quarters, getting through three horses and falling several times. He stopped the hounds at 5.30, riding back nineteen miles to the kennels by 10 p.m. Sitting down to dinner at 10.50, he arrived at 12.30 at the Hunt Ball at Market Harborough, where he was cheered to the echo, stayed two hours and hunted the next day.[7]

W. Bromley Davenport, Cheshire landowner and MP, hunted with the Quorn. He was short-sighted, and out hunting he wore a black coat and white stock like a parson. In Parliament, he helped found the Charity Organisation Society. A visitor to the Quorn who followed him found himself jumping fences bigger than he'd ever jumped before, arriving first at the check. 'How did *you* get here?' someone asked. 'I followed that parson,' replied the visitor, pointing at Bromley Davenport.[8]

In Bromley Davenport's 'Dream of an Old Meltonian', describing a run with the Quorn in Sir Richard Sutton's time, being brave out hunting becomes a moral obligation.

> Shun the gap of deception – the hand gate of guile;
> Oh! avoid them! for there, see the crowd is contending
> Ignoble the object – ill-mannered the throng,
> Shun the miry lane, falsehood, with turns never ending,
> Ride straight for truth's timber – no matter how strong.

Sir Charles Mordaunt, who thought Bromley Davenport the bravest short-sighted rider he'd ever seen, remembered him reining back his horse a mere five yards to charge a locked gate, taking a ghastly fall and being carried unconscious on a hurdle to the nearest farmhouse.[9]

The justification for hunting shifted. Yes, said Scrutator (Mr Horlock, MFH), hunting was open to all classes and, yes, it kept the gentry in the country. But hunting should really be defended on its own merits, above all because it promoted manliness.[10]

Manliness was partly a matter of 'nerve'. Nerve, said Whyte-Melville, was 'a moral quality, the result of education, sentiment, self-respect and certain high aspirations of the intellect'.[11] It was destroyed by drink, which engendered 'funk'. *Market Harborough* contains lurid descriptions of hunting bachelors drinking brandy and soda nightly out of 'glasses the size of stable-buckets'. When it comes to the morning their nerve has gone.

Manliness was also close to godliness. For the Muscular Christians Charles Kingsley and Thomas Hughes the two were almost interchangeable. Kingsley, who was vicar of Eversley in Hampshire, hunted with the Garth. He thought he detected a distinct improvement in fox hunters' morals. 'I remark now, that with hounds, and in fast company, I never hear an oath,' he told his friend Hughes in 1857. Kingsley thought the popularity of Hughes's book, *Tom Brown's Schooldays*, was another sign of progress. He met a very fast fellow out hunting who said: 'If I had had such a book in my boyhood, I should have been a better man now!' 'Isn't it a comfort,' Kingsley told Hughes, 'to see that fellows are in a humour to take it in?'[12]

Swearing, gambling and drunkenness became taboo. The Marquess of Hastings, Master of the Quorn 1866–8, lost £120,000 on the Derby, breakfasted on mackerel bones cooked in gin, and kept the field waiting when he had a hangover. (Once he was asked to blow his horn. 'Impossible,' he replied, 'do you want to see me sick in sight of the whole field?') This was standard Regency behaviour, but the Victorians were shocked. His tenants twice presented him with Bibles but he didn't take the hint and died at twenty-six.[13]

Lord Wilton, King of the Meltonians, was said to have orgies on a yacht, but in his case 'vice' was redeemed by Evangelicalism.

> Whilst on his switch-tailed bay, with wandering eye
> Attenuated Wilton canters by.

His character, how difficult to know
A compound of psalm tunes and Tally-ho! . . .

An amorous lover with a saintly twist,
And now a jockey, now an organist.

Wilton was a very fine horseman, famous for his 'hands' or touch on a horse's mouth, which was said to be so good that he could hold a pulling horse with a pack-thread.[14]

Earl Spencer, who became Master of the Pytchley in 1861 at twenty-six, was a bold rider with a loose seat, clinging to the back of his saddle when he jumped. Known as the Red Earl because of his long red beard, he disciplined the thrusting 'Pytchley Wild Boys', who pressed so close to hounds that Charles Payne the huntsman had taken to galloping between coverts to shake them off. (Spencer once turned round to tell off some galloping thrusters, only to find himself addressing a herd of thundering shorthorns.) Spencer rarely swore, using sarcasm instead. When knocked over jumping a fence he remarked: 'I am very much obliged to you, sir; upon my word I am. *Did you come far to do this?*'[15]

The moral reformation of the hunting field coincided with the withdrawal of the hunting clergyman.

Sporting parsons were commonplace in the early nineteenth century. When Mr Chute was Master of the Vine (1790–1842) a majority of the followers were clergymen, rich and unbeneficed, conspicuous in their black coats and white stocks.

Devon was a haven of hunting parsons. In the 1830s twenty clergymen in the diocese of Exeter kept hounds, including the great Jack Russell. When Henry Phillpotts was appointed Bishop of Exeter in 1831 he came across a pack of hounds pursued by a large number of riders in black coats. 'Alas!' said he. 'This neighbourhood must have been visited by some fearful epidemic. I never saw so many men in mourning before.' Phillpotts, a high church martinet, charged Russell with neglecting his duties and ordered him to give up his hounds. Russell took no notice, and went on hunting his own

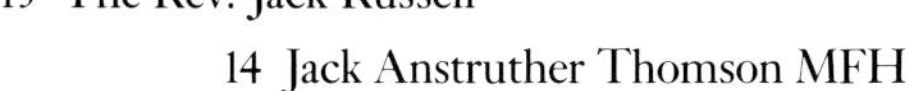

13 The Rev. Jack Russell

14 Jack Anstruther Thomson MFH

15 Hunting house party at Badminton, 1857. Jack Anstruther Thomson (*back row, fourth from left*) stands next to the Duke and Duchess of Beaufort.

16 William Goodall, Belvoir Huntsman 1843-69. Lord Henry Bentinck thought Goodall the greatest huntsman of his day.

hounds until he was seventy-six. He had his favourite hunters made into armchairs, complete with four legs and hoofs on castors. He lived on to become a national institution, famed for his powers of endurance and his breed of fox terriers.[16]

The moral revolution that swept the hunting field was also sweeping through the Church. Hunting parsons were in retreat – to the dismay of the Rev. J. Austen-Leigh, who thought they improved the moral climate of the hunting field. Bottle-nosed, black-booted sporting parsons were mourned by Surtees; exemplary parish priests, he thought they did far more towards 'promoting real religion and happiness among the people than all the cant, the mock humility, pretended abstinence and humbug that characterize the rising generation of ecclesiastics'.[17]

Parsons stopped giving out the week's meets in church. A clergyman who came out with the Belvoir in scarlet in 1857 was reprimanded by the Duke of Rutland. Bishops gave their hunting clergy a hard time, though some determined clergymen gave as good as they got. There was the story of the parson who was told off for hunting by Bishop Wilberforce of Oxford. 'Bye-the-bye,' he replied, 'I saw your lordship's name in the list of those who attended the last State ball.' 'Quite true,' said Wilberforce, 'but I assure you I am never in the same room with the dancers.' 'Just my case, my Lord, I am rarely in the same field with the hounds.'

A hunting parson was soon no more acceptable than a pregnant smoker today. 'The world at large,' wrote Anthony Trollope, 'is very prone to condemn the hunting parson . . . and, for myself, I am not prepared to say that the world is wrong.'[18]

Plenty of parsons still hunted nevertheless. In Leicestershire in the 1860s at least seven 'sporting parsons of the old school' still hunted regularly with Mr Tailby in the Billesdon or South Quorn country.

The best Leicestershire parson across country was the Rev. Cave Humfrey, the model for the sporting Parson Dove in Whyte-Melville's *Market Harborough*. 'Why, the very way he folded his neckcloth was suggestive of Newmarket; and no scarlet coat that was ever turned out by Poole looked so like hunting as that well-cut unassuming black.' In real life, Humfrey had his critics. Riding home from hunting one day, he and a companion passed a magnificent Dissenting chapel recently built in Humfrey's parish. 'I call that a monument to foxhunting!' said the companion. 'What do you mean?' asked Humfrey. 'I mean that when the parson hunts four days a week, they're pretty sure to build a Dissenting chapel.'[19]

One way round the difficulty was to hunt by accident. Parsons didn't go to the meet; they went riding for their health and just happened to fall in with the hunt. This was the kind of hunting at which Charles Kingsley excelled. Here he describes a scene which seems almost to leap out of a Victorian Christmas card:

> I had just done my work, and seen my poor, and dinner was coming on the table yesterday – just four o'clock – when the bow-wows appeared on the top of the Mount, trying my patch of gorse; so I jumped up, left the cook shrieking, and off. He wasn't there, but I knew where he was, for I keep a pretty good register of foxes (ain't they my parishioners, and parts of my flock?); and, as the poor fellows had had a blank day, they were very thankful to find themselves in five minutes going like mad. We had an hour and a half of it – scent breast high as the dew began to rise (bleak north-easter – always good weather), and if we had not crossed a second fox, should have killed him in the open; as it was we lost him after sunset, after the fiercest grind I have had this nine years, and I went back to my dinner. The old horse behaved beautifully; he is not fast, but in the enclosed woodlands he can live up to anyone and earned great honour by leaping in and out of the Loddon; only four more doing it, and one receiving a mucker.[20]

Very few women had hunted in the first half of the nineteenth century. The hard-drinking bachelor hunt clubs of the 1820s weren't suited to ladies. Young ladies were expected to sit about indoors, in blissful and refined ignorance of life below stairs, out of doors or below the waist, preserving their complexions and child-bearing faculties for their future husbands.

Surtees thought women a bore out hunting. 'A man does not like riding before them, or leaving them in the lurch; and even if they do "go along" the whole field is kept in alarm lest an accident happen.' Then there was the danger of running out of conversation in the evening if one spent the whole day with the ladies. It was possible to have too much of a good thing. Ladies should canter to the meet and home again to work up an appetite for luncheon.[21]

The side-saddle of 1820 had hardly changed since Catherine de Medici's invention of the second horn or pommel two hundred years before. It wasn't geared to the new, fast hunting: jumping at speed was almost impossible, even if you hung on to the back of the saddle.

Modesty dictated long, flowing skirts, very decorative but lethal. Breeches on a woman were voted indecent; even carrying a whip was frowned upon. Mrs Turner Farley, who hunted for fifty years with Assheton Smith, the only lady to whom he gave his hunt button, wore a compromise between decency and comfort: tight breeches beneath a white petticoat with a lace flounce. Her habits were made of fine face-cloth with a full flowing skirt, and a feather hung from the side of her hat.[22] Long skirts and voluminous petticoats could get tangled in the horse's feet while cantering, or trap the rider in the saddle if the horse fell. The mid-century fashion for sewing lead shot into the hem of the skirt to weigh it down didn't make habits any safer.

Women like Mrs Turner Farley who hunted in spite of these handicaps had to be keen. 'When women do ride,' said Surtees, 'they generally ride like the very devil,' often putting the men to shame.[23]

Wives and daughters of MFHs were expected to 'go', often wearing scarlet. In 1840 Delabere Blaine told a story of Lady Rowley, wife of Sir William Rowley MFH, who galloped up towards the end of a hard run as he was trying to wrench open a gate. 'For Heaven's sake, gentlemen, get out of the way,' she shouted, and leapt the gate, leaving the unfortunate Blaine with no alternative but to follow suit. The incident was the more shaming because Lady Rowley was 'at this time rather far advanced in her pregnancy'.[24]

The ladies in Surtees's novels can certainly 'go': Miss de Glancey in *Ask Mamma*, Angelena Blunt in *Young Tom Hall* and, best of all, Lucy Glitters, cigar-smoking ex-circus equestrienne and female whipper-in. Apart from the sympathetic Lucy, hunting women in Surtees are adventuresses and 'tuft hunters', more interested in catching men than foxes.

In the 1860s side-saddle riding was transformed by the 'leaping head', the downward-curving horn which holds the left thigh in place. It gave the rider a very secure seat, making jumping practicable. It encouraged women to ride with a long rein and light hands, interfering very little with the horse's mouth. But the side-saddle

Page from Anstruther Thomson's Hunting Diary, 1865

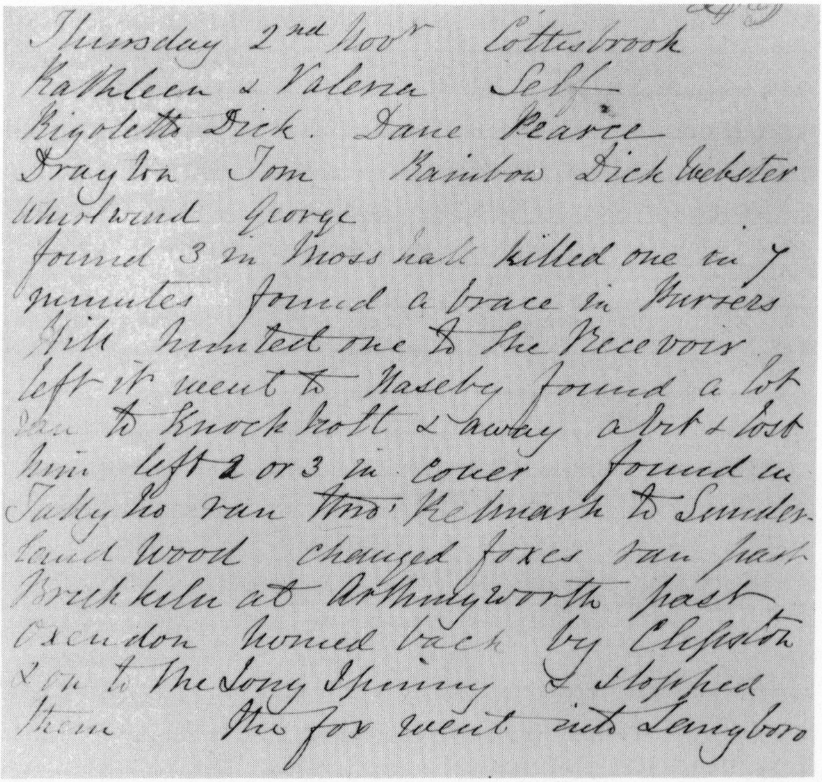
Thursday 2nd Novr Cottesbrook
Kathleen & Valeria Self
Rigoletto Dick. Dane Pearce
Drayton Tom Rainbow Dick Webster
Whirlwind George
found 3 in Moss hall killed one in 7
minutes found a brace in Pursers
Hill hunted one to the Reservoir
left it went to Naseby found a lot
ran to Knockholt & away a bit & lost
him left 2 or 3 in cover found in
Tally ho ran thro' Kelmarsh to Sunder-
land Wood changed foxes ran past
Brickkiln at Arthingworth past
Oxendon turned back by Clipston
& on to the Long Spinney & stopped
them the fox went into Langboro

rider has little leg-power and can't push the horse into its jumps; ladies tended to gallop at their fences and hope for the best. 'They are too apt,' said Whyte-Melville, 'to "chance it" at the fences, encouraging with voice and whip the haste that in the last few strides it is judicious to repress.' Frequent falls were the result.

Though women were more secure in the saddle than men, when the horse fell they were far less likely to be thrown clear. Whyte-Melville thought it twenty to one in the man's favour each time he fell, 'whereas with her the odds are all the other way, and it is almost twenty to one she must be hurt . . . It turns one sick,' he wrote, 'to think of her dainty head between a horse's hind-legs, or of those cruel pommels bruising her delicate ribs and bosom.'[25]

One of the first ladies across country in the new saddle was Skittles (Catherine Walters), some of whose adventures were incorporated by Surtees into Lucy Glitters's later career in *Mr Facey Romford's Hounds* (1865).[26] A beautiful horsewoman, Skittles started as an equestrian tart in Rotten Row, and came to hunt with the Quorn during Lord Stamford's mastership (1856–63), where she was piloted by the rough-rider Jem Mason. Skittles was a pioneer of the safety skirt – the habit skirt which came off at the waist in an emergency rather than hanging the rider from the saddle. She once left her skirt in a bullfinch, and was stamping about in a white petticoat and jack boots. The cry went up for a 'married man' to come to her rescue. 'Are you a married man?' they asked a confirmed clerical bachelor. He was not amused.

With the Quorn, Skittles caused offence to Lady Stamford, herself a gamekeeper's daughter with a murky past, who forced her husband to ban Skittles from the hunt. To which Skittles is alleged to have responded: 'I don't know what right Lady Stamford has to object to me. She's not even the head of our profession – Lady Cardigan is.' (Adeline de Horsey, second wife of the hero of Balaclava, was another equestrian courtesan who made the peerage.)

Skittles then went out with the neighbouring Billesdon, and some of the field asked Mr Tailby the Master to take his hounds home in protest. He refused, saying, 'The hunting field is open to all the world . . . I am not the censor of the morality of the hunting field.' But what really saved Skittles was her tact and warm-heartedness. 'I never hear any complaints of her conduct in the hunting field,' wrote Mr Tailby in his diary, 'or that she is in any way objectionable to the ladies who come out.'[27] Aided by her many gentleman friends, Skittles soon found her way back to the Quorn.

Most scarlet women weren't so lucky. In the 1850s and 1860s they were banished from the field. It was the duty of the MFH, wrote Scrutator in 1865, to exclude 'women who are known to belong to a certain class'. This was the more necessary because more and more *ladies* were hunting. It was an insult to the ladies present, said Scrutator, if men brought their mistresses out. The hunting field was the preserve of virtue. It was no longer a kind of demimonde where moral distinctions were blurred. No, the MFH must send the 'lost one' home immediately under threat of taking hounds home himself. The Victorians had pulled up the ladder linking vice and virtue. Vice was firmly excluded.[28]

Hunting ladies were encouraged by moral reformers because they helped raise the tone. In a sense they filled the gap left by the retreating hunting parson. They acted as moral air fresheners. The presence of ladies, thought Trollope, meant that hunting was no longer associated with 'horsiness'. 'That a man may hunt without drinking or swearing, and may possess a nag or two without any propensity to sell it or them for double their value, is now beginning to be understood. The oftener that women are seen to be "out", the more will such improved feelings prevail.'[29]

Adultery was outlawed. No MFH could hope to get away with it. Earl Fitzhardinge, Master of the Berkeley since 1807 and still a rake, brought a new mistress to Cheltenham, his hunting centre, in about 1850. She 'flaunted in the High Street and Promenade, bedizened in finery, and in the shops talked with a loud voice of the sport "our hounds were having"'. This was too much for the respectable citizens of Cheltenham, already stirred up by an Evangelical vicar. Fitzhardinge was sent to Coventry by the town; when his mistress's unfortunate husband fell off out hunting the field whipped on his horse and laughed at him, grounded and covered in mud.[30]

Then in 1856 there was the Cheshire Difficulty. The Master, Captain Arthur Mainwaring, was discovered to have written an indiscreet letter to a married woman. When he refused to resign, landowners banned him from their coverts, and the subscribers withheld the subscription. Mainwaring was forced to quit by the newly formed Masters of Foxhounds Committee of Boodle's club.[31]

The hunting lady had acquired a new image. Whyte-Melville's heroines have nothing in common with Surtees's adventuresses except a passion for hunting. Girls like Cissy Dove in *Market Harborough* are clear-skinned, wholesome and virginal.

CHAPTER FOUR

The National Sport

'If it is to retain its vigour, it must never become the privilege of any particular class. Like all other really good things it is either national or else it is nothing.'

LORD WILLOUGHBY DE BROKE, 1920

Towards the end of *Handley Cross* Jorrocks is summoned before a Commission of Lunacy. A jury of London merchants finds his passion for hunting insane and commits him to a lunatic asylum. Surtees was making a serious point. Sober businesslike merchants and lawyers, respectful of property rights and used to saving time and money, couldn't see the point of hunting. What was a hunt, after all, but a gang of men in red coats who rode about the country booted and spurred, cracking whips, committing trespass and forming a riotous assembly?

Disapproval from outsiders wasn't new. Moral reformers had mounted a campaign against rural sports around 1700, pillorying sportsmen as intemperate, extravagant and irresponsible.[1]

Outsider opposition in the 1840s was especially formidable because it was mixed up with politics. Cobden and Bright, radical spokesmen for Manchester merchants, campaigned against the Corn Laws, poured scorn on the squires and attacked hunting as an anachronistic feudal sport, out of place in the age of commerce. If the squires went on hunting, warned Cobden, they would become like the hidalgos of Madrid or the noblesse of France, a backward-looking aristocracy pushed out of politics. 'All that posterity will know of these,' thundered Bright, 'will be commemorated to them upon a marble tablet in some obscure parish church.'[2]

Fox hunters usually tried to keep sport out of politics. 'Never interfere with politics,' was Colonel Cook's advice to the MFH in 1826; 'when you turn politician, give up your hounds.'[3] But Prime Minister Robert Peel's repeal of the Corn Laws in 1846 was too much. Tory hunting squires accused Peel the textile manufacturer's son of selling out to Cobden and Bright.

Peel's downfall was engineered by Lord Henry Bentinck's brother, Lord George Bentinck. He was the last man to wear hunting pink in the House of Commons. Disraeli described him arriving at the House after hunting all day in Hampshire with Assheton Smith 'clad in a white great-coat which softened, but did not conceal, the scarlet hunting coat'.

Bentinck mobilized Tory backwoodsmen to break Peel's government. Disraeli described the fateful division, when Peel sat watching his followers troop out to vote against him. 'The Manners, the Somersets, the Bentincks, and the Lennoxes, passed before him' – the Protectionists represented the cream of hunting England.[4] Hunting, as Cobden predicted, was drawn into the Great Sulk.

Tempers flared on the hunting field. Peel's son went out hunting with the Warwickshire and asked Squire Little the name of his horse. 'Name, do you want to know his name? I call him "Apostate" after your – father.'[5]

Peel's son had an even worse time with the Atherstone. In 1851 the mob attacked a dinner of Protectionist farmers in Tamworth. Young Peel infuriated the farmers in the Atherstone country by writing to *The Times* defending the mob. Out hunting a furious farmer warned him off his land. 'If you were a gentleman I would horsewhip you,' said young Peel. 'Two can play at that,' replied the farmer. Soon afterwards Peel's son announced his retirement from hunting, and sold all his horses at Tattersall's.[6]

Free trade was coupled with the threat posed by railways. Delmé Radcliffe had nightmares about the invasion of the countryside by steam-powered shopkeepers. Railways, he wrote, were 'a monster, which will rend the vitals of those by whom it has been fostered'; they would cut up the country, 'transforming the rural soil into one vast gridiron', and make hunting impossible.[7] Lord Redesdale resigned as Master of the Heythrop in 1853 in protest at a railway coming through the country. The Warwickshire Hunt succeeded in stopping the London and North Western railway going through their fifteen-acre covert of Ladbroke Gorse.

Railways, warned Surtees, made it too easy for the gentry to leave their homes for London. Superfluous cash was sucked into the metropolis and spent on luxuries rather than subscribed to the hunt. 'The present generation,' he complained, 'do not subscribe to hounds as their fathers did.'

Delmé Radcliffe thought railways would make England like Ireland, a nation of absentee landlords. 'The evil of absenteeism, so fatal to the sister country, is already shedding its sickening hues over the fading, but not yet departed glory of old England.'[8] By draining the gentry into London, railways would desolate the countryside, warned Harry Hieover. The peasantry would return to barbarism. 'It is seeing the habits and occasionally being brought in contact with the gentleman, that tends to soften the rudeness of the boor ... [and] teaches a proper deference towards them.'[9]

Harry Hieover was wrong. By making it easier for the gentry to escape, the railways made country life more bearable. Though the gentry went to London, they always bought return tickets. Surtees became a railway enthusiast, addressing detailed 'Hints to Railway Travellers and Country Visitors to London' in 1851. Tickets, said Surtees, should be carried in the glove or waistcoat pocket, and held out on demand like a hand at cards.

Railway companies laid on hunting specials, provided horse boxes and offered special fares for fox hunters and hounds. Urban fox hunters steamed out into the countryside on local lines. 'We have become more luxurious and idle,' said Scrutator, 'preferring a first-class carriage for ourselves, and a loose-box for our hunter.'

The journalist Cornelius Tongue, who wrote as 'Cecil', compiled a Fox Hunter's Guide in 1850–1: a hunting Bradshaw, listing the meets of each hunt, and their distance from railway stations.

Jorrocks thought 'the two best covert hacks in the world' were the Euston and Great Northern Stations. Railways transformed London hunting. Cockney sportsmen no longer rode out from the City at daybreak to hunt with the Surrey. Croydon, once the Melton of the South, was engulfed in railway-led suburbia.

By 1854 railways had brought twenty-four packs of foxhounds within reach of the Londoner. South of the Thames, the Garth, Sussex, and Crawley and Horsham were within easy reach. North of the Thames, Londoners went out with the Essex or the Old Berkeley, which hunted four days a week in Betjeman's metroland: Rickmansworth, Amersham, Hemel Hempstead were all convenient stops on the Metropolitan Line.

The Midlands were also within reach. Trains from Euston took you to Bletchley, within hacking distance of meets of Mr Selby Lowndes's Whaddon Chase. In the 1880s a 7.30 train from Euston got you to Rugby by 9.34. If you caught the 7.15 from King's Cross you reached Melton Mowbray at 10.32.

Stag hunting was designed for city businessmen. The carted deer guaranteed a gallop, and staghounds met conveniently late, at 11.30 or 12.00: a 9.30 train from Euston reached Leighton Buzzard at 10.24, in good time for meets of Lord Rothschild's Staghounds. The Great Western Railway laid on a special train from Paddington on Tuesdays and Fridays for meets of the Royal Buckhounds.

Most London fox hunters kept their horses at livery where they hunted. Livery cost about thirty shillings a week; the Hunt Hotel, Leighton Buzzard, charged twenty-six shillings a week in the 1884–5 season.[10]

Midlands hunting centres on main lines boomed. Rugby was within half an hour by train of meets of the Pytchley, Warwickshire and Atherstone. Leamington, two and a half hours from London and an hour from Birmingham, combined the attractions of a spa town with access to Midlands packs like the Atherstone. The Atherstone had gone through a bad patch under Mr Applethwaite in the 1830s, when hunting men talked of 'a minute with the "tart"', which didn't sound as if long runs were the rule; it revived under the brilliant Mastership of Jack Anstruther Thomson (1847–55).[11]

The pack which really cashed in on the Leamington market was the Warwickshire North. Mr Baker the Master (1855–62) built his kennels a mile from the town, making the hunt the town's pack, and the town in exchange coughed up for it. Businessmen from Coventry also hunted with the North Warwickshire. When Cecil went out with Mr Baker in 1861, the meet was at Coventry railway station for the especial gratification of the distressed weavers, thirty to forty thousand of whom turned out to see the hunt.

Railways brought trainloads of anonymous fox hunters from the towns. Businessmen no longer needed to buy country houses in order to hunt. Cecil regularly came across Midlands fields of two to three hundred on his hunting tours in the 1860s. Out with the Meynell he could name only a handful of gentry and peers – 'who comprised the remaining two hundred or so I cannot say'.[12]

Discipline became a major problem. The Field Master, whose job it is to keep the field in order, dates from the railway era. In 1848 Surtees proposed an officer he called the Station Master, charged with marshalling the field, stopping horsemen riding over hounds at checks, and keeping them quiet when the huntsman made his cast.[13]

Hunting literature was addressed to the new audience of urban fox hunters. Authors like Harry Hieover, Delabere Blaine or Whyte-Melville wrote about the technique and etiquette of riding to hounds, rather than the 'science' of hunting hounds.

John Leech, a nervous rider who hunted with the Puckeridge, filled *Punch* with cartoons of pouting hunting maidens pounding their wimpish admirers, of fat whinging farmers and ludicrous Frenchmen whose idea of *la chasse* was killing a fox in cover without a hunt. 'One has only to glance at [*Punch*],' wrote Hippolyte Taine, who toured England in the 1860s, 'to realize how completely national is the taste for horseflesh and for dangerous riding to hounds.'[14]

*

Trollope called fox hunting the 'national sport'. Hunting, he claimed, was unique to Britain. 'We are to the manner born; till we think about it and dwell upon it the thing does not seem strange to us.' Foreigners accustomed to 'the enclosures of France, the vine and olive terraces of Tuscany, or the narrowly-watched fields of Lombardy', couldn't understand why British farmers put up with crowds of horsemen trampling fields and breaking fences.[15] Trollope even wrote a novel to prove the point: the plot of the *American Senator* turns on a visiting American's ignorance of hunting conventions, leading the American to support the case of a vulpicidal farmer.

Fox hunting had actually been established in America almost as long as it had in Britain. And in 1836 Lord Chesterfield had founded the Rome Hunt. Richard Cobden (of all people) went out with them in 1847. English whips drew the ruins of aqueducts and tombs in the Campagna in regular Melton style. Pope Pius IX later tried to ban the hunt when an Englishman was killed. To reduce the danger it was agreed that the Master should be preceded by a peasant with an axe, cutting down the obstacles in front of the field.[16]

Trollope was lucky not to be killed out hunting. He was very heavy, but always rode cheap horses. Too short-sighted to see hounds turning, or even to see the fence in front of him, he either followed someone or rode at a fence convinced he might be going into a horse pond or a gravel pit. He jumped into both. But from the time he first hunted as a young clerk with the Post Office in Ireland in the 1840s, hunting was a duty and a passion for him.

In the 1870s Trollope lived in London, and hunted three days a week, first with Mr Selby Lowndes and later with the Essex. 'Getting up at six o'clock in November to go down to Bletchley by an early train is not in itself pleasant,' he wrote (and how right he was); but at least the train got him from his house in Montagu Square to the Midlands by eleven o'clock.[17]

He often included hunting scenes in his novels. Lizzie Eustace hunts; so do Phineas Finn and Madame Max Goesler. In Lord Chiltern (*Phineas Redux*), Trollope sketched the character of the MFH who, officer-like, never gives reasons for his decisions. Unlike

Surtees or Whyte-Melville, Trollope wasn't very knowledgeable about hounds or hunting technique. Serious fox hunters dismissed his hunting scenes as superficial. Maybe they are; but in this respect, too, Trollope spoke for the urban fox hunter.

Trollope claimed hunting had an effect on the national character. It was a force for social equality. By no means all fox hunters were squires and farmers. On the contrary, said Trollope, hunting was open to all classes above the level of wage labourers. The field included 'attorneys, country bankers, doctors, apothecaries, maltsters, millers, butchers, bakers, innkeepers, auctioneers, graziers, builders, retired officers, judges home from India, barristers who take weekly holidays, stockbrokers, newspaper editors, artists, and sailors'.

Hunting made 'all classes for a time equal in the country'; out hunting aristocracy was not 'exclusive and over-bearing' as it was in the town. Trollope claimed that 'this feeling of out-of-door equality has spread from the hunting-field through all the relations of country life, creating a freedom of manner and an openness of countenance . . . which do not exist in the intercourse between man and man in cities'.[18]

Cobden reluctantly agreed, blaming the failure of his dreamed-of bourgeois revolution on the snobbishness and toadyism of the middle classes. 'We are,' he despaired, 'a servile, aristocracy-loving, lord-ridden people.'[19] Because it offered opportunities for hobnobbing with the aristocracy, hunting helped cement the middle class–aristocratic alliance which blocked his dream of a bourgeois state.

Some conservatives welcomed this alliance. T. F. Dale, a sporting journalist writing in 1899, thought hunting performed the role often attributed to Victorian public schools: educating the middle classes in aristocratic values. Hunting taught the middle classes the aristocratic virtues of dash and endurance; it formed them into a governing race capable of ruling Britain's vast empire of mixed races.[20]

Businessmen from the Potteries went out with the North Staffordshire, which contained relatively few landowners and farmers,

CHAPTER FIVE

Blood Sports and Barbarians

For I looked into its pages and I read
the book of fate,
And saw Fox Hunting abolished by an
order of the State.

W. BROMLEY DAVENPORT,
Lowesby Hall, *c.* 1853

The English National Sport consisted of people on horses chasing a pack of hounds chasing foxes to their death. Sportsmen couldn't expect to go about this unmolested.

Eighteenth-century England had been a nation of pet-lovers. Jeremy Bentham the Radical philosopher had a much-loved cat. Bentham suggested that animals might have rights like people. The question to ask, he wrote in 1789, was not 'Can they reason?' nor 'Can they talk?' but 'Can they suffer?'[1]

When Beckford's book on hunting came out in 1781, reviewers pounced on him for cruelty not to foxes but to hounds – he recommended flogging and hanging young hounds.

John Lawrence, who also argued for animal rights, was a republican admirer of the French Revolution and advocate of the rights of man. In his Philosophical Treatise on horses (1796) Lawrence accused fox hunters of cruelty, not to their prey, but to their horses. An opponent of hare hunting, he thought fox hunting was justified by the need to control a bloodthirsty predator.[2]

Lord Erskine introduced a bill outlawing cruelty to animals in

1809. He argued that man had a God-given dominion over the natural world. Animals had been created for man's use and comfort. Man's dominion was a moral trust. Animals should never be abused by man.[3]

Serious-minded sportsmen argued that hunters and foxes were among the animals created by God for the use of man. Robert Vyner MFH dedicated his book of 1841 to the fox. 'Nothing,' he wrote, 'bespeaks the presence of Divine providence more than the animals which the Almighty has destined for the use of man' – particularly animals contributing to 'those innocent amusements, which were without doubt kindly given to [man], to lighten the burden of his toils, which he is doomed to undergo in this life.'[4]

The Society for the Prevention of Cruelty to Animals came into being in 1824. The Evangelical William Wilberforce was one of the founders. Its purpose was to extend and enforce the revolution in morals begun by Richard Martin's Act of 1822. Martin's Act, the first piece of anti-cruelty legislation, banned cruel practices to cattle. It was widened in 1835 to outlaw bull and bear baiting, cock fighting and dog fighting.

'No one who condemns bull baiting can consistently defend fox hunting,' declared the pro-bull-baiting William Windham in a debate in the Commons in 1800. Consistently or not, Parliament banned bull baiting while tolerating fox hunting. 'A man of ten thousand a year may worry a fox as much as he pleases,' said Sidney Smith in 1809, 'and a poor labourer is carried before a magistrate for paying sixpence to see an exhibition of courage between a dog and a bear!'[5]

The SPCA derived much of its income from the subscriptions of fox-hunting country gentlemen. Queen Victoria was a patron of the SPCA, and in 1840 she gave it the royal prefix. She was hardly going to lend her name to a society which campaigned against the field sports Albert so enjoyed. There was a rather awkward moment at the RSPCA general meeting in 1840, when someone from the floor asked 'the nobles and gentlemen on the platform, who declaimed upon the subject of cruelty to animals, how many hunters they had in their stables, and how many had been ridden to death for their amusement?'[6]

Evangelicals campaigning against cruelty to animals weren't usually concerned with animals *as such*. They were far more interested in the morals of the wrongdoers. Over eighty per cent of the prosecutions filed by the RSPCA under Martin's Act were against the working classes. The commonest offences were against horses and cattle, abused by butchers and drovers.

The RSPCA modelled their organization of inspectors on the recently formed police. For Evangelicals cruelty to animals was like trouser-clad women dragging trucks on hands and knees in mines, or factory women doping their new-born babies and going to work with milk streaming from their breasts. It was symptomatic of terrifying social chaos.[7]

Fox hunting in Victorian England certainly didn't threaten the social order. Nor did it depend on witnessing an animal's suffering and death. What mattered was how you went during the hunt, not whether you saw the kill.

In George III's reign Beckford had insisted, 'Sport is but a secondary consideration with a true fox hunter:- The first is, *the killing of the fox*.' Elaborate funeral rituals underlined the point. The dead fox was treed (hung from the bough of a tree) while the hounds bayed the death song around it. The hero of the day was the rider first up at the death, who was rewarded with the fox's brush – even though he hadn't been near hounds during the entire hunt. Sporting artists like Rowlandson did a thriving trade in pictures of the death, the huntsman holding the fox's carcase aloft above the baying pack.

But by the 1820s priorities had definitely changed. The new hunting mystique stressed *sport* – meaning doing something needless for its own sake – rather than killing. Unlike foreigners and particularly Frenchmen, the British enjoyed hunting for its own sake. Fox hunters guffawed at the story told by Colonel Cook in 1826, and often repeated, of the Frenchman out hunting in England. When the fox was killed by mobbing without a hunt, the Frenchman rode up to the Master, took off his hat and exclaimed, 'Sir! I congratulate you on catching him so soon and with so little trouble.'[8]

Other nations might hunt, declared Harry Hieover in 1853, but always for an animal's flesh or fur. 'Render his flesh distasteful to them, his horn, sinews or skin valueless, and these ostensibly eager and daring hunters would no more follow the chase than would a Leicestershire man run by himself on foot a couple of miles across country, or along the road from Kirby gate.'[9]

The elaborate funerary rites were dropped. Queen Victoria's vulpine subjects were given very simple funerals. The huntsman seized the dead fox, cut off the brush, pads and mask, held up the carcase before the baying pack and threw it to them to eat. Commercially successful Victorian painters sold pictures of horses and hounds at the meet, not at the death. Landseer revelled in death and filled his canvasses with tongue-lolling carcases. But he painted stags, not fox hunting. The death of the fox, wrote Trollope, was no more visible than the death of 'the wasp that is crushed without remorse by a lady's fan'.[10]

In 1839 the Society for the Prevention of Cruelty to Animals gave a prize to an essay attacking hunting as a cruel sport. The author, the Rev. John Styles, was known in Evangelical circles for his tract on the immoral and anti-Christian tendency of the stage. Grantley Berkeley MFH wrote a reply, dismissing Styles's essay as ridiculous and exposing his alleged ignorance of natural history. The judge of the essay competition admitted privately to Berkeley that Styles's essay won a prize because, of all the rubbish submitted, it was the least ridiculous.[11]

Styles's essay caused quite a flutter because it was one of the first publications to charge hunting of cruelty to *foxes*. In 1869 the historian Edward Freeman took time off from his five-volume *History of the Norman Conquest* to write an article for the *Fortnightly* on 'The Morality of Field Sports'.

Fox hunting, argued Freeman, wasn't concerned with getting rid of a verminous animal as quickly as possible. Far from it – hunting caused *needless* suffering in the interests of 'sport'.

Freeman wasn't against killing as such. He wasn't vegetarian.

Killing in defence of life or property or for food he allowed. Shooting was legitimate. But hunting couldn't be defended, because it was needless.

The fact that foxes were artificially preserved in order to be hunted underlined his point. Fox hunters, said Freeman, had somehow succeeded in getting away with an upside-down morality: the life of the fox was sacred, except when it was killed with the prescribed amount of wanton cruelty. Hence the absurdity that any farmer who shot a fox for the legitimate purpose of protecting his hens was damned.[12]

Freeman was answered in the *Fortnightly* by Trollope. But Trollope didn't really face up to the question of needless cruelty. Instead he stressed the social advantages of hunting. 'A minimum of suffering,' he said, 'produces a maximum of recreation.' One fox keeps a hundred horsemen happy.[13]

A Liberal and a good hater, Freeman was unimpressed. He enjoyed stopping the hunt riding over his land in Somerset. 'Drove out hunters,' he would write in his diary. Relations didn't improve when a member of the hunt, taking him for a gardener, offered him five shillings as a sweetener. Freeman thought fox hunters overbearing and intolerant. To call hunting manly was absurd: it was cowardly to torture a defenceless animal and foolhardy to risk one's neck for no adequate cause.

Nor was Freeman a lover of foxes. To the objection that without hunting foxes would become extinct he replied, with remorseless consistency, that he didn't care. 'The fox, like the wolf, is a beast which must and ought to die out before the advance of civilization.'[14]

Freeman's indifference to the fate of the fox species was the weak point in his argument. It cost him the support of the growing number of conservationists. The historian Macaulay in 1848 had welcomed the extermination of wolves, wild cats and fen eagles as a sign of the progress of civilization.[15] By the 1870s, however, the disappearance of rare breeds was causing concern. The Association for the Protection of British Birds was founded in 1870, and the first statutes protecting wild birds from egg collectors followed soon after.

Baily's Magazine claimed in 1885 that hunting was responsible for the survival of the fox species. The taboo on vulpicide had provided the kind of protection for the fox that people now called for in relation to rare breeds. It was all very well for Freeman to argue that 'directly you preserve a thing from being killed by anyone, in order that it may be despatched by a privileged few, you abolish sport, and set up cruelty and artificiality in its place'. In fact, the *artificiality* of hunting had kept foxes alive.[16]

In 1884 a National Sports Protection and Defence Association was formed. It changed its name in 1885 to the Field Sports Protection and Encouragement Association, broadening the defence to include hunting, shooting, fishing, racing and coursing.[17]

Sportsmen were becoming more cruelty-conscious. In 1875 'Brooksby', alias Captain Pennell-Elmhirst, Leicestershire correspondent to the *Field*, registered 'A Protest Against Butchery' – meaning digging foxes from their earths when they went to ground and bolting them for the hounds to kill. It was, he wrote, 'a crying enormity, a disgrace to a noble sport, and should be put down as rigorously as vivisection'.[18]

Charles Darwin noted in 1875 that 'the gentlemen of England are humane, so long as their own sports are not considered, which entail a hundred- or thousand-fold more suffering than the experiments of physiologists'. Vivisection was far worse, in the eyes of sportsmen, than bolting a fox when it ran to ground. Insistence on killing above ground merely underlined Freeman's point that hunting was an artificial sport, not a necessary form of pest control. To dig or not to dig was, as the Duke of Beaufort put it in the *Badminton Library*, the decision of the Master alone. 'Let us hope that he may usually incline to mercy.'[19]

Henry Salt founded the Humanitarian League in 1891. A vegetarian, a freethinker and a socialist, Salt was far more extreme than Freeman. He also had more of a sense of humour. He excelled at baiting heavy-footed sporting journalists.

Salt popularized the term 'blood sports' – in itself a stroke of genius. One of his most effective tactics was to condemn field sportsmen out of their own mouths. He published a collection of extracts from the *Eton College Chronicle* reporting the Eton Beagles: a record of '"blooded" hounds and of the hare "broken up", or crawling "dead-beat", "absolutely stiff", "so done that she could not stand"'. He then wrote a spoof article called 'The Beagler Boy' purporting to save a gallant school sport from extinction which was accepted by *Horse and Hound* and the rest of the sporting press, neatly demonstrating that 'there is nothing too fatuous to be seriously accepted as argument by the upholders of blood sports'.

Salt caricatured fox hunters. They were unthinking savages who baptized their children in the blood of a butchered fox. They believed that man was a superior being, separated by a deep gulf from inferior animals. This, claimed Salt, was a primitive Christian myth, exploded by recent science. In particular, he cited Darwin.

Darwin's theory of evolution had put paid to the old idea of a man-centred universe. 'Man in his arrogance thinks himself a great work worthy the interposition of a deity,' Darwin had written in 1838. 'More humble and I believe truer to consider him created from animals.' This was the message of *The Origin of Species*. If man was indeed descended from animals, he could hardly claim that they were created by God for his enjoyment. In Darwin's world animals shared human feelings such as pleasure and pain; they could also reason and communicate.

Darwin himself was a keen shot as a boy and at Cambridge. He gave up shooting because he thought it cruel, but nevertheless supported vivisection. Henry Salt, however, thought *all* killing was wrong. He believed in animal rights. Universal kinship was a biological fact: killing animals was murder.

Faced with the argument that without hunting foxes would not exist, Salt would reply, rather grandly, that 'existence cannot be compared with non-existence'. In other words, we can know whether existence is good or bad, but of non-existence we know nothing.[20]

The Humanitarian League's most successful campaign was directed against the Royal Buckhounds.

Since the eighteenth century the Buckhounds had hunted the

carted stag, which came to the meet in a van and was caught again at the end of the day. The Rev. J. Stratton, a Wokingham parson, worked tirelessly for ten years, walking miles to collect evidence of cruelty.

Stratton and the Humanitarian League argued that stag hunting was a 'spurious sport' involving entirely unnecessary suffering. Stratton wasn't consistent. He saw nothing wrong with fox hunting, for instance. And spurious sports were in some ways less cruel than necessary sports. During Lord Ribblesdale's three seasons as Master (1892–5), a total of five stags were killed, all by accident.

There were other reasons for abolishing the Buckhounds. 'Wire in Middlesex, the villa in Berks, the pheasant in Bucks,' ruined their country. Worse, they were a political liability. When Mr Gladstone appointed Lord Ribblesdale Master (the appointment was political) it was already plain that the Buckhounds were 'under sentence of dissolution, if not of death . . . They cost the taxpayer money – hunting the carted deer was cruel – hunting generally was associated with Tory principles.' The end was only delayed by Queen Victoria's fondness for having a Master of the Buckhounds at court (though according to Salt she privately considered the Buckhounds cruel). When Victoria died the Buckhounds were scrapped, ostensibly on grounds of economy.[21]

The humanitarians of the 1890s were easily caricatured. Lady Florence Dixie, who wrote a pamphlet on 'The Horrors of Sport', kept a menagerie of wild animals which she exercised along the banks of the Thames. Once her jaguar escaped, causing consternation to the citizens of Windsor. Sister of the Marquess of Queensberry, who denounced Oscar Wilde, she and her husband Sir Alexander Dixie were known as Sir Always and Lady Sometimes Tipsy. An extreme feminist, she cut her hair like a boy, wore a knee-length tartan kilt (this was 1880) and, worse, rode cross-saddle.

Florence Dixie was in her youth a 'female Nimrod', one of the 'cream of the cream in the shire of the shires'. So was Lady Warwick, Edward VII's Darling Daisy, who also converted to anti-blood sports. It was easy to sneer; as an old Melton hand remarked, 'When women lose their nerve, they find out as hunting is cruel.'[22]

Salt was the kind of figure fox hunters loved to laugh at. He lived the simple life in Surrey, tearing up his Eton gown (he'd been a master) to tie up his creepers; he refused to employ servants and his friends were vegetarians and left-wing intellectuals like Shaw and Edward Carpenter.

Humanitarians were portrayed in the sporting press as morbid and effeminate sentimentalists, sedentary and physically feeble city-dwellers. Gluttons for lobster and turtle soup, their opposition to the manly sports was symptomatic of a decline in national vigour.[23] Bromley Davenport had nightmares about the future, when oysters would be eaten with anaesthetics, and stoats charged with murdering rabbits, when the National Sport would be banned and the nation itself undermined by a channel tunnel.[24]

Uneasy at the charge of cruelty, fox hunters took refuge in ridicule. They responded in much the same way to radical politicians like John Bright and Joseph Chamberlain, who attacked the aristocracy and their monopoly of landownership.

In his Unauthorized Programme of 1885 Chamberlain called for the division of land into smallholdings – the creation of an English peasantry. 'Black-coated, gamp-umbrellaed, cotton-gloved' political missionaries came out from Birmingham to Warwickshire villages to convert the agricultural labourer.[25]

Chamberlain's Three Acres and a Cow would mean more grass and many more fences to jump, said Brooksby. The Duke of Beaufort dreaded the day when, the land being given over to Chamberlain and wantonness, the gun not the horn would sound the death knell of the fox.[26]

John Bright's speeches could hardly be taken seriously. After all, this was 'the same Mr John Bright who, in speaking about the Pytchley Hounds, disclosed his abysmal ignorance by actually pronouncing the word P*i*tchley, instead of P*y*tchley'. A Radical was merely 'a person whose motto was "Down with everything", and who certainly could not be trusted with a gun in his hand within shooting distance of a fox'.[27]

In fact Radicals stood for a new and potent ideal of the countryside: a compound of Wordsworth's religion of nature and Henry

George's ideas about common ownership of land. What moral right had idle, pink-faced peers to lay claim to vast tracts of England? Radicals believed God gave the land to the people. Aristocrats must pay ransom.

It was a romantic ideal with a lot to offer the urban educated classes: it made the countryside immediately accessible. They campaigned for footpaths, went fell walking and Alpine climbing. Alone and on foot they communed with nature.

The sporting classes were dimly aware of Henry George, whose ideas inspired Chamberlain's Three Acres and a Cow. *Baily's* thought a Henry-George-inspired system of smallholdings the biggest threat to sport in England.[28] But Henry George prompted little heart-searching among aristocrats. England could show few landed introverts to rival Tolstoy who, in *Resurrection* (1899), agonized over landownership and the moral basis of aristocracy.

Surtees rarely describes the countryside through which his characters hunt. And the leather-bound, gilt-edged hunting journals assiduously kept by Victorian sportsmen contain bald records of wind and weather, coverts drawn and runs taken by long-dead foxes. The same phrases – 'a good/poor day's sport', 'not a good scenting day', 'sorry to say I lamed my gee' – occur again and again.

George Wyndham, Tory politician and lover of Romance literature, didn't go hunting to admire the view. For him a good day's hunting was 'a romance, comparable only to fighting' – jumping fences, keeping in front (he was very competitive), getting wet and tired. The exhilaration was physical, not spiritual.

> I have steeped my body and brain in wind and rain. For I hunted five days last week and four this and always got soaked to the skin. But in the ancient riding-coat, leather breeches and boots this does a man good. He becomes a hot, happy, soppy, sweaty animal with a blithe heart and no mind. So I cannot write lucid prose or undulating verse.[29]

'I know many sportsmen,' wrote George Bernard Shaw, 'and none of them are ferocious. I know several humanitarians; and they are all ferocious.' Hunting society in the 1880s and 1890s was Barbarian in Matthew Arnold's sense of the word: aristocratic, pleasure-loving, good-looking and kind. Barbarians had a 'peculiar serenity', which Arnold put down to 'their never having had any ideas to trouble them'.[30]

The king of the Barbarians was Henry Chaplin, Squire of Blankney in Lincolnshire. Chaplin succeeded Lord Henry Bentinck as Master of the Burton, which he hunted on and off from 1865 to 1885. He worshipped Lord Henry, whom he thought 'the best brain ever given to the breeding of hounds'. When Chaplin became MP for Lincolnshire in 1868 Lord Henry helped him write his speeches.

But Chaplin was very different from the workaholic water-drinking Lord Henry. 'All my life,' said Chaplin, 'I have lived according to a very simple plan. It is always to have what I like, when I like it, and as much of it as I like.' He was a tremendous trencherman and weighed eighteen stone. When he rang the bell in his dining room the butler brought in not one but six bottles of claret. He hunted the Burton six days a week at his own expense. After late night sittings in the House of Commons he hired special trains to take him from King's Cross straight to the meet next morning. 'When our Harry is broke,' said the Duke of Westminster, 'all the crowned heads of Europe ought to give him a hundred thousand pounds a year in order that he may show them how to spend their money.' He did go broke, and in 1892 Blankney was sold.[31]

Barbarians started young. 'We are not allowed to hunt more than three times a week,' said one of the children of the eighth Duke of Beaufort, 'till we are five years old.'[32]

Education wasn't allowed to get in the way of hunting. Hunting was rife among Oxford undergraduates. The University statute forbidding undergraduates to keep horses without leave from the College authorities was widely overlooked; in any case, you could get round it by hiring a horse. On hunting mornings at least twenty hired hacks jostled in Oriel Lane, waiting for Christ Church undergraduates to finish their breakfasts. In 1852 the Royal Commission on the University had condemned the extravagance – a day's hunting cost at least four guineas – and called on College authorities to keep much stricter control over undergraduate hunting.

Walter Long, who was at Christ Church in the 1870s, thought the authorities were still far too lax. Undergraduates came out in force with the Bicester, the Heythrop, the South Oxfordshire, and the Old Berkshire – dubbed the Old Blasphemers on account of the language of Mr Tom Duffield, Master 1867–75. The University Drag went out two afternoons a week. Mr Bayne, the Senior Censor at Christ Church, offered no objection to undergraduates hunting, so long as their parents didn't disapprove. He drew the line only at fox hunters' anti-social habit of summoning their servants in college by blowing a hunting horn. At New College in the 1890s the undergraduate Willoughby de Broke was advised by a well-meaning don to work for honours. 'It would mean reading seven hours a day . . . How was I to hunt if I were to read seven hours a day? . . . I could hunt once a week perhaps, in the afternoon, he said.'[33] That was enough. Willoughby took a third at the second attempt.

Barbarians worshipped the horse. Chaplin spent hours in the stables, fed his horses with carrots and sugar and talked to them like dogs. In the Commons he drew horses on his Order Paper. The stable, wrote the Duke of Beaufort, 'should be as sweet and clean as a house'. The Sunday morning ritual of stable inspection, offering up scrubbed carrots from a silver tray, was an act of worship. When the art critic Vernon Lee visited Jack Anstruther Thomson's family at Charleton in Fife in the 1880s, she found them 'entirely equestrian. I use that word because *horsy* would convey a wrong impression. You would as soon have called a centaur *horsy*.'[34]

Barbarians called each other nicknames and played practical jokes. Mid-Victorian earnestness dissolved in laughter. Surtees, whose coarseness had embarrassed his contemporaries, was adored by Barbarians. Chaplin read Jorrocks aloud to his children, tears of laughter streaming down his face.

Mid-Victorian Melton had been sober and dull. Hunting was work, and late nights were taboo. When Lady Augusta (Gussy) Fane first went there in 1879 there was no gambling or dancing. There wasn't even a hunt ball, only 'a tiresome dance called the Primrose Ball, a semi-political affair got up by Sir Herbert Praed'. Soon Melton was all horseplay and jokes. For her thirtieth birthday in 1890 Lady Augusta held a midnight steeplechase. The heroes of the Quorn raced across country with ladies' nightdresses over their scarlet coats. The next Sunday the parson took as his text, 'Have no fellowship with the works of darkness but rather reprove them,' and the whole congregation fell about laughing.[35]

Bay Middleton, who looked after the Empress of Austria out hunting, had a 'playful habit' of seizing the tails of people's evening coats after dinner and ripping them up the back. Captain Chicken Hartopp filled a ticket collector's hat with water and clapped it on the man's head. 'He were always doing things like that on people who couldn't retaliate for a joke, and then throw them a sovereign.'[36]

Margot Tennant crashed over the fences, determined to be in front at all costs, her admirers pursuing her like a string of onions. Peter Flower, who wanted to marry her, once rode a horse upstairs, where it got stuck and was then renamed First Flight. After 1894 when Margot married the politician Henry Asquith, she sold her horses and stopped hunting. Gussy Fane asked her the name of a useful-looking hunter she was selling. 'I call him Henry,' said Margot, 'he is so safe!'

The older generation tut-tutted. The Earl of Wilton was shocked (the old hypocrite) by two young ladies he saw hunting. 'I am sure you will not believe it,' said he, 'but I saw the ankle of one of those young ladies; and, besides that, I heard one of them call her horse a *devil*, and distinctly heard the other say "*damn*"!'[37]

More ladies were certainly hunting, going better than ever before. In about 1875 an improved type of safety skirt was introduced. Known as the 'fig leaf', it was tailored rather than voluminous and, like the earlier safety skirt, came off at the waist in an emergency. Mrs Arthur, one of the first ladies to wear it in the shires, was cut by her female neighbours for riding in such indecent clothes.

In 1884 the Quorn made the safety skirt compulsory: 'better a live lady in breeches than a dead one in a habit'. Lady Augusta first met Madame de Clermont Tonnerre out with the Quorn sitting on the grass without her skirt, which had been left on her saddle when she took a toss over a fence. She was far too modest to think of running after her horse in breeches and boots.[38]

The first female MFH after Lady Salisbury and the Hatfield Hunt in the eighteenth century was Victoria, Countess of Yarborough at the Brocklesby, 1875–80. Lady Yarborough was a skilled and tactful Field Master. Like Lady Salisbury, however, she only got the job because her husband died young. She was regent for her son, who took over the hereditary mastership when he came of age.

Lady Yarborough wore 'just a suspicion of scarlet waistcoat' beneath her 'dainty habit'. In 1886 the leading ladies of the Cottesmore turned up at the opening meet in red coats. The gentlemen were not amused.

After dining at Windsor, Daisy Warwick (who usually hunted with the Quorn) left before breakfast clad in her red coat to go hunting with the Essex. Queen Victoria watched her go, peeping behind her bedroom curtains. 'How fast,' said the Queen. 'How very fast.'[39]

There were limits, however. Ladies didn't ride cross-saddle. Mrs Nannie O'Donoghue, who wrote a manual called *Ladies on Horseback*, explained why not. 'There are many things which a woman may legitimately admire, and, in a certain sense, *envy*, yet with which she should never desire to meddle, unless she is ambitious to merge her womanhood in the semblance of man. The cross-saddle is one of these.'[40]

Margot Tennant hunted in Leicestershire but her friends were intellectual politicians and well-read women belonging to the clique known as the 'Souls'. Most Barbarians would have felt distinctly uncomfortable at Souls' parties. 'I do not see why I should break my neck because a dog chooses to run after a nasty smell,' said Arthur Balfour, fastidious leader of the Souls and Tory Prime Minister.

Sir William Eden, father of Anthony Eden, was Master of the South Durham, and a watercolourist and would-be aesthete. He gave up the hounds in 1890 because of the people. 'They never used their eyes . . . Whisky and water, horses and cigars, and occasionally a pretty woman, that was their taste, that was the sum-total of their education.'[41]

Aesthetes defined themselves in antithesis to fox hunting. Osbert Sitwell did a brilliant demolition job on his rich Londesborough cousins, their lives dedicated to 'fun' and killing. 'They were scarcely at ease out of the saddle, and tended to fall asleep if they entered a house and sat down for a moment, except at meals.'[42]

Gerald Berners, aesthete and composer who had his fantail pigeons dyed bright colours, was brought up in Shropshire in the 1890s by his mother, a conventional Victorian and dedicated fox hunter. As a boy he hated riding, which frightened him. He was forced to do it because it was manly. 'Why,' he wondered, 'was it considered unmanly to cling to the pommels of the saddle when it seemed such a very obvious thing to do? Why was it manly to kill a rook or a rabbit or even to ill-treat a cat, while it was unmanly to hurt a dog or a horse, who were much larger and apparently better able to retaliate? Why were music and painting held to be effeminate when all the greatest composers and musicians had been men?'[43]

CHAPTER SIX

'Ware Wire

'I think, sir, that Sir Robert Peel's Bill will stop you, though I cannot.'

LORD SOUTHAMPTON, MFH, to a farmer overriding hounds, *c.* 1845

The fun at Melton in the 1880s was exceptional. Elsewhere there was despondency. Farmers struggled to survive agricultural depression. Hunt subscriptions shrank. Morale was low.

The agricultural depression of 1878–96 came at the end of a long mid-century boom. Since the 1850s high farm prices had encouraged farmers to plough up more and more land for wheat. Hunts in the corn countries in the east were mainly plough. In the 1850s Bromley Davenport had nightmares of hunting with the York and Ainsty (Nasty) 'in a land devoid of grass'.

Trollope described the successful hunting farmer in the 1860s. 'He wears a thick black coat, dark brown breeches, and top boots, very white in colour, or of a very dark mahogany.' Then there was the ostentatious farmer who subscribed ten or fifteen guineas and wore a scarlet coat.[1] Robert George Luxton, head of the Luxton clan of North Devon farmers, farmed two thousand acres, borrowing heavily to invest in drainage and new machinery. Through the influence of his crony and patron, the Earl of Portsmouth, he became Master of the Eggesford Hunt 1854–8.[2]

Farmers formed the bulk of the county electorate, and hunting could sometimes swing elections. In Shropshire at the 1868 election

17 The Brocklesby Rallywood, 1843. Eighty years later his genes were in half the hounds of England.

18 Victoria Lady Yarborough, Master of the Brocklesby 1875-80

19 Will Dale, Huntsman of the Brocklesby, in 1895, the year the famous dog pack was sold

20 Hunting scene by Randolph Caldecott, *c.* 1880

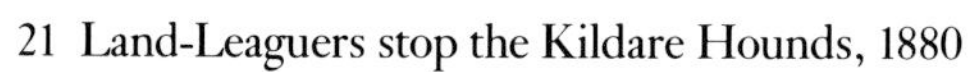

21 Land-Leaguers stop the Kildare Hounds, 1880

the Tory candidate, Colonel Corbett, had difficulty making himself heard. When he said he'd been chairman of the County Lunatic Asylum he was laughed down. Then he announced he'd been Master of the Shropshire hounds in the 1850s. 'This in a county where every little farmer or landowner was a true sportsman, was universally accepted as an amply sufficient proof of capacity for political affairs.' The Colonel was cheered, and won the seat.[3]

Where farmers didn't hunt, relations weren't quite so cordial. In Leicestershire, fences of thick, rusty, relatively jumpable wire appeared in about 1860. Even worse was the farmers' new practice of running a single concealed strand of wire through a hedge to make it stockproof. In 1863 the Duke of Rutland pronounced that unless the wire was done away with, there would be no more hunting in Leicestershire. On behalf of the farmers, E. A. Paget retorted that fox hunters must pay if they wanted farmers to take down wire fences. A compromise emerged. Farmers took down wire at their own expense, receiving hidden payments from hunts in the form of contributions to the prize money at agricultural shows.[4]

Cattle in Northamptonshire were struck by rinderpest or plague in 1865–6. Farmers hung up slaughtered carcases in the fields and put up double gates to keep out the hunt, for they were convinced the plague was spread by hounds crossing their land. They petitioned Jack Anstruther Thomson, Master of the Pytchley, to stop hunting. Next day Anstruther Thomson received a petition with three times as many signatures asking him to go on. He went on hunting.[5]

In the 1868 election the two North Leicestershire parliamentary seats were contested by two Conservatives – Lord John Manners, son of the Duke of Rutland, and S. W. Clowes, ex-Master of the Quorn (1863–6) and son-in-law of Sir Richard Sutton – and a local independent, C. H. Frewen. Frewen campaigned against the Rutland influence and fox hunting. He wrote a letter to the local paper, attacking Clowes, who owned no land in the county: 'If he should be dragged in to represent the fox-hunting interest, why then, the sooner fox hunting is put an end to the better, – and if he should happen to get in some of us intend to do our best to clear the country of foxes, *which can very easily be done*.' In the event,

Frewen's letter contributed to his own defeat. But his outburst had been prompted by the strength of anti-hunting feeling among Leicestershire farmers.[6]

Many hunting farmers prospered into the 1870s. Hunting fitted naturally into their lives, and they didn't even need to dress the part. Mr Fairbrother, a Warwickshire tenant of Lord Willoughby de Broke, wore a pork pie hat out hunting, with a stick-up collar, blue bird's eye cravat, dark-grey tail coat with side pockets and large flaps, cotton corduroy breeches in 'gosling green', and boots with brown tops. 'On non-hunting days the upper man was the same, but the top boots would be replaced by pigskin leggings and walking boots with no toe-caps.'[7]

John Calvertt took the lease on two farms on Crown estates near Shipton-under-Wychwood, Oxfordshire in 1875. Calvertt hunted with the Heythrop. The Master, Albert Brassey (1873–1918), rich son of the railway contractor, lavished hospitality on the hunt. At the opening meet Brassey provided lunch of champagne and pheasant for a thousand guests. Calvertt brought his wife and daughters to see the local nobs. The hunt found a fox on Calvertt's farm, and Brassey gave him the brush. At the hunt steeplechase in

Inchdairnie, *24th Aug.*, 1886.

A Dinner, given by Captain Cheape, to the Keepers, &c., West Fife Hunt, will take place in the City Arms Hotel, Dunfermline, on the 30th inst., at which your presence is desired.

Dinner at 2-30 o'clock.

Yours truly,

A Reply will oblige. JIM BEAVAN.

the spring Brassey dispensed champagne to farmers. In the summer Calvertt visited Badminton Kennels, was shown round the house and rode the Marquis of Worcester's polo pony.

Hunting was a genuine social ladder in the countryside, linking farmers like Calvertt to their superiors in a way that the Conservative Association or Primrose League couldn't equal. Not that Calvertt was altogether deferential. He approved of his neighbour, Mr Marmaduke Matthews, who once stopped the Duke of Beaufort riding over his wheat. The Duke asked if he knew who he was. 'Yes,' said Matthews, 'you are the Duke of Beaufort – I am "Duke" Matthews!'

The summer of 1878 was wet, and 1879 was worse. In his diary, Calvertt railed at 'the most cursed, ruinous weather on record' – no sun, rain for weeks on end, the land too wet to work and then a worthless harvest. The agricultural depression had begun. Calvertt watched his neighbours resign their leases, selling their stock at knock-down prices. News reached him of ruined farmers committing suicide. Further east it was even wetter. From Lincolnshire he heard news of 'floods, wrecks and ruin'. In the winter of 1879–80 Calvertt hunted over a country ruined by wet. Sheep and cattle were dying in the fields, killed by rot caused by grazing the sodden land.

More wet summers followed. Bankrupt neighbours sold up, and land prices tumbled as farms glutted the market. Calvertt recorded floods and sprouting barley in 1880, wet harvests in 1881 and 1882, and in 1883 a harvest of 'Muck and Water' – 'to the ruin of thousands who cultivate the soil of Cloudy, Foggy, Blighty, Rainy, *uncertain*, Old England!!!'[8]

Cheap wheat from the North American prairies flooded the English market, and prices crashed. When the Corn Laws were repealed in 1846 Assheton Smith had remarked, 'So much the better, for then I shall hunt over a grass country.' After 1878 his words came true. In Britain as a whole the area under wheat shrank from 3.6 million acres in 1874 to a low of 1.4 million in 1895. By 1900 the York and Ainsty was at least half grass. In the Warwickshire grass increased to two-thirds of the country.[9]

John Calvertt went on hunting throughout the depression, and Mr Brassey still held his champagne meets. In 1882–3 Calvertt hunted thirty-two days, and in 1883–4 he had a record fifty-two days' hunting. But Calvertt got generous rent remissions from the Crown. Not all farmers were so lucky.

In March 1876 and again in January 1878 Elizabeth, Empress of Austria came to Northamptonshire to hunt with Lord Spencer and the Pytchley. She carried a black fan out hunting to protect herself from onlookers, she drank beer and – worse – she smoked (when she lit a cigar after dinner at Althorp Lady Spencer sent for a screen). Rather mad and probably anorexic, she often kept the field waiting for an hour while she dressed, an elaborate procedure which involved her being sewn first into a chamois body stocking and then into her habit. Skilfully piloted by Bay Middleton, she could certainly go. 'Remember,' she told Bay, 'I do not mind the falls, but I will not scratch my face.'[10]

Royalty brought fields of five hundred. Fifteen thousand spectators turned up at the meet on the Empress's last day. After a bad patch in the early seventies, the Pytchley boomed. Will Goodall, huntsman 1874–95, was a legend in his lifetime and 'White-collared Will and his galloping whips' showed sport the hunt has probably never equalled since.

There were tensions, however. Herbert Langham, who was Master 1878–90, ran out of cash. One day in 1885 the whip turned up at the meet on a bicycle with the news that the bailiffs wouldn't let the hunt horses out of the kennels. In 1890 Spencer came to the rescue, becoming Master for the third and last time. So vast were the Pytchley fields that Spencer tried meeting at 9.30, which wasn't a success. He also tried to prevent Brooksby from reporting the Pytchley in the *Field*.

Brooksby had moved from Leicestershire to Northamptonshire in 1886, and his hunting reports added to the Pytchley's unwelcome popularity. He eventually agreed to stop naming names because it encouraged jealous riding; but the *Field* insisted that their readers wanted to read Brooksby's Pytchley reports and, whether Spencer liked it or not, they must continue to supply that want.[11]

Side-saddle elegance. By Kit Anstruther Thomson.

Too many people came out with the Belvoir too. Agricultural depression weakened and destroyed the squires and farmers who had formerly made up the backbone of the hunt. In the great Goodall's day, the Belvoir had been a family party of the Duke of Rutland. In the 1870s it became 'a mob in scarlet and black, not unwilling to ride over both hounds and huntsmen'. T. F. Dale, who wrote a history of the Belvoir in 1899, blamed the middle classes. Hunting in the 1870s, he wrote, 'was making long strides towards the great and dangerous popularity which it enjoys today. The immense diffusion of wealth, the decrease of the Puritan prejudice against sport, tended to set the middle classes free from the limits which public opinion had imposed upon them.'[12]

The Quorn was over-subscribed as well. The depression coincided with the reign of Tom Firr, who was huntsman 1872–97. Firr was a very able man, often compared to Mr Gladstone. People said he could have become prime minister; fortunately he was brought up as a huntsman instead.

Hunting the Quorn hounds five days a week with three or four hundred horsemen riding hell-for-leather at your back was not an easy job. Rather than allow hounds to worry out the fox's line, Leicestershire huntsmen were forced to use the galloping cast: they lifted hounds when they checked and cast forward at a gallop.

Firr was the greatest of the galloping huntsmen. He had nerves of steel. He went with the best, and the best of the Meltonians were very good indeed. Brooksby thought you couldn't claim to have 'seen' a run unless you'd been in the same field with hounds all the way. When asked where he'd seen a certain run, Captain Greene replied: 'I saw it in my usual place, seventeen yards to the right of Ruby.' (Ruby was a hound.) When Firr couldn't out-ride the thrusters, he outwitted them. Once he was pestered by a man from the Belvoir who overrode hounds and interfered when he was casting. Firr rode up to a fearful place with a huge ditch on the far side and made his horse refuse. 'I wish Captain Smith were out,' he said loudly. 'He'd give me a lead.' Whereupon the thruster rode at the fence and disappeared.[13]

The huge fields which flocked to the Quorn to follow Firr were not popular with farmers, struggling to survive the slump. Leicestershire farmers' resentment boiled over in 1878, when Mr Tailby announced his resignation as Master of the Billesdon Hunt.

The Billesdon had originally formed part of the Quorn, and had been hunted by Mr Tailby since 1856. In 1878 Mr Coupland, Master of the Quorn and a Liverpool shipper, claimed the country back for the Quorn. Most of the Billesdon landowners supported him. Another shipping magnate, Sir Bache Cunard – husband of Emerald, famous society hostess – made an offer to hunt Tailby's country separately. He was backed by the Billesdon farmers, who didn't want the Quorn hordes trampling over their land.

The dispute was referred to the MFHs' committee at Boodle's club, which ruled in favour of Coupland. But the Billesdon farmers had never heard of Boodle's – 'What we wanted to know was, who Mr Boodle were anyway?' – and didn't see what it had to do with them. A meeting of farmers resolved to stick to Sir Bache, warning Coupland that if he hunted over their land they would sue for trespass. When Sir Bache refused to stand down, there was nothing that Boodle's could do. 'Can Boodle's,' asked *Baily's*, 'stop actions for trespass? Can they cause wire to be removed, and prevent gates being locked and the hinges turned down? Can they prevent foxes being killed?'

Lord Spencer intervened with a compromise. Cunard was to hunt the country, while recognizing the Quorn's legal right. In 1919, on the death of Cunard's successor, Mr Fernie, the Quorn finally relinquished its claim to what then became the Fernie country.[14]

This wasn't a clearcut victory for the Billesdon farmers over their landlords, as most of the landowners came round to the Cunard party. But the farmers had certainly won a share in the right to decide who hunted the country. As occupiers of the land they held the whip hand, whatever Boodle's might say. Depression strengthened them, as no landlord now dared evict.

One consequence of the Billesdon row was that the MFHs moved out of Boodle's club. In 1881 the Duke of Beaufort invited all MFHs to form an association, the Masters of Foxhounds Association, to settle hunt disputes.[15]

Wire reappeared during the 1880s. Ugly barbed wire fences also sprang up. This time the wire was here to stay.

Wire fencing cost about a tenth as much as timber, mainly because it required less labour. There was no wire in the Heythrop, a country of great estates. In the Pytchley the big estates were wire-free, but barbed wire went up where there were no big landowners.[16] The dairy farms and small fields of the North Staffordshire were riddled with it, even on tenanted land. Here

PAST AND PRESENT. A SPORTSMAN'S DIARY OF 1837.

"Glorious Run to-day! Drew Tod's Gorse—a sure find. Took a splendid Line. Big Jumping, mostly Timber."

PAST AND PRESENT. A SPORTSMAN'S DIARY OF 1897.

"Wretched Sport! No Foxes in the Country! Found late in the Afternoon at Tod's Gorse, but could not ride a Yard for Wire. Several Hounds Killed on the Railway."

G. D. Armour on wire, *Punch*, 1897

very few farmers hunted and the wire question wasn't brought home to them in the way it would have been if they themselves had hunted.

The Duke of Sutherland, Master of the North Staffordshire 1874–1903, set up a wire fund to build hunt jumps in wire fences and imported skilled fencers from Warwickshire to show his tenants how to strengthen their fences without wire. Other hunts took similar measures, setting up wire committees and paying for wire to be taken down. In the shires, wire was taken down in the autumn, after the autumn fatstock sales. Permanent wire was signposted.[17]

But wire had a deeper meaning. Putting up wire was, for a farmer, like voting Liberal or shooting foxes. It was a gesture of dissent. Non-interference with the landlord's sport was part of the deal for the tenant farmer. As A. G. Street recalled of pre-1914 Wiltshire, 'With a hunting landlord an absence of wire was more important than good farming.'[18]

Deference was breaking down. When young Sir Francis Burdett had a fall over a stake-and-bound fence and got tangled up with his horse in a ditch, Mr Brewitt, a farmer, came to the rescue. Alfred Brocklehurst, a Quorn wag, jumped the fence and yelled back over his shoulder: 'You d–d fool, Brewitt; you d–d fool; why don't you sit on his head till he lowers your rent!' In fact, Burdett wasn't Brewitt's landlord, which rather spoils the story.[19]

Where old tenants were forced to quit by the depression, their successors were less likely to put up with the hunt. In Essex wheat farmers on heavy clay were clobbered by falling prices, and old tenants, many of whom had been on the same estate for generations, were replaced by 'foreigners' – Scotsmen, Cornishmen and 'the deuce knows who', cattle ranchers and dairy farmers. Before the 1880s tenants who didn't like the hunt 'dare not object, or their farm would soon change tenants, and they would have looked in vain for another farm'. The new tenants were much less easily cowed.[20]

Brooksby thought the pageantry of hunting helped keep farmers sweet. The hunt was a spectacle, a blaze of scarlet, shining leather and burnished steel. 'The brave gentlemen who take part in the pageant are really performing a public duty, viz., popularizing fox hunting and maintaining its place in public esteem. What would the Lord Mayor be, but for the Lord Mayor's show?' Brooksby had been to India, and seen how the Raj used glitter and show to maintain its popularity. Red coats did much the same for fox hunting. 'A farmer will take pride and pleasure in the passage of the gay throng across his land, who would give anything but a cordial welcome to a bevy of riders merely loosing off their superfluous energy over his farm.'[21]

Since the early nineteenth century hunts had compensated farmers for fox damage to poultry and hunt damage to crops. Farmers' claims shot up in the 1880s. Poultry claims, wrote the Duke of Beaufort in 1885, 'increase and multiply to a degree that threatens to make it one of the heaviest items in the expense of keeping hounds'. The Meynell, for instance, which was paying out £150–200 a year on poultry claims between 1873 and 1883, paid over £500 most years between 1885 and 1900. Worried by rising damage claims, late-nineteenth-century authorities stoutly denied that foxes killed lambs – in contrast with many of today's fox hunters, who insist that lamb-eating foxes would be wiped out by farmers in the absence of hunting.[22]

Fewer farmers hunted. Hunting men worried about a shortage of foxes. Lord Willoughby de Broke, Master of the Warwickshire, recalled in 1884 how a hundred farmers used to come out on Fridays, riding horses worth £150 or £200. Bad times meant that fewer farmers joined them now, and this he thought accounted for the recent 'dearth of foxes, more or less'. Farmers, he always said, were the best fox preservers.[23]

Angry farmers at the Meynell threatened to wipe out foxes. In 1888 Reginald Chandos-Pole resigned as Master when the committee tried to stop him hunting six days a week, two with his private pack. Chandos-Pole was popular with the farmers, and they were furious when he went. 'It's all up with the Meynell now,' said one, 'they'll get no more foxes.' Under the new Master, Hamar Bass, a brewer, the Meynell went into sharp decline. Bass, though rich, was lazy and often ill. The shortage of foxes combined with wire to cause a fall-off of subscribers. A meeting largely attended by tenant farmers attempted to get rid of Bass in 1897. Bass finally went in 1898, complaining bitterly about how badly he had been treated. A dirge of 1901, allegedly sung by an old farmer, blamed the Meynell's decline squarely on the farmers.

> Oh, what were trampled pastures, and, oh, what was damaged wheat,
> Or poultry raised and fattened which the foxes used to eat?
> Oh what were broken fences, what was stock all gone astray?
> Great houses bought our produce then, great stables used our hay.
> Who mangled them and tangled them and rolled them in the mire?
> *We* killed the goose with golden eggs with thrice-accursed wire.[24]

In fact, fox numbers seem to have risen during the depression years. Hunt records show a marked upward trend in foxes killed. At the Warwickshire, the average number of foxes killed or run to ground per day out in the 1870s was around 0.8. In 1888–9 the daily average shot up to 1.5, and held up at around 1.2 through the 1890s. At the North Staffordshire the pattern was much the same. Poor sport was recorded in the 1870s, when the daily average of foxes killed or run to ground was 0.8 or below. In the 1880s sport picked up. The daily average peaked at 1.4 in 1883–4, remaining high through the 1890s. The Brocklesby, which did well in the 1870s, killing or running to ground a daily average of between 1.0 and 1.2 foxes, did even better after 1884. The average daily score climbed steadily for a decade, peaking in 1894–5 with 1.6 foxes killed or run to ground.

The increase in kills is probably symptomatic of a rising fox population. The depression brought changes in habitat which probably had more influence on fox numbers than the guns of angry farmers. More wasteland and rough grazing coupled with overgrown hedges provided ideal conditions for animals like field voles, sustaining a bigger fox population.[25]

Young Farmer No. 1. "WELL, CHARLEY—HAVE YOU HAD MUCH SHOOTING LATELY?"
Young Farmer No. 2. "WHY, NO; WHAT WITH HUNTING TWO DAYS A WEEK AND COURSING TWO DAYS, I DON'T GET MUCH TIME TO GO OUT WITH A GUN."

John Leech mocks farmers' complaints of agricultural distress, 1851

The 1880 Ground Game Act, giving tenant farmers the right to shoot hares and rabbits, made little difference to fox numbers. Hunting men's fears that tenant farmers would extinguish rabbits, thus emptying the fox's larder, proved exaggerated. As *Baily's* pointed out in 1881, foxes flourished in the Midlands where rabbits and hares were anyway rare. Thinning swollen rabbit and hare populations sometimes improved hunts' sport. In Warwickshire, for example, before the Ground Game Act hounds had to hunt through hundreds of hares; after 1880 far fewer hares crossed the fox's scent.[26]

Farmers emerged as a force to be reckoned with. Gentry-dominated hunt committees could not count on farmers' automatic support. It wasn't enough for the Master to give champagne at the opening meet and say good morning. Farmers wanted *control* over their hunting.

Farmers rebelled against gentry dominance at the Vale of the White Horse in 1884. C. A. R. Hoare, the Master, was a rich banker and, according to Lord Bathurst, 'a big, stout, rather common-looking man'. The farmers loved him. He asked them to shooting parties with lots to eat and drink, gave them Christmas presents and horses, lent them money, and – the sin no real fox hunter could forgive – often stopped in the middle of a day's hunting to eat a large lunch at a farmhouse, leaving the hounds to wait outside. As if this wasn't enough, he had an affair – and a child – with the underage Beatrice Sumner, daughter of the Master of the Cotswold, which ended up in the courts.

In January 1884 the committee sacked him. But the committee only spoke for the landowners. Six hundred farmers signed a petition protesting against Hoare's dismissal. When Hoare turned up at a meet at Ashton Keynes the farmers welcomed him with flags and banners reading 'Mr Hoare the Farmers' Friend', and 'Hoare for ever'. The landowners decided to split the country. Led by Lord Bathurst, they formed a separate hunt, the VWH (Cirencester), leaving Hoare to carry on with his farmer friends in the Cricklade side of the country.[27]

Farmers versus landowners was also the line-up in the notorious row which blew up at the Puckeridge in 1885. The Puckeridge was a three-day-a-week country in Hertfordshire and Essex with a lot of plough which was badly hit by the depression. Its Masters were usually bankers or brewers. The Calvert family who founded it in 1755 were brewers, and since 1800 it had been dominated by the wealthy Quaker cousinhood of Hanburys, Barclays and Hoares. (Why do Quakers feature so prominently as MFHs?) During the Mastership of the banker Robert Gosling subscriptions dwindled from £1,500 in 1875 to about £750 in 1885, when Gosling handed in his resignation. The landowners in the Monday and Wednesday countries persuaded him to stay and hunt their side of the country only. The farmers in the Saturday country, most of whom were related to the powerful Sworder family, declared Home Rule, putting up their own MFH, a bookmaker's son called Swindell.

In 1889 the dispute was referred to the Masters of Foxhounds Association, who ruled that the Puckeridge should be hunted as one country. A general meeting in 1890 elected Swindell Master of the whole country. This time the Goslingites seceded and went on hunting their side of the country as the Herts and Essex Hunt. War broke out. Swindellites galloped through woods the Herts and Essex was about to draw, blowing their horns. Anticipating the tactics of the antis of today, they made elaborate plans to lure the Herts and Essex on a drag into a wood, where they put up trip wires behind the jumps and hid, waiting to hit the Herts and Essex on the head as they fell off (the plan misfired). In 1893 the MFHA again intervened, and in 1894 the country was reunited under an outsider, Lancelot Bathurst.[28]

Splitting a country was one way of meeting farmers' grievances. It reduced the size of fields, increased the number of meets, cut overheads and subscriptions, and often gave farmers more power. The Billesdon, Puckeridge and VWH rows were noisy instances of a process that was going on throughout the depression. Between 1875 and 1893 the number of hunts increased from 135 to 158.[29] On the Borders, for instance, two new packs were carved out of outlying parts of the Duke of Buccleuch's country: the Jedforest in 1884 and Mr Scott Plummer's, later the Lauderdale, in 1889. Both were far more closely rooted to the farming community than the Duke's, which was the lairds' pack.

Hunts looked for ways of conciliating farmers. Subscribers were strongly encouraged to buy their horses' oats and hay locally. 'I will go so far to say this,' declared Lord Willoughby de Broke at a hunt dinner in 1890, 'that a man who goes out hunting and feeds his horses on that abominable mixture called foreign oats – (laughter) – or beds them on that nasty stuff called moss litter – (laughter) – should not be allowed to go hunting at all. (Hear, hear.)'[30]

Hunt custom had never really helped farmers before, and it probably didn't help much now. Lord Lonsdale, Master of the Quorn 1893–8, did all he could to make subscribers buy their oats and hay directly from farmers. But it didn't work. Grooms wanted the best for their horses, which wasn't necessarily what farmers had to sell; owners wanted credit and farmers wanted cash. Neither could do without the middlemen, and corn merchants stayed in business. In Rutland the agreement to buy locally was upset by the grooms. They demanded a shilling a quarter commission on local farmers' oats, and if this was refused they condemned the forage as bad.[31]

A far more effective device was the cap, a daily tariff levied on non-subscribers. It raised funds for poultry or damage and at the same time limited numbers. In 1892 the Whaddon Chase charged one guinea. In 1893 all the Leicestershire hunts agreed to charge a cap of two pounds. Other hunts limited fields by charging a minimum subscription, ranging from three to thirty guineas.[32]

Capping has been seen as a symbolic parting of the ways: the abandonment of the ideal that hunting was open to all.[33] In practice, however, hunting had never been open to all. The need for a horse excluded all but the richer elements in rural society. And farmers were always exempt from capping or subscriptions. In so far as capping was designed to help farmers it was a move towards a more democratic organization.

Capping was linked to another change: the admission of farmers to hunt committees. The Warwickshire, for instance, set up a committee mainly composed of farmers to deal with poultry and damage claims in 1888. Four farmers joined the Quorn Committee in 1887, and four joined the Meynell in 1889.[34]

Hunting was no longer dominated by the gentry; the farmers were beginning to come into their own. In 1890 H. P. Cobb, the Radical MP for Warwickshire, attacked the hunt in a bid for farmers' votes. Sir Charles Mordaunt effectively ridiculed his claims at a hunt dinner.

> Gentlemen, we have heard something about there being discontent with regard to the most popular and unselfish amusement in England. The fact is, gentlemen, that what little discontent we have heard of has been invented and manufactured by Mr Cobb to suit

his own purposes, which are entirely unconnected with hunting. (A Voice: 'No politics,' and applause.) . . . Mr Cobb . . . has shown lamentable ignorance – ('No') – of this noble science – (Hear, hear) – a science far too noble for him to grasp, and much too great. (A Voice: 'Cobb's no fox hunter.') If Mr Cobb wants to understand something more about hunting, let him come out with the Warwickshire hounds. (Hear, hear and laughter.) But I am reminded that it is very possible that he cannot ride. (Laughter.)[35]

22 Meet of the Hambledon Hounds, 1892.

23 Lord Willoughby de Broke, Master of the Warwickshire 1876-1900, with Archibald. By Trood.

24 Kate and Mary Russell, daughters of Lord de Clifford, dressed for hunting, 1853

25 'A rum one to follow, a bad one to beat'

CHAPTER SEVEN

The Image of War

'Idiotically elated, I stood there with
my finger in my right ear and emitted
a series of "view-halloas" (a gesture
which ought to win the approval of
people who still regard war as a form
of outdoor sport). Having thus failed
to commit suicide, I proceeded to
occupy the trench – that is to say I
sat down on the firestep, very much out
of breath, and hoped to God the
Germans wouldn't come back again.'

SIEGFRIED SASSOON,
Memoirs of an Infantry Officer, 1930

Fox hunters claimed that the Battle of Waterloo was won on the hunting fields of Leicestershire. Hunting was regarded as training for war, and anyone who opposed it was downright unpatriotic.

The Duke of Wellington hunted a lot, and he was worshipped by fox hunters. Delmé Radcliffe drooled over the Iron Duke, calling him a 'demi-god'. Wellington was said to prefer fox hunters as aides-de-camp because they knew how to ride straight across a country and 'were equally willing to charge a big place or an enemy'. The Duke apparently thought Assheton Smith would have made one of the best cavalry officers in Europe. In fact, Assheton Smith was doing something far more important – throughout Wellington's wars he was busy hunting the Quorn. '*Voici, messieurs, le premier chasseur d'Angleterre*,' said Napoleon when introduced to Assheton Smith in 1802 during the Peace of Amiens.

In the Peninsula campaign Wellington kept his own hounds and often hunted them himself. One of his ADCs was the fox-hunting Marquess of Worcester, later seventh Duke of Beaufort MFH. In Charles Lever's novel *Charles O'Malley* (1840) the Iron Duke is portrayed taking part in a Peninsula fox hunt – stern, masterful and preoccupied. In real life, at Salamanca in 1812, Wellington was riding along the line with his staff under fire from French artillery when two greyhounds appeared in pursuit of a hare. Wellington instantly gave the view halloa and went after them at full speed, to the amazement of the foreign generals. Nor did he stop until he saw the hare killed, when he returned and resumed command as if nothing had happened. One day in October 1813 when Wellington wasn't out, hounds killed a fox in the enemy's position, and the French opened fire. Only when the Master advanced with a white handkerchief was he allowed to bring hounds back.[1]

Thomas Graham, Lord Lynedoch, who commanded a division in the Peninsula and hunted with Wellington's hounds, had hunted in Leicestershire since the 1770s. Dubbed by Napoleon 'that daring old man', he often said he would never have been the soldier he was had he not been a hunting man. As a boy Lynedoch was so keen that he overrode hounds and himself caught the fox in a river.[2]

Linking hunting with patriotism was a clever move, calculated to wrongfoot opponents of the sport. Dating from the French wars of the 1790s, the argument gained in strength with Wellington's victories. Wellington's officers went out hunting in regimental scarlet coats. After Waterloo the scarlet coat stuck, underlining the military connection. The case for hunting as training for war stuck too. Without hunting, wrote Colonel Cook in 1826, the breed of men would degenerate. 'Instead of the hardy, open-hearted, liberal-minded Briton, you would see nothing but an effeminate race, that would only meet once a year at a *grande battue*, to shoot a tame pheasant, and that would be the only *chasse* in England.'[3]

In fact, where hunting was concerned the Iron Duke was a tin god. Wellington killed only one fox in Portugal in 1812–13 and that was by mobbing. At home, he was a generous subscriber. 'Get what you can,' he told his local pack, 'and put my name down for the difference.' The difference turned out to be six hundred pounds a year, and he paid up cheerfully for several years. But Wellington was a poor horseman. 'I have never seen a man with less idea of riding,' wrote Surtees. 'His seat is unsightly in the extreme, and few men get more falls in the course of a year.' A Frenchman took a house near Strathfieldsaye solely in order to follow 'Old Waterloo' out hunting with the Garth and watch him 'rolling in the dust', which he often did three or four times a day.[4]

Out hunting Wellington wore kerseymere breeches, a lilac silk waistcoat and Wellington boots. He hunted, he explained, from *noblesse oblige*. 'Nothing the people of this country like so much,' he said, 'as to see their great men take part in their amusements. The aristocracy will commit a great error if they ever fail to mix freely with their neighbours.'[5]

Hunting was arguably a liability to the cavalry. Wellington's cavalry officers treated military campaigns as an extension of the fox hunting they did all winter. The results were sometimes disastrous. As the French cavalry commander Excelmann remarked: 'Your horses are the finest in the world, and your men ride better than any continental soldiers. The great deficiency is in your officers who . . . seem to be impressed by the conviction that [they] can dash or ride over everything; as if the art of war were precisely the same as that of fox hunting.'

Wellington ticked off his cavalry officers in the Peninsula for their trick of galloping at everything and never manoeuvring before the enemy. The superiority of English horses he thought made matters worse; the French cavalry was more manageable precisely because their horses were poorer than the English hunters.[6]

At Waterloo the galloping cavalry almost brought it off. Spear-headed by the Scots Greys, the Union Brigade charged and smashed the advancing French infantry. Charge! Charge! Hurrah! Hurrah! The trouble was that once their blood was up they were unstoppable. Ignoring the rally, the Union Brigade galloped on into the main French position where they were surrounded. Of the three hundred men of the Scots Greys, twenty-one survived.

This was the 'cavalry spirit': the sort of courage that led men on horses to perform desperate deeds against overwhelming odds. Its peacetime equivalent was what hunting men called 'pluck' or 'nerve'; the physical experience that came closest to a cavalry charge, combining extremes of fear and exhilaration, was a quick burst over fences in Leicestershire.

The cavalry spirit was instilled by a code of honour. The honour of officers in 1815 has been described as 'a matter of comportment, of exposure to risk, of acceptance of death if it should come, of private satisfaction – if it should not – of having fulfilled an unwritten code'.[7] The code of Nimrod's Melton was very similar. It was all about exposure to risk, being seen to be brave, speaking the language and wearing the dandified uniform of a caste. Duelling was part of the code; it depended on the gentleman's understanding that the man in the wrong owned up before the fight. Grantley Berkeley thought that duelling ceased to work when the diffusion of wealth made it impossible to tell who was a gentleman.[8]

Meltonians and officers observed the same etiquette. Getting off one's horse in the field was *mal vu* both at war and in Leicestershire; and if anyone fell, either in battle or when hounds were running, one should never stop to help.

Hunting was, in the poet Somerville's words, the 'Image of war without its guilt'; it was Jorrocks who added, 'only five-and-twenty per cent of its danger', a gloss Meltonians would have disputed. For them danger was the essence of the sport, though honour dictated that they should never mention it. Apart from Jorrocks, 'funkers' are usually cads in nineteenth-century literature; and we hear very little about fear or injuries caused by falls.

The cavalry spirit triumphed in 1854 at Balaclava. In obedience to a disastrously confused order conveyed by Captain Nolan, Lord Cardigan led the charge of the Light Brigade straight into the main

Russian guns. Of 673 men only 195 survived the ride – first at a steady trot, and eventually at a gallop – into the jaws of death. '*C'est magnifique mais ce n'est pas la guerre*,' said the French General Bosquet.

In fact it was more like Leicestershire. Lord George Paget, who led the second line of the Light Brigade, cigar clamped in mouth throughout (the charge was over in ten minutes) compared it to 'the finest run in Leicestershire'.

When Cardigan reached the Russian guns, he was 'thrown out', and lost his brigade; making no attempt to rally his troops, he rode back alone. On entering the Russian battery one officer 'brought his hand to the ear, and delivered a shrill "Tally-ho!" which hurled forward the hitherto well-ordered line and broke it up into racing horsemen'. Another officer owed his life to his Irish hunter which was schooled to jump big when he halloaed; when he gave the command it jumped on top of a Russian who was about to put a lance through him.[9]

Kinglake, the Liberal historian of the Crimean, blamed Balaclava on the system which gave commands to elderly aristocratic fools like Cardigan who had no experience of war. Cardigan had bought his way up from cornet to lieutenant colonel in six years at a cost of twenty-eight thousand pounds. The charge of the Light Brigade was also an indictment of aristocratic Melton where Cardigan was king. 'If hunting be the image of war,' wrote Whyte-Melville, 'Lord Cardigan certainly loved the reflection next to the reality.'[10]

In Nimrod's *Quarterly* article on the Quorn it is Cardigan who gallops on past the man who falls in the ditch, for 'the pace is too good to afford help'. A bully and a martinet, Cardigan fought duels and adored uniforms. He married as his second wife his mistress Adeline de Horsey, with whom he'd lived adulterously for eighteen months. This was the woman Skittles called 'the head of our profession'. Cardigan had a strong sense of caste. 'Here goes the last of the Brudenells!' he declared as he set off into the jaws of death. He could be appalling towards his tenants. Charles Payne, the Pytchley huntsman, was about to dig out a fox on Deene when Cardigan ordered him to stop.

> 'He has been killing some lambs, my Lord, and the tenants are complaining.'
>
> 'Tenants complaining?' shouted Cardigan. 'The land is mine, the woods are mine, and the tenants are mine; and my tenants are not in the habit of complaining about anything.'[11]

Officers could always get leave to hunt. Jack Anstruther Thomson once dined with Cardigan's 11th Hussars at Hounslow. There was a hard frost, but at three a.m. it began to rain. They all wanted to hunt, but as a watering parade was ordered for the morning they needed to ask Cardigan for leave. Thomson knocked on Cardigan's door and found him sitting on the side of his bed with his hair standing on end, not having slept a wink since they had made such a row all night. But all he said was, 'Certainly, certainly.'

Anstruther Thomson was so dedicated to hunting that when in 1841 his regiment was ordered to India he exchanged into the 13th Light Dragoons; he hunted various regimental packs – his colonel whipped in to him at Ipswich and he had two colonels as whips in Ireland – selling out to take the Atherstone in 1847.[12]

After the Crimean War, cavalry officers still spent most of the winter hunting. Hunting, said the cavalry, taught officers their most important skills: 'a quick eye, knowledge of the country, the requisite dash, and *going straight*'. In the 1870s officers who could afford it could hunt six days a week – as long as they went round their stables once during the day. In addition, cavalry officers took two and a half months' leave, usually during the hunting season.[13]

When regiments went to Ireland they bought hounds locally. In 1864, for example, the 10th Royal Hussars bought a pack in Cashel. With Captain the Hon. C. C. Molyneux as huntsman, Lord Valentia and Private Thomas Bowkett as whips, capital sport was shown in the Golden Valley of Tipperary. There were hounds with the cavalry in the Crimea, where the jackals gave better runs than the foxes.

Foxhounds were sent out to regiments stationed in India, where they hunted jackal. Pig-sticking in India didn't use hounds, but it was organized on the same lines as English fox hunting. The country of a 'Tent Club' was sacrosanct, the role of the club's honorary secretary very similar to the MFH at home. In Shanghai they hunted paper.[14]

At home, officers were usually welcomed out hunting. The 10th Hussars, stationed in Yorkshire in 1861, found that 'there was nothing more calculated to endear them to the people of that county than by turning out in large numbers at all the meets of the foxhounds'. In 1855 the seventeen-year-old Evelyn Wood went out with Mr Farquharson's hounds with his arm in a sling, having been wounded in the Crimea. His horse ran away with him, charged into the hounds and killed three. Farquharson used strong language. But when someone explained about the Crimea, Farquharson dropped the limp hound he was examining, bowed and took off his hat to Wood with the words, 'As many times, sir, as ever you like.'[15]

Critics argued that the army hunted too much. In the 1870s admirers of Prussia and supporters of Cardwell's Liberal army reforms blamed hunting for perpetuating army amateurism and inefficiency. English cavalry officers were astonishingly ignorant of the art of war; they spent too much time hunting and not enough on military instruction. Regimental duties and field training were neglected. The 9th Lancers, for example, crammed their training in mounted and dismounted duties in scouting, reconnaissance, commands and signals into four days. Because of hunting, cavalry regiments were dispersed around the country in small detachments, typically the troop, the smallest unit of all.[16]

By scrapping the purchase of commissions in 1871, Cardwell hoped to open up the army to middle-class talent. Social exclusiveness was most pronounced in the cavalry, largely because the cavalry was so expensive. In addition to heavy regimental expenses, cavalry officers were expected to pay for hunting out of their private incomes. In the 1850s Evelyn Wood found a private income of three hundred pounds sufficient to meet all regimental subscriptions and keep a third horse for hunting, 'which indeed was practically enforced by public opinion'. By 1903 an officer needed an income of six or seven hundred pounds, closing the cavalry to all but the rich. The expense of the cavalry reinforced its amateurism: because cavalry officers were so rich they tended not to take the army seriously as a profession.[17]

Hunting did have its military uses, however. Mid-nineteenth-century fox hunters rode with the natural seat – short stirrup, leg bent, back straight. This was much more secure than the artificial seat affected by fox hunters earlier in the century: they rode leaning well back with their legs stretched out straight in front of them so that it was impossible to grip above the knee.

The natural seat was also stronger than the military seat known as 'tongs across a wall' which the cavalry had used since 1815. Cavalrymen were taught to hold the leg absolutely straight so that the heel was in a perpendicular line with the point of the shoulder. To prevent 'clinging', the man's leg below the knee was brought away from the horse; he was taught to ride entirely by balancing on his fork, sitting at the trot. This riding-school seat was adopted at the insistence of the Prince Regent, a passionate admirer of all things Prussian. Military riding had been imported from France and Germany since the late seventeenth century. But tongs across a wall was both painful and insecure. Jumping was almost impossible, and

The military seat, *c.* 1850

if the horse bolted (as it was likely to do in a charge) the man lost his balance and fell off.

Captain Nolan of Balaclava fame, probably the best military horseman of his day, urged the cavalry to take up the natural hunting seat. No cavalry officer, wrote Nolan, would dream of riding across country like a foreign riding master. Nolan once showed some foreign officers an English hunting print of a rider jumping a fence with his hand in his breeches pocket and a glass in his eye. They burst out laughing, saying, 'As if we are such fools as to believe any man ever took a jump like that with his hand in his pocket! No, no! Englishmen may be cool fellows, but none of them can do that.'[18]

'If we Englishmen are as a body the finest horsemen in the world,' asked the cavalryman Valentine Baker, 'why should we not act upon our superior knowledge, instead of imitating those who are confessedly inferior to ourselves?' Why not, indeed? In the 1850s the cavalry adopted the natural hunting seat. A riding manual of the time claimed a victory for English empiricism over continental rationalism.[19]

During the Franco-Prussian War an English militia officer served on the staff of the French General Bourbaki. At Belfort in 1871 the general sent two ADCs across a valley with an important order. The Englishman watched them go slowly round by road. 'Will you allow me to go with that order, sir?' he asked. Getting his Irish hunter by the head, he galloped straight across country, taking the fences in his stride, delivered the order before the others and reported back. 'Do English officers always take orders in that way?' asked the General. 'Yes, sir,' said the Englishman, 'they always go the nearest way with them.'[20]

The cavalry's confidence in the hunting seat was sapped nevertheless by the success of the manège-trained Prussian cavalry in the Franco-Prussian war. After 1871 English military riding was once more dominated by continental influences. The Cavalry Riding School at Canterbury concentrated exclusively on showing up a good ride of *haut école* animals.[21] Just how wrong they were to turn their backs on hunting and outdoor schooling would be made only too clear by the Boer War.

Throughout the nineteenth century the cavalry was mounted chiefly on hunters. Usually containing a large proportion of Thoroughbred blood, their average height increased from about 14 hands 3 inches in 1800 to 15 hands 2½ inches by 1900. Part-Thoroughbred hunters were superior in many respects to the heavier horses used by continental armies: unbeatable, for example, in a flying approach march followed by a charge.[22]

Army remounts were all bought on the open market. There was no government stud, with its distasteful overtones of continental absolutism. Until the formation of the Army Remount Establishment in 1887, individual regiments were responsible for buying their own horses. The type of horses bought depended on the commanding officer's preference. Fox-hunting officers in both light and heavy cavalry regiments preferred big horses and big men to match.

The distinction between the two types of cavalry became blurred; as Valentine Baker put it, 'we have no real light cavalry in the British service'. Jack Anstruther Thomson, who was 6′ 2½″ high and weighed sixteen stone, was a light cavalryman. Light cavalry regiments (hussars, light dragoons, lancers) were more fashionable and aristocratic; heavy cavalry officers, whose expenses were higher, were often the sons of rich merchants.

Despite government studs light cavalry assimilated itself to heavy cavalry in continental armies too. There hunting had nothing to do with it. The real problem was that to the cavalryman the functions of light cavalry – reconnaissance, skirmishing – were contemptible beside the charge which, though properly the role of heavy cavalry, was the consummation of his purpose in life.[23]

British horses suffered terribly in the South African War. Of the 518,800 horses provided for the campaign, 347,000 (67 per cent) were lost.

The big hunters that the cavalry brought out with them were quite unfit for the South African campaign. They were bred 'to carry a man in a burst over a big hunting country' and for the last fifty years breeders had ignored stamina and temper. Accustomed to a pampered peacetime existence of routine and plenty – three corn feeds daily plus as much hay as they could eat – they couldn't survive on South African rations: an average of eight pounds of corn daily and sometimes no hay. Hunters were soon abandoned in favour of smaller and tougher breeds bought from the empire and abroad.

Horseflesh was squandered through amateurism and ignorance. Cavalry officers dismissed horsemastership as a dreary chore best left to the men, just as at home it was up to the groom to keep one's hunters' legs on.

Ignorance was compounded by etiquette. The cavalry were notorious for giving their horses sore backs. By contrast with the artillery, they treated their horses like machines. The cavalryman must never walk anywhere or be seen off his horse.[24] Hadn't the Prince Imperial been stabbed to death by Zulus in 1879 when he got off his horse in the elephant grass for a pee?

The cavalry learned their lesson. 'Look after the horses first, the men next, the officers last,' became the cavalryman's golden rule. Standards improved as officers became more professional after the Boer War, and by 1914 British cavalry horsemastership was as good as any in Europe.

The cavalry made not a single knee-to-knee charge throughout the South African War. They were useful only when they exchanged their swords and lances for rifles, fighting like mounted riflemen. The Boer War could hardly have been more different from Leicestershire. In some ways it was like hill hunting, particularly during the final phase of guerrilla warfare:

> As dawn broke some signs of departing Boers, the scent perhaps taking the form of an outspan or information from local natives, then a dragging hunt after wheel tracks and more native information, till from the top of some prominent kopje a pair of Zeiss glasses gives a glimpse of a line of wagons trekking ten miles distant. Then tally-ho, and away, and the jaded horses have to go best pace over miles and miles of undulating

> veldt. And then from scent to view as the Boer convoy comes into sight a mile or two away. Our men spread out and go full gallop as they ride from 'view to a death in the morning'. 'Who-oop!' the hunt is over and the prey is ours – perhaps a dozen prisoners with as many Mausers, some wagons, and a few useful teams of oxen.[25]

Hunting was certainly training for this kind of war. In his book *Pink and Scarlet* (1900), the mounted infantryman Lieutenant Colonel E. A. H. Alderson argued that hunting was the next best thing to active service: it took up the fighting education of the young officer where the barrack square and the drill field left off. Alderson showed how each stage of a day's hunting had its equivalent in war. Riding to the meet gave an officer an eye for country, watching hounds draw trained him in 'use of ground', while the hunt itself – the battle – was training in initiative. Even dressing for hunting was valuable. Putting on exquisite pink and white to gallop through mud taught the officer to set an example to his men, and to see that they themselves were well turned out.

Alderson was an enthusiastic supporter of the Staff College Drag at Camberley. The Drag had been founded in 1870 when E. B. Hamley, the military historian, was Staff College Commandant. Hamley hunted regularly. It was said that he would as soon find a student reading Jorrocks as his own *Operations of War*, and he once sacked a student who couldn't ride. By demonstrating that Staff College wasn't all book learning, the Drag helped to break down prejudice and improve the type of officer applying. After the Boer War Evelyn Wood applied for a Treasury grant to restart the Drag – the hounds had been put down during the war – on the grounds that 'the most gifted Staff officer is useless in the Field unless he is at home in the saddle'. He got two hundred pounds.[26]

After the Boer War officers hunted less than before. Controversy raged over the cavalry role. The Cavalry School of strategists, led by John French and Douglas Haig, championed the *arme blanche*.

The cavalry, they thought, should stick to steel (swords and lances), relying for its effect on shock. If you gave the cavalry rifles, they would lose the cavalry spirit and become mere mounted infantrymen. Training for the charge was the more vital because this was the area where the Germans excelled. Before 1914 80 per cent of cavalry training time was devoted to preparing for the charge. Meanwhile, the German army made hunting with State foxhounds compulsory.[27]

In the First World War more horses were used to less effect than ever before. Hunters provided half the cavalry remounts for the British Expeditionary Force. During the retreat from Mons (August 1914) Allenby's cavalry division effectively deployed mounted infantry skills to shield British troops from German attack. But after autumn 1914, as both sides settled into the stalemate of trench warfare, cavalry as such had nothing to do. Only in the Middle East, against the militarily backward Turks, did conventional cavalry tactics pay off.

French and Haig were both fox hunters and cavalrymen, and they clung to the *arme blanche*. The war would be over when the cavalry broke through the enemy line and reaped the fruits of victory – à Berlin! Throughout the war the cavalry expensively waited, massed behind the point of each great attack, poised for the breakthrough that never came. Not until the autumn of 1918 did the British smash through the German lines; and then there was no need for cavalry to persuade the Germans to surrender.[28]

Even so, frustrated cavalry commanders seized the long-awaited opportunity to advance. Robert Hartman took part in one attack with the 11th Hussars. His horse jumped a trench, landed on a bomb but galloped on unscathed; the 11th Hussars then captured a village. 'With élan, éclat, panache and drawn swords we charged into the village to find that two Australian photographers had been there for an hour, waiting to take a film of our arrival.' On 11 November 1918 Hartman was ordered to pursue the retreating German army. He refused. 'I knew well enough what was wanted: a picturesque end to the war, a cavalry charge. But I was not going to risk the life of a single man or horse in my squadron on what was probably to be the last day of hostilities.' Against barbed wire and machine guns the *arme blanche* was not even a gesture, it was suicide.[29]

'The horse,' wrote J. F. C. Fuller in 1920, 'is doomed; it is no longer an argument of fire-arms *versus* the *arme blanche*, but of a change in the element of movement itself.' Only if the cavalry exchanged their horses for tanks would mobility be restored to war. The cavalry spirit must be reborn in a tank.[30]

Choleric colonels fumed in the Cavalry Club. But it was no good. Mechanization was irresistible; and hunting was no longer the image of war.

Officers still hunted, of course. In England hunting went on throughout the 1914–18 war. 'What on earth are officers home from the front going to do with their time, if there is no hunting for them?' asked Lord Lonsdale, wartime Master of the Cottesmore. Hunting may have played its part in welding together the divisions of Kitchener's new army. But perhaps the real reasons for going on through the war had little to do with the war effort. As C. S. Forester suggested, fox hunters didn't believe the war to be nearly so serious as the suspension of hunting.[31]

Lord Carrington, later head of NATO, joined the Grenadier Guards in 1939. His commanding officer told him to remember two things. 'On no account are you to marry until you are twenty-five: and you are to hunt in Leicestershire at least two days a week.'[32]

CHAPTER EIGHT

Ireland

'Landlord and tenant, the red coat and the broad cloth, have met at the cover-side in amicable warfare long before "equalizing" theories had inoculated the brain with fixity of tenure as the panacea for all our country's ills. Their "fixity of tenure" was in the saddle, the only "eviction" thought of, of the fox.'

BERNARD FITZPATRICK,
Irish Sport and Sportsmen, 1878

Mr John Power brought a pack of foxhounds from Tipperary in 1797 to found the Kilkenny Hunt Club. Hounds have always been kept in Ireland, but the Kilkenny was the first hunt club of Anglo-Irish gentry, and John Power was among the first to bring the new-style fox hunting to Ireland.

John Power hunted a vast unenclosed country. In the early days he met at daybreak with about twenty fellow enthusiasts and walked his fox to death. He imported fast English hounds, preserved foxes and planted gorse coverts. The Kilkenny Hunt Club met for two weeks in November and February at Rice's Hotel. In 1815 it guaranteed John Power a subscription of six hundred pounds. He was clever and good company, though a moderate drinker. A staunch Whig and supporter of Catholic Emancipation, he was made a baronet in 1836. 'I wish every Tory was rolled out flat!' he exclaimed as he led a tired horse up Tory Hill at the end of a long hunt.

The Kilkenny Hunt Club climaxed around 1830. John Power's son started a craze for 'lepping', and Kilkenny became Ireland's Melton, the headquarters of Irish hunting. Hard-riding, hard-drinking Irish squires thronged the dining room at Rice's Hotel. The Marquess of Waterford, a Meltonian who had literally painted the town of Melton red, rode his horse up the stairs of Rice's Hotel and jumped over the dining room table. When it was too hard to hunt he practised marksmanship, shooting out the eyes of family portraits.[1]

When members of the Kilkenny went home, they spread the word about the new style of hunting, setting up various county hunt clubs which raised subscriptions to pay for county packs. Colonel William Wrixon turned his family pack in Cork into the Duhallow Hunt Club, and Colonel Pigott formed the Wexford Hunt Club in 1810. In about 1813 the gentlemen who kept private packs in Meath amalgamated to form the Clonghill Hunt Club, which became the Meath in 1832. The Club's twelve members subscribed £360. John Power's most brilliant protégé was probably John Watson of Ballydarton, who founded what later became the Carlow in 1808.

In Galway a hunt club was formed by Robert Parsons Persse, Master 1803–29. His hounds came from his uncle, Burton Persse, the 'Irish Meynell', who hunted Galway until 1803 and dressed his servants in orange plush. Persse's hunt was dubbed the Blazers – no one really knows why. One very Irish explanation is that after a joint meet with the Ormond Hunt, Persse's followers set fire to their hosts' house. Another story, thought to be more likely, is that the hunt was called after the 'ruby locks' of two of its members.[2]

East Galway was hunted by a private pack kept from 1791 to 1829 by Colonel Giles Eyre of Eyre Court, 'the man for Galway':

> To keep game cocks – to hunt the fox,
> To drink in punch the Solway,
> With debts galore, but fun far more;
> Oh! that's the man for Galway.

The original of Charles Lever's *Charles O'Malley*, Eyre lived like a petty prince. He could hardly write, but he managed to sign sufficient bills to 'thatch Lough Coultra Castle' and exhaust his enormous fortune. His hounds, which were crossed with bloodhound and mastiff, once ate a drunken huntsman in their kennels.[3]

Fox hunting prospered best where the Anglo-Irish were strong. Near Dublin, for instance, a relatively dense gentry population was swelled by townsmen, soldiers and viceregal staff. Dublin's own pack was the Wards, which hunted carted stags over the same country as the Meath. It was formed in 1830 when two Dublin merchants' packs amalgamated, switching from bagged foxes to carted stags. Two other fashionable and prosperous packs could be reached easily from Dublin: the Kildare and the Meath.

The 'killing' Kildare soon ousted the Kilkenny as premier pack. Founded in 1793, the Kildare was really made by Sir John Kennedy of Johnstown. Sir John was Master 1814–41. He not only helped pay off the hunt's debts (in 1808 the Kildare had been driven to charging 1*s*.8*d*. field money) but he also planted thirty-one gorse coverts in the Kildare's bare, unwooded country. Members of the Kildare Hunt Club were enthusiastic fox preservers. 'We . . . have heard with great regret,' they wrote on one occasion, 'that Mr Digby's butler has shot a fox, and we hope that Mr Digby will take such steps as will prevent said butler from again perpetrating a similar crime while in his employment.' 'Mr Digby has heard with great regret,' came back the reply, 'of the offence committed by his butler, and begs to inform the members of the Kildare Hunt Club that he has discharged said butler.'[4]

The territory hunted by the Kildare was dominated by landlords. No ancient hunts seem to have survived here. Early this century, Edith Somerville and Violet Martin made a special expedition to the west to visit a foot pack of trencher-fed black-and-tan Kerry Beagles. The beagles hunted on Sundays after mass. Cheered on by a crowd of countrymen on foot, the beagles needed no huntsman.[5] Foot packs of harriers with traditions stretching back to the sixteenth century proliferated in three areas: Ennis in County Clare; the drumlin belt of Fermanagh, Cavan and Monaghan; and Kerry and Cork.

County Cork now contains mounted harriers, which in good Irish fashion hunt foxes. The fourteen or so packs of mounted harriers are farmers' packs or town packs, often fed on butchers' offal and patronized by shopkeepers.[6] They may descend from the hounds kept by Irish middlemen or land agents, about whom Arthur Young was so rude in the 1770s: 'these men very generally were the masters of packs of wretched hounds, with which they wasted their time and money, and it is a notorious fact that they are the hardest drinkers in Ireland'.[7]

Cork is a county without a dominant landlord family. The eastern limit of mounted harrier country is sharply defined by the Marquess of Waterford's estates in County Waterford.

The Anglo-Irish before the Famine inhabited an *ancien régime* world of absenteeism, appalling transport, indebtedness and drunken 'Waterford capers'. Hordes of black-coated, hungry peasants swarmed outside, clutching at survival. The number of smallholdings multiplied as rack-renting middlemen subdivided holdings. In 1840 70 per cent of Irish holdings were under eleven acres. Humanity Dick Martin, King of Connemara, who owned two hundred thousand heavily-encumbered acres, fed the countryside from his kitchens at Ballinahinch, forty miles of beggars lining his avenues. He died in poverty in Boulogne in 1834.

Seven years after Martin's death, Anthony Trollope went to Ireland to work for the Post Office. Trollope took up hunting, and he was struck by the gulf between the Anglo-Irish and Irish. 'Five-and-twenty cousins in red coats and top-boots' made up the field of the Mayo hunt described by Trollope in *The Kellys and the O'Kellys* (1848). When the villain, a drunken Irish Protestant, rides over a hound, one of the Anglo-Irish remarks: 'He's as much business here as a cow in a drawing room.' 'But what can we do?' asks another. 'One can't turn him off the land; if he choses to come, he must.' 'Why, yes, if he will come he must. But then, if he insists on doing so, he may be horsewhipped; he may be ridden over; he may be kicked; and he may be told that he's a low, vulgar, paltry scoundrel; and, if he repeats his visits, that's the treatment he'll probably receive.'

People who trod on hounds weren't treated quite like that in England.

Irish and Anglo-Irish were separated by far more than class. The Anglo-Irish turned in on themselves and married each other; as Edith Somerville put it – herself a member of a much-married cousinhood – there was no choice but 'to love your neighbour – or, at all events, to marry her'. Humbler Anglo-Irish families marked themselves off from the Irish by cloaking their origins in fake genealogy obligingly endorsed by *Burke's Landed Gentry of Ireland*.[8]

Hunting gave the gentry something to do, discouraging absenteeism. No one suggested that it was open to all in Ireland. Field money was charged from 1808, when the Kildare started a cap. Nor did the Anglo-Irish need to make their hunting seem respectable. Hunting in Ireland produced nothing to match England's Victorian flood of sporting journalism. There was no attempt to give hunting in Ireland the moral dimension that Trollope and Whyte-Melville gave it in England.

Hunting in Ireland faced things much worse than middle-class disapproval. The sport of the Anglo-Irish was hampered by agrarian unrest, which erupted all too easily into violence and terrorism.

Most packs stopped hunting during the Famine of 1845–51. Subscriptions dried up, and hunts went into debt. Some landlords were ruined by the Famine. The Martins of Ross in Connemara, who made every effort to feed their starving tenants, were forced by crippling rates and unpaid rents to mortgage their estates out of existence.

When Engels went to Ireland in 1856 he found the landowners living the life of O'Riley. 'Of mixed blood, mostly tall, strong handsome chaps, they all wear enormous moustaches under colossal Roman noses, give themselves the sham military airs of retired colonels, travel around the country after all sorts of pleasures, and, if one makes an inquiry, they haven't a penny, are laden with debts and live in dread of the Encumbered Estates Court.'[9]

For unscrupulous landlords, the Famine gave a long-sought

opportunity to consolidate holdings, which had been reduced to uneconomic size by constant subdivision under the pressure of a growing population. In the west mass evictions were commonplace. In Cork, for example, the number of holdings under fifteen acres was cut by more than half, and the population fell by one quarter. Broken by starvation, tenants offered no resistance. Usually they received neither compensation nor even money for emigration.[10]

When the Famine was over, Irish agriculture boomed. It was increasingly an export industry, supplying England with butter and meat. Ireland's grass became the envy of England.

Ireland became the breeding ground of hunters. Irish horses, said Whyte-Melville, had not a drop of Clydesdale blood. Schooled to jump banks in a snaffle by Irish horsebreakers, who possessed a natural affinity with horses – in spite of their outrageously shabby turn-out – Irish hunters found Leicestershire fences child's play. In the 1870s they were good value, a hundred to two hundred pounds for a first-class jumper up to thirteen stone.[11]

The Kildare, which almost went bankrupt after the Famine, was made solvent by Lord Mayo, Master 1857–62. Though he served as Tory Irish Chief Secretary, Mayo was popular with all classes: 'a certain strong-handed policy, very intelligible, even if directed in unpopular channels, never alienated the affections of the many admirers who, knowing Lord Mayo, were forced to be proud of him as an Irishman and sportsman'. Kildare had more resident gentry than any other county. By 1876 income from subscriptions and field money combined to cover costs of about two thousand pounds; there were 138 subscribers, and an average field of 150.[12]

The adjoining Meath languished until 1851, when the great Sam Reynell began his twenty-year Mastership. Like Sir John Kennedy at the Kildare, Reynell made the country, planting gorse coverts in a vast sea of grass – sixty miles by thirty of strongly fenced cattle ranches. The Hunt Club subscription increased to twelve hundred pounds (which still wasn't enough). The Wards, which hunted stags over the same country as the Meath, prospered too. After the Crimean War the English garrison in Dublin had given up their own staghounds, subscribing two hundred pounds to the Wards instead. The Wards agreed to hunt an extra day, changing its name to Ward Union. Dublin stag hunters came out on special trains provided by the Midland Great Western Line.

Down in County Waterford, the Marquess of Waterford made his family pack. He came home to Waterford in about 1844 after an unsuccessful Mastership in Tipperary. His ambition to turn the Tipperary into the Leicestershire of Ireland had been foiled by 'outrages', culminating in the burning of the hunt kennels. 'This annoyed his lordship so much, he gave up in disgust.' In Waterford, where he owned forty thousand acres and took no subscription, he had trouble at first stocking the country. 1848 was a year of agrarian troubles, and the Marquess, who was a Tory, had his foxes poached. By 1859, however, when he was killed out hunting, he had built up a good stock of foxes. His funeral was vast and Irish, and 'never was one followed to the grave by more *truly* sorrowful men'.[13]

In Galway the Blazers flourished under Burton Persse (1852–85). When Isaac Bell was Master (1903–8), he took his hounds to cub some outlying woodlands which hadn't been hunted since Persse's day. The woods were full of countrymen, old men with sticks who said they hadn't heard the hounds for years and years and 'pined for it once before they died'. They told him 'what a wonderful huntsman was Burton Persse, and that he had blooded every one of them as children and drilled them in hunting'. They found a litter of cubs, and then moved silently through the wood, following the system Persse had taught them. 'Whenever hounds had crossed a ride, they lined up in it and gently tapped their staves to prevent the cub returning to his foil, thus keeping him always in the quarter ahead.'[14]

Many hunts languished. The Westmeath stopped for about a decade after the Famine. When it restarted in 1853 there was a shortage of foxes, a high turnover of Masters, and no more than thirty followers. Falling subscriptions compelled the Ballymacad to give up from 1856 to 1885. 'How can I manage to feed the hounds,' scrawled the huntsman, 'unless I get some money amongst you old gentlemen?'[15] Lord Drogheda kept the Erno going through the

Famine, but he got little support, and in 1850 he gave up. The Erno amalgamated with the Queen's County in 1854.

Hunting stopped in West Carbery, near Skibbereen, notorious during the Famine for ghastly scenes of death and destitution (the population fell by 36 per cent). The Limerick very nearly became extinct after the Famine too. There was a scant subscription, a wretched pack of hounds, coverts in disrepair and hardly a fox to be found. In 1861 it was rescued by Sir David Roche, who imported English hounds and 146 foxes.

Fox hunting stopped in Roscommon in the 1870s. The county had been hunted since the 1740s by the de Freynes of French Park. By the 1850s they had run out of foxes, which were killed by Irish keepers desperate to preserve pheasants and lacking the knack of keeping foxes too. Roscommon formed a pack of staghounds instead.[16]

The natural scarcity of foxes in Ireland meant that hunting was always vulnerable to sabotage. In Ireland it was a far more artificial sport than in England. Foxes were poisoned near Cork in the 1870s. Mr Meredith, Master of the Kilkenny and 'now best forgotten', retired in 1870 in very unpleasant circumstances and when the hunt advertised for a new Master there was no reply for months.[17]

Landlord–tenant relations were breaking down. Irish landowners have been blamed for not investing in agricultural improvements during the boom.[18] But Irish landed society wasn't capitalist in the way that England was. It had more in common with Russia. The Anglo-Irish were colonists: their country houses had 'a blank look, the windows staring across the country, like blind eyes . . . looking out across the country which they possessed, but never owned'.[19]

At best, landowners were benevolent patriarchs, dispensing food and rough justice. Every big house had its back door, the haunt of hangers-on living out of the kitchens, shadowy, self-appointed servants, beggars, hereditary pipe-smokers. At Ross in the 1860s the household got through a sheep a week and a cow a month; there was cream, turf, timber and game in abundance. 'But after all these followed the Saturday night labour bill, and the fact remains . . . that these free fruits of the earth are heavily paid for, that convenience is mistaken for economy, and that farming is, for the average gentleman, more of an occupation than an income.'[20] It was a world more familiar to Tolstoy than, say, to the Duke of Rutland.

Agrarian tensions snapped during the agricultural depression after 1878. The Irish party now had Parnell as leader, 'a grim, disdainful Master, whose pack never dared to get closer to him than the length of his thong; but he laid them on the line, and they ran it like wolves'.[21] In 1879 the Land War began. When landlords evicted for non-payment of rent, they weren't allowed to get away with it. Tenants maimed cattle, fired into houses at night and boycotted landlords and land-grabbers.

Fox hunting was an obvious target. The fact that so many MFHs and hunt servants were English didn't help. Nor were republican American agitators impressed by the sport of kings. 'Small wonder,' wrote *Baily's*, 'if a sport which originated among the aristocracy of the land, and which, though broad and tolerant as the British Constitution itself, had always a most patrician savour about it, should be looked upon with suspicion, which all too soon turned to aversion.'

Hounds were poisoned or stoned, foxes poisoned and coverts burned. Most packs stopped hunting during the 1881–2 season. Things were better in the east, but even in Meath, where hunting went on throughout the season, *Baily's* found 'the old feeling of security and matter-of-courseness of the chase somewhat wanting'. Several packs went under. The Roscommon staghounds went into liquidation, selling their deer and hounds. The Limerick, the Ormond and the Muskerry sold their hounds. Tipperary was only rescued from the same fate by Richard Burke, who became Master in 1887 having married a rich American wife. When Lord Waterford's hounds were stoned in the middle of the 1881–2 season, he left Ireland and finished the season at Badminton, his wife's home. The country was unhunted from 1884 to 1900.[22]

The Land War in Galway was described by Trollope in *The Land-Leaguers* (1884), his unfinished last novel. Each covert the hunt intends to draw is filled with crowds of countrymen. The Master takes hounds off to a covert ten miles away. He finds the Land-Leaguers have got here first too. The Master loses his temper and tries to ride down the crowd. The kennels are burned in retaliation. 'He was aware now, though he never had thought of it before, by how weak a hold his right of hunting the country was held. He and his hounds could go into any covert; but so also could any other man, with or without hounds. To disturb a fox, three or four men would suffice ... The occupation of his life was over.'

Despite the Land War, Lord Spencer and Bay Middleton brought the Empress of Austria to hunt with the Meath and the Wards in 1879. English fox hunters flitted over to Dublin like snipe when it froze too hard to hunt in the shires. As Irish viceroy in 1882–5, during the later phases of the Land War, Spencer hunted regularly. It was from Irish banks that he got his ugly habit of clinging to the back of the saddle while jumping. The Dublin season began after Christmas, and in Spencer's reign balls at the castle always ended early, at one a.m., because of hunting the next day.

Chicken Hartopp, Leicestershire practical joker and pugilist, was Master of the Kilkenny 1880–2. He would offer Land-Leaguers his right hand; if they refused it, he responded, 'So you'd rather have this, then,' and brandished his vast left fist in their faces. Captain 'Jock' Trotter, Scottish Master of the Meath 1878–88, rode four horses a day and hunted six days a week. The agricultural depression cut into the rents on his Border farms and forced him to give up, leaving the hunt badly in debt.[23]

Baily's reported diminished hostility towards hunting in 1888–9.[24] A lawyer turned up at Ballydarton, home of Robert Watson, Master of the Carlow and Island 1869–1904, known as the 'Old Master'. The lawyer saw a typical Irish country house with pillars in front and a long, straggling, untidy avenue. He told the Old Master, who was about to go hunting, that he had a claim to Rockingham castle. 'Young man,' said Watson, 'what would I be wanting with an English castle, when I have Ballydarton and the best hounds in Ireland?' And he rode off.[25]

Robert Watson's son John became Master of the Meath 1891–1904. Life in Meath revolved round the hunt. 'What do you do in Meath in the summer?' someone asked. 'We just wait for the winter,' replied Lady Fingall.[26]

John Watson hunted the Meath hounds himself five days a week. On the sixth day he went out with the Ward Union. Watson was a 'terrible man', 6′4″ high, cruel to his horses, dour, hard and silent. He refused to drive to meets, insisting that motor cars spoiled hunting. He hated women out hunting. 'I wish they'd go home and do their knitting,' he would mutter. Lady Fingall once rode home with him. He spoke to her only once, pointing with his whip at some lambs in a field. 'Look at those damned lambs.' And that was all. Only one woman ever got the better of him. She overrode hounds. 'Woman! Go home,' he roared. 'Go home yourself,' she replied, 'you damned son of a bald-headed Carlow onion.' Watson died in 1908 of a 'strained heart'.

The Meath in Watson's day was certainly smart. Tuesdays and Fridays in the Dublin country attracted fields of four to five hundred. Lady Fingall, whose husband was Master before Watson, hated hunting except for the clothes, which she adored. She bought them in London – hat at Lock's, boots at Peal and figure-hugging habit made by Busvine. When dressing she always put her hat and net on first. Her maid found her one morning sitting in the bath wearing nothing but a top hat.[27]

Galway too was smart. Ikey Bell, the young American Master of the Blazers, thought little had changed since Giles Eyre's time. Anglo-Irish squires still talked hunting, shooting, fishing and bullocks. During the hunting season they wore pink at dinner, and the MFH took over from the High Sheriff as guest of honour at parties and functions. Bell drove to meets in gum boots with a gun and his top boots in the dogcart, hoping to shoot a snipe on the way.[28]

The grandest hunt ball was held by the Kilkenny, which recovered from near extinction during the Land War under the Mastership of Sir Hercules (Herky) Langrishe, 1890–1908. The dancing was opened at ten o'clock, when Lord and Lady Ormonde appeared like royalty, she in a tiara, and danced a quadrille with Herky and Lady Langrishe, who also wore a tiara.[29]

But this was the last fling of the Anglo-Irish. Gladstone's conversion to Home Rule in 1886 had begun the great betrayal of the Anglo-Irish 'garrison'.

The Conservatives responded with a policy of killing Home Rule by kindness, buying out landowners and handing over land and cash to the Irish peasants. George Wyndham, a hunting Tory Chief Secretary, offered landlords a cash bonus of 12 per cent over and above the price of the holding. Almost half the arable land of Ireland was sold to tenants under the 1903 Wyndham Act. By 1914 three-quarters of tenants had bought their holdings.

Shortly after the Act, George Wyndham wandered into the gaming rooms at Monte Carlo. 'George! George! The bonus!' called out a once-broke Irish peer, pointing to the pile of notes and counters in front of him.[30] Land purchase was a bonanza for the Anglo-Irish. But it left those who stayed at home with little else to do but hunt. There's something a little too frantic, desperate even, about the hunt balls, the who-whoops, the hunting six days a week. It's all a bit *après nous le déluge*.

'When those rascals in Parliament took our land from us,' said Mrs Knox, 'we thought we should have some peace, now we're both beggared and bothered!'[31] Mrs Knox, grandmother of Flurry Knox, is the real hero of Edith Somerville and Martin Ross's stories of an Irish RM. 'A rag bag held together by diamond brooches', she eats filthy food off priceless silver, quotes Virgil and has hunted hounds herself. Despite land purchase, her ex-tenants still look to her as their landlord.

The Irish RM stories, published between 1899 and 1915, tell of Mrs Knox and her grandson Flurry, Master of a pack of hounds in the west of Ireland. Mrs Knox and Flurry belong to the clan of Knoxes, Black Protestants spread upwards and downwards in county society, who are endlessly fighting and marrying each other. The Clan Knox goes hunting in force with Flurry, 'its more aristocratic members dingily respectable in black coats and tall hats that went impartially to weddings, funerals and hunts'. But there is also 'a humbler squireen element in tweeds and flat-brimmed pot-hats, and a good muster of farmers, men of the spare, black-muzzled, west of Ireland type, on horses that ranged from the cart mare, clipped trace high, to shaggy and leggy three-year-olds, none of them hunters, but all of them able to hunt'.[32]

The hunting described in the Irish RM stories certainly isn't smart. It's based on the recently revived West Carbery Hunt in West Cork, where Edith Somerville was Master from 1903. The country is rough and boggy. It rains all the time. Flurry Knox MFH is first seen in a cloudburst: 'His gloveless hands were red and wet, the rain ran down his nose, and his covert coat was soaked to a sodden brown.' You can *feel* the wet.

Hunting with Flurry is wild and woolly – breathless scrambling over heather, rocks and bogs. When Lady Susan, the Englishwoman in *The Silver Fox* (1897), sees Irish countrymen digging for a fox with more enthusiasm than science, she feels 'much as a devout clergyman might feel at beholding a low travesty of the Church service'. Major Yeates, the Irish RM, is always keen to go home as soon as possible, and 'conscious not only of a nervous system, but of the anatomical fact that I possessed large, round legs'.

The raw material for the Irish RM was supplied by Edith Somerville. Here she is, breathless and full of gusto, describing a day with a neighbouring pack:

> The fox took us over awful country, heather, and rocks, and bogs, and we had to ride just about as hard as the horses could leg it, for the hounds were racing with their heads up on a red-hot scent. An adorable Kerry baigle (Naygress, I think), was leading them, and her yowls were enough to tear the very heart out of you – like the most piercing old woman at a funeral! It was all we could do to keep them in sight over that breakneck country, but we did it somehow, and after about twenty-five minutes they checked suddenly, and began to rage round a huge cairn of stones. A. [her brother]

> was off in an instant and shoved his crop into a hole between the stones, and before you could say 'shnipes', out jumped the fox into the very jaws of the whole pack! They were so taken by surprise that while they were snapping right and left, he had darted like lightning between their legs.
>
> But he beat us. In less than a hundred yards there were two big rocks, and he wriggled in between them just as Naygress made a grab at his brush! . . . I am glad when a good fox gets away, but I must admit that A. and I could have cried.[33]

Edith's real-life experiences were given an anti-heroic, comic twist by Violet Martin. She wrote as Martin Ross – she was a Martin of Ross in Connemara, living with her mother in the dilapidated house that was all that remained of the Martins' once-great estates, ruined by the Famine. Edith later recalled how rigorously she and Martin tried to purge their work of anything approaching 'that intolerable adjective "rollicking"'.

They were deliberately abandoning Victorian convention. As Edith put it, 'The hunting people of Handley Cross, like Lever's dragoons, were always at full gallop. With Surtees, as with Lever, everyone is "all out", there is nothing in hand – save perhaps a pair of duelling pistols or a tandem whip – and the height of the spirits is only equalled by the tallness of the hero's talk.' Somerville and Ross brought a new realism to hunting writing.

Their being women helped. The Frenchman who thought their book was called 'Some Reminiscences of an Irish Harem' wasn't entirely off the mark. Somerville and Ross were New Women of the 1890s, rebelling against Trollope's weeping heroines and John Leech's feeble females, 'turbaned and crinolined, wholly idiotic, flying with an equal terror from bulls and mice, ogling Lord Dundreary and his whiskers, being scored off by rude little boys'.[34]

CHAPTER NINE

The Plutocrats

Broke! broke! broke!
Are the lords of this cold, clay land;
And slender's the chance that the
money lost
Will ever come back to hand.
Annals of the Warwickshire Hunt, 1896

Hugh Lowther, the Yellow Earl of Lonsdale, was Master of the Quorn 1893–8. A showman and a stickler for etiquette, Lonsdale was a compulsive spender. In spite of an allowance from his coal-rich estates of over eighty thousand pounds a year, his main aim in life was to get more and more out of his trustees. 'I am the last of the Lowthers,' he cried, which was quite untrue. Cigar almost permanently in mouth (his cigar bill of three thousand pounds a year was exactly covered by the subscription he took from the Quorn), he breakfasted on a glass of brandy and half a bottle of white wine. He boasted he could crush a horse's ribs between his legs. He dressed his hunt servants in white leather breeches and mounted them on hog-maned chestnut Thoroughbreds. Eighty-four of his hunters were sold for 18,228 guineas at Tattersall's in 1898. At the Quorn he issued a new hunt button with the letter 'Q' surmounted by a lavish Lonsdale coronet. Rebellious subscribers cut off their old buttons and refused to sew on the new ones. Whenever the field annoyed him – which was often – he sent the hounds home. On one occasion when hounds circled three times, Lonsdale, on the third lap, overtook riders on the second lap. They were overriding hounds, he said, and went home. Next day he received a telegram saying, 'Entirely approve of your action – Wilhelm R & I.'[1]

Gilbert Greenall, a very rich brewer, was made Master of the Belvoir in 1896, on the retirement of the seventh Duke of Rutland. He kept the hunt going in the ducal style to which it was accustomed, paying eighteen thousand pounds for hunt horses and, like Lonsdale, dressing his hunt staff in leathers. He employed a man who did nothing else but clean hunt servants' breeches.

In the shires the MFH was a figure of considerable importance. A conscientious MFH like Greenall was popular, supporting local charities. He succeeded in eliminating wire from the Belvoir by dividing the country into districts, each with a local man in charge.[2] Lonsdale too excelled at organization, and Lady Lonsdale knew every Quorn farmer's wife and children by name. Farmers got a brace of pheasants and a haunch of venison at Christmas, and Lonsdale encouraged subscribers to buy forage from them. He also ordered the Quorn's two hundred or so second horsemen to stick to the roads, rather than larking over the fields.

Agriculture enjoyed a revival after 1900. The nagsman J. H. Marshall remembered an Edwardian childhood at Hickling in the Quorn and Belvoir countries. His father farmed three hundred acres, and had a standing order to find Lord Lonsdale twelve chestnut horses every twelve months. At Hickling there were great joints of meat running with gravy, Stilton cheeses made on the farm soaked with port, brass handles counter-sunk in the stable doors, and mounted foxes' masks on the walls.[3]

In the Vale of Aylesbury, Lord Rothschild and his brother Mr Leo de Rothschild appealed to the followers of their family pack of staghounds in 1908: 'We beg that they will in every way conform to the wishes of the Field Master, and, further, we should take it as a compliment if the etiquette of hunting dress were more carefully observed.' *Baily's* circularized MFHs and found them unanimously in agreement. Farmers, it was said, would be more likely to put up with broken fences and squashed crops if the damage was done by redcoats not rat-catchers. One Midlands Master insisted that twenty-five-guinea subscribers come out in scarlet swallow tails with two inches of waistcoat showing below, leather breeches and top boots, 'the tops to be of a pink hue of a depth not exceeding three inches'. Another insisted that ten-guinea subscribers be differentiated from twenty-five-guinea men 'to the extent of wearing a billycock [bowler] hat, or low top hat of plain felt with no gloss on it'.

A new etiquette was invented for the motor car, by now the rich man's covert hack. Motors were allowed by most Masters at the meet (though at the Pytchley Lord Annaly only allowed them within half a mile). Because of their allegedly disastrous effect on scent they were banned everywhere from following the hunt.[4]

Tom Firr retired as Quorn huntsman in 1897 after a bad fall. The Quorn went into decline. Sport was changing. Like reared pheasant shooting, smart hunting was now a matter of competitive killing. What mattered was how many foxes were killed, not how they were hunted. Midlands masters advertised bags of seventy brace or more a season where before thirty brace had been respectable. In 1906 the Pytchley killed a record 208 foxes. The shires were stuffed with foxes, many of them such miserable specimens that they took very little killing. Six foxes a day was quite normal, or twelve during cub hunting.[5]

Too many foxes made the shire huntsman's job easier. To satisfy the field of competitive riders, the main concern was to provide a gallop – by any means. If his hounds checked, the huntsman lifted them at the gallop and picked up another fox. Frequent changes of foxes were accepted as characteristic of hunting in the shires. 'If you run twenty minutes in Leicestershire,' remarked an Edwardian guidebook, 'it is more than an even chance that you have hunted two foxes at least.'[6]

One of the best of the galloping huntsmen was Arthur Thatcher at the Cottesmore. His partnership with Evan Hanbury MFH, a rich brewer (1900–7), was a blaze of glory. Famed for his 'methods of barbarism', Thatcher was death on foxes.

In 1904, however, Lord Lonsdale, one of the biggest landowners in the Cottesmore country, sent Thatcher a stiff letter. Quoting Lord Henry Bentinck, Lonsdale accused Thatcher of using his hounds like draghounds not foxhounds. 'You go from halloa to halloa . . . you pay no attention to the position or attitude of sheep or cattle, and when once you are at fault, instead of working out your line and making your ground good, you gallop away on the off-chance of hitting some strange line, which is ruination to your hounds.' Thatcher went on to be huntsman of the Fernie, and in 1912 Henry Higginson, an American MFH, found him up to the same tricks. Nor was Thatcher above letting a fox out of a box if he feared a blank day. He swore by boxes rather than bags, which he thought made the fox smellier, spoiling the hounds for wild foxes.

Thatcher had his supporters, however. According to Isaac Bell Thatcher knew exactly what he was doing. If he gave a pack more galloping and lifting than he thought good for them, their next day out would be on the unfashionable side of the country, where he left them alone and made them work out the line for themselves.[7]

Lonsdale wasn't without critics himself. He gave his men whistles and ordered them not to halloa; if anyone halloaed a fox the hounds were stopped, sometimes losing the only hunt of the day. He also had 'a maddening trick' of interfering with his huntsman when hounds checked. Declaring they were on the line of a hare, he would order his huntsman to cast back, thus often ruining a good run.

> Lord Lonsdale came up at this minute
> To make us all think
> He'd been in it:
> As a matter of fact, though is it quite fair?
> He really thought we were hunting a hare![8]

Hound-breeding fashions didn't help sport. Critics blamed the Peterborough Hound Show. Since its foundation in 1888, Peterborough had promoted an obsession with breeding for looks. Lord Henry Bentinck had bred for working qualities, rarely commenting

Lord Lonsdale at a Quorn meet

on looks. Bone he dismissed as 'that useless appendage'. Peterborough entries were bred for bone. Legs must at all costs be straight. The 'Belvoir type' – big, straight-legged and Belvoir tan – was all the rage, fetching big money and Peterborough prizes.

The Peterborough style of breeding was reinforced by the governing kennels. The Beaufort, Brocklesby and Fitzwilliam were hereditary packs hunting flattish plough countries. Inheriting in middle age, their Masters didn't want very fast hounds. The Dukes of Beaufort were always their own huntsmen, and they bred slow hounds rather like themselves, 'big-boned, handsome and great line hunters'. The ninth Duke of Beaufort, Master 1899–1924, weighed twenty stone and never jumped.[9]

During Gilbert Greenall's Mastership the Belvoir was premier kennel, visited in summer by scores of masters, 'standing against the wall in the big yard, with pencils and a green-covered Belvoir hound list in hand . . . making notes against every hound after inspection'.[10] The Belvoir hounds were poor workers, however. Frank Gillard, huntsman 1870–96, left the hounds in a bad way.

The sixth Duke of Rutland had been Master 1869–88, but he rarely hunted, and Gillard was in effect his own Master and secretary. Gillard bought the hunt horses, engaged the servants, organized each day's hunting, controlled the field and dealt with poultry and damage claims, supervised hound breeding and entertained visiting MFHs. He wrote up each day's hunting in his diary, kept up a substantial correspondence, and visited the Duke each evening after hunting.

The seventh Duke of Rutland, who succeeded as Master in 1888, liked shooting better than hunting. Gillard, who far preferred kennel management to hunting as he became older, got up to tricks like bag foxes and 'touching' foxes. Earth-stoppers were given a mysterious substance known as 'Gillard's mixture' and told to stop the fox in its earth. When hounds came to draw, the earth-stoppers bolted the fox and gave it a dollop of mixture (exactly how this was done history doesn't relate). Hunting 'touched' foxes ruined the hounds. They got slack, allegedly going home at lunchtime of their own accord.

Greenall, who was only thirty when he took over in 1896, inherited an impossible position. The hounds and kennels were still the Duke's, 'and he didn't forget it neither'. The dog hounds went from bad to worse. Many of the bitches sent by MFHs to Belvoir proved barren, and it was rumoured that 'they weren't put to the dogs they was supposed to be, and often as not weren't served at all'. Belvoir kennel management was attacked in the *Field* by Charles McNeill, Master of the Grafton. Greenall resigned soon after.[11]

Ikey Bell, another critic of Belvoir blood, thought the craze for bone led to faults such as 'knuckling over' at the knee and pigeon-toes. Hounds became heavy-limbed, broad-chested and slow. Hunting qualities were ignored. What was gained in looks was lost in stamina and drive. Kennels lost their individuality as they competed to conform to the Belvoir type.

The exception was the Pytchley. Frank Freeman, who became huntsman in 1906, was given a free hand to breed what he liked by Lord Annaly, Master 1902–14. Freeman took over a kennel of Peterborough winners, big but soft, bred by Mr Wroughton (1894–1902), the last Pytchley Master to wear a top hat. He put down many of Wroughton's hounds, and bred his own pack of small, fast Pytchley bitches.

The Pytchley in the Freeman-Annaly era was probably the best of the shire packs. Market Harborough was more crowded than Melton Mowbray. Annaly dressed his hunt servants in a deep Padua scarlet instead of ordinary bright red, and ordered second horsemen to wear their employer's livery.

Freeman had a single-minded dedication. Guy Paget, Freeman's biographer, who hunted with him in 1908–12, often riding home with him, recalled how, if he'd lost his fox, he would be silent for miles, answering only in monosyllables, and then: 'I know why I lost him. Did you see Playful two fields before we checked?' Then field by field, hound by hound, he argued the case, Fox v. Freeman. Freeman was often compared to Tom Firr, and Brooksby, who hunted with both, rated Freeman the better fox-killing huntsman and Firr the better horseman. Firr also had more personality and wit.[12] Professional huntsmen like Firr, Freeman and Thatcher were beneficiaries of the shires' prejudice against MFHs hunting their own hounds.

Many of the old gentry had either sold up or stopped hunting since the agricultural depression of the late 1870s and 1880s. In 1878, wrote the historian of the Meynell, there had begun 'that steady flow of new blood into the country, which has gone on ever since . . . This practically worked a revolution, and gradually a plutocracy took the place of the squirearchy.'[13]

'The feudal system,' declared *Baily's* in 1906, 'is as extinct as the dodo.' The historian T. F. Dale, whose books track the decline of aristocratic packs, suggested that hunting might fill the gap left by the death of feudalism. The decay of the gentry meant that 'the link between the farmer and the governing classes was broken', hence recent governments' neglect of agriculture's interests. In the shires, however, hunting brought influential 'strangers' – MPs, peers and businessmen – into direct contact with farmers and their interests. 'Hunting,' argued Dale, 'is the farmers' best instrument of power, and indeed stands between him and social and political insignificance.'[14]

Not all farmers agreed. In 1911 farmers in the Bicester country formed a Farmers Hunt Union. At a meeting in Buckingham in 1912 they demanded a tariff of a pound per horse from fox hunters who neither owned nor occupied land in the country, together with a 'rent' from the hunt of a shilling per acre. The sporting press was not impressed. The union's proposals threatened to change the whole basis of hunting, thundered the *Country Gentleman*: 'to substitute compulsion for good will, and the despotic order of cold commercialism for that bond of sympathy and close understanding . . . between agriculturists and the hunting community'. Rent of a shilling an acre would cripple hunts financially. The Bicester's 500,000 acres would be liable to a rent bill of £25,000. Yet the Buckingham dairy farmers had a real grievance. Why should they put up with vast Bicester fields of Londoners, many of whom paid no subscription?[15]

Baily's bristles with gloomy articles lamenting the decay of hunting in the provinces. The official histories commissioned by many hunts in about 1900 were obituary notices for a vanished golden age. Georgina Bowers, *Punch*'s lady artist, entitled her picture book of 1889 *Hunting in Hard Times*.

Hunting costs had risen. In the 1860s the cost of hunting a provincial country was reckoned at £600 for each day in the week hounds went out; by 1900 this had become between £750 and £1,000 per day. Agricultural incomes had fallen, squeezing hunt subscriptions. At the Burton on the sodden ploughs of Lincolnshire the Master's guarantee slumped from £1,200 in the early 1870s to £300 in 1884. The hunt gave up altogether for the season of 1888–9. Lord Yarborough's rents also slumped, and in 1895 with 'a terrible wrench' he sold the famous Brocklesby dog pack with its hound list going back to 1746. In 1879 the joint Masters of the Craven in Berkshire resigned after two anxious years, when the committee came nowhere near meeting its commitment of £1,650.[16]

Rich Masters were at a premium. Sometimes big-spending ones were heirs to old money. Lord Willoughby de Broke, eighteenth baron, was Master of the Warwickshire 1876–1900. Probably the most hot-tempered MFH of his day, he hunted hounds himself. He took over a moderate pack, and bred it up into a famous pack of Peterborough winners, pouring money into the hunt at a time when rents were squeezed.

> There was a young 'feller' called Broke,
> Who was 'broke' when the Foxhounds he took,
> But when he was Master
> The money flew faster
> Than he could tear cheques from his book.[17]

In the north east hunting was floated on coal. John Straker, founder of a dynasty of coal-owning equestrians, took the Tynedale, and over a long Mastership (1883–1937) made it the Leicestershire of the north. In 1896 Lewis Priestman, a Newcastle colliery owner, resuscitated the Braes of Derwent, which had been languishing since the demise of an earlier generation of coal-owner Masters, the Cowens.

Down in Dorset, at the Blackmoor Vale, Merthyr Guest hunted six days a week and took no subscription (1883–1900). A son of the ironmaster J. J. Guest, Merthyr married an even richer wife, Lady Theodora, daughter of the Marquess of Westminster. He kept eighty grey horses for himself and his hunt servants.[18]

The Cheshire had been split into the North and South Cheshire in 1877. Both packs were linked to the exclusive Tarporley Hunt Club, which fought a losing battle against Barbarians invading from Liverpool and Manchester in the north and east. In 1906 the two hunts were united under Bendor, fabulously wealthy Duke of Westminster. Bendor gave up in 1911, taking hounds and hunters to the South of France where he formed a wild boar hunt. *The Times* published an article entitled 'From Fox to Boar', hinting at disloyalty to the national sport.[19]

Rich Masters like Bendor could cause problems. Quarrels broke out. On hunt committees declining gentlefolk cohabited uneasily with the new rich, accustomed to what *Baily's* called business or City authority, where every little detail is booked as important. There was a rapid turnover of Masters. In the 1860s ten years or more had been the usual term. Now Masters often resigned after only two or three seasons. H. W. Selby Lowndes, younger son of Mr Selby Lowndes whose family had hunted the Whaddon Chase since the eighteenth century, was one of the new poor. He wrote bitterly in his diary:

> The present-day young man with a good big banking account takes hounds. He attends the Rugby hound sales, gives fabulous prices for hounds entirely for their looks – work being quite a secondary consideration. The same with his horses. He fills his stables in a similar manner, and even fuller is his wardrobe. The usual result is that he resigns in three years, heartily sick of the whole thing.[20]

Hound breeding suffered from lack of continuity and expertise. Despite increased costs two-day-a-week countries often killed no more than thirty foxes a season which, even at a conservative estimate of £750 per day, worked out at an expensive £50 a fox. The attempt to bring the provinces up to the standards of Leicestershire led not to better sport but to increased and unnecessary show.[21]

Many of the new rich preferred shooting to hunting. Reared pheasant shooting was glamourized by Edward VII and the Big Shots – competitive record-breakers like Lords Ripon and Walsingham. Lord Ripon, who was about the best, killed a total of 556,813 head of game between 1873 and 1923. Edward VII was too heavy to ride, and anyway 'Tum-tum' didn't like missing his luncheon.

Shooting was also the sport of the Edwardian businessman, middle-aged and overweight. Tracts of hunting country within fifty miles of London were given over to businessmen's syndicate shoots. If foxes were in surplus in the shires, they were almost extinct in the home counties.

Gamekeeping boomed. Since 1850 keepers had been equipped with breech-loading guns and strychnine. On syndicate shoots, where there was no resident landowner in charge, keepers ruled like petty tyrants. Acts of extraordinary cruelty and vandalism were perpetrated in the name of the fat, low-flying pheasant. Rare predators like polecats and buzzards were wiped out altogether. Religious war was waged against foxes.

To keep the hunt happy, keepers provided bagged foxes. These were sometimes imported from Germany. Another device was to kill vixens with litters and rear the cubs in captivity. But bagged foxes like reared pheasants were poor sport, often collapsing exhausted after a field or so. They were also peculiarly prone to mange. Mange became endemic among foxes, and hunting men held keepers responsible.[22]

The East Kent, a run-down provincial pack spoiled by too many Masters, was taken over by H. W. Selby Lowndes in 1900. Over a thirty-year mastership he made it solvent, popular and deadly. He killed between twenty-four and thirty-seven and a half brace of foxes each season from 1900 to 1910.

Selby Lowndes was not a rich man. He had hunted in the shires and didn't like what he saw there. He'd learned his hunting as Master of the Bilsdale (1897–1900), the trencher-fed farmers' pack in the Yorkshire Dales. Here he found 'sportsmen in the best sense of the word. They have a great knowledge of woodcraft and venery, and a keenness and endurance, both on horseback and on foot, which is refreshing to those of us who deplore the luxury and "fashion" which has crept into the chase.' At the East Kent he tried to encourage active interest among farmers and landowners. He also introduced new blood into the pack: the Welsh cross from Sir Edward Curre, producing some of the most effective hounds ever seen in East Kent.[23]

As a breeder of hounds, Sir Edward Curre ranks with Hugo Meynell or Lord Henry Bentinck. At Itton Court in Monmouthshire (1896–1930) Curre bred and popularized the Welsh cross, 'the most important single development in the history of modern hound breeding'.[24] It was also the most controversial.

The *pure* rough-coated Welsh hound had survived in remote Welsh-speaking Glamorganshire packs such as the Glonyer or Bwlfa. The Gelligaer was another pack of Welsh hounds. According to *Baily's Hunting Directory* it was a difficult country to hunt, 'being principally on coal measures'. On Snowdonia the Jones family had hunted their private foot pack of Welsh Fell hounds, the Ynsfor, since 1765, wearing their hunt uniform of local undyed brown tweed known as Brytwyn Llewd. Major Evan Bowen Jones, Master 1901–40, fought in the Boer War. Soon after, he called on an old lady in the hills for a cup of tea. 'I've been away at the war,' he said. 'Well indeed,' she replied, 'and has there been a war?'[25]

Curre hunted with long-established Welsh hill packs like Mr Thomas Williams's Glog, near Pontypridd, selecting stallion hounds to cross with his English bitches. The result was a hound that was the antithesis of the big, tan Belvoir type. 'I wanted a hound that had drive and voice and speed,' said Curre. 'I wanted them all of a type, without the woolly Welsh coat – which to me was unsightly – and I wanted them *white*, so that I could see them in the distance.'[26]

On the Scottish Border Jacob Robson, Master 1879–1919, used a cross with long-haired fell hounds to breed a killing hill pack. Like John Peel, Robson wore a grey coat. In 1897–8 he killed fifty-five brace of foxes with only twenty-seven hounds and four horses. 'Did the Pytchley or the Quorn do better than this with their studs of forty horses and sixty couple of hounds, ninety couple of whelps at walk and a large staff of servants?' asked *Baily's*. 'We doubt it.' Will Ogilvie the Border poet made the same point in verse.

> Here is no ponderous pride,
> Here is no swagger, no place for the swell,
> But a handful of fellows who'll ride
> A fox to his death over upland and fell
> Where a hundred good foxes have died.[27]

Sir Edward Curre's Welsh cross soon infiltrated orthodox kennels. In 1907 Charles McNeill took the Grafton, then in a bad way, and used hounds from Curre to breed a famous working pack. Isaac Bell, who became Master of the Kilkenny in 1908, took hounds from Itton Court back to Ireland. After the Great War Bell used the same stock to breed a pack at the South and West Wilts (1925–34). He became a leading advocate of the Welsh cross. So did A. H. Higginson MFH, a fellow American who perhaps shared Bell's scepticism about genealogy.

Another Welsh enthusiast was Sir Ian Heathcoat Amory, Master of the Tiverton in Devon 1910–30, and breeder of Tiverton Actor 1922, a stallion hound whose genes penetrated most good packs. 'There are in England two schools of hound breeding,' said Amory, 'one of which is trying to breed hounds which are good-looking and sometimes kill foxes, and the other to breed hounds which kill foxes and are sometimes good-looking. I prefer the latter sort.'[28] Not everyone agreed. Aristocratic MFHs, guardians of orthodox bloodlines, looked on with disgust at Curre's bastard Welsh cross.

The aristocratic reaction against the Welsh cross was led by Earl Bathurst and the nineteenth Lord Willoughby de Broke, who had succeeded his father as Warwickshire MFH in 1900. Diehard Tories to the tips of their blue-blooded fingers, they saw the Welsh cross as the canine equivalent of Lloyd George – a demonic threat to the old aristocratic order.

In 1909 Lloyd George, as Chancellor of the Exchequer, had introduced his People's Budget, proposing super tax and land valuation, and made speeches attacking the Duke of Westminster. Nervous jokes were cracked in the shires. In 1909 Winston Churchill, then much hated for deserting to the Liberals, had a fall out with the Quorn. 'What's the damage?' asked Alfred Brocklehurst, the Quornite wit. 'He broke his collarbone,' was the reply. 'Good Lord! Is that all? Pity it wasn't his – jaw!'[29]

In 1911, Willoughby de Broke plunged into active politics in the House of Lords. 'I have been brought up in the midst of stock breeding of all kinds all my life,' he declared in a debate on second chamber reform, 'and I am prepared to defend the hereditary principle . . . whether the principle is applied to Peers or whether it is applied to foxhounds.' He led the revolt of the Diehard peers, who preferred to die in the last ditch rather than let through the Parliament Bill curtailing the Lords' veto. When charged with disloyalty to his leader, Lord Lansdowne, he replied: 'As Master of Hounds I don't like killing a fox without my huntsman, but it is better than losing my hounds.'[30]

In the House of Lords the Diehards were defeated. They couldn't stop Lloyd George. His Land Campaign of 1913–14 aimed to capture the counties for the Liberals by setting farmers and agricultural labourers against landowners. Whole fields of mangold-wurzels, said Lloyd George, had been devoured by clouds of hungry pheasants. At least hunting was kept out of the argument. Margot Asquith, the Prime Minister's wife, had hunted in Leicestershire in her youth. 'Promise me,' she implored Lloyd George, 'you won't mention fox hunting in your land speeches.' He didn't.[31]

After the Great War the Diehards fought back. Baulked in their bid for an aristocratic comeback in politics, the least they could do was to preserve the aristocratic principle in the foxhound.

Hound breeding was Lord Bathurst's life. Alfred Munnings,

who painted him, remembered him in a coat of exquisite, faded geranium pink, watching his hounds, 'lips apart, in a sort of living ecstasy'.[32] In 1926 Bathurst spoke out. The Welsh cross was 'a blot on the escutcheon, a *mésalliance*, a marriage without quarterings'. In short, the Welsh cross had no grandparents. For Bathurst the breeding of foxhounds, like the breeding of racehorses (and peers), was governed by a golden rule: always breed from an animal whose pedigree traced back by as many direct lines as possible to famous ancestors.[33] Bathurst's coup was to ban the Welsh cross from the Foxhound Kennel Stud Book.

The FKSB had been published by the Masters of Foxhounds Association since 1886. (Earlier volumes were compiled by Robert Vyner in 1841 and Cornelius Tongue in 1866.) Since 1886 the FKSB had been edited by the Rev. Cecil Legard, vicar of Cottesbrooke in Northamptonshire 1887–1920. Legard, who dressed like a Regency parson in frocked coat, winged collar and tall hat, was known as 'Your Oiliness' on account of his love for lords. He professed to hate tobacco smoke, once making a group of farmers put out their pipes in a railway carriage. When two peers passed puffing cigars, Legard leaped up and followed them into a smoker. Later, one of the farmers put his head into the smoker, saying, 'I see the smoke of the lord is savoury to the priest's nostrils.'[34]

Despite Legard's snobbishness, his policy as editor of the FKSB had been merely to list the hounds entered annually by recognized packs. There was nothing to stop a pack from registering Welsh-cross hounds like any others, and many did. Bathurst, however, succeeded in introducing a new rule into the constitution of the Masters of Foxhounds Association. Rule twenty-eight stipulates that for hounds to qualify for registration, 'their sires and dams, or both their grand-sires and both their grand-dams must have been registered in the Foxhound Kennel Stud Book'.

Snobbery was triumphant. The English foxhound was now a member of a closed caste; rather than *Burke's Peerage*, the FKSB was now a canine *Almanac de Gotha*. Distinguished new packs like Sir Alfred Goodson's brilliant College Valley, which has a fell cross, or Sir John Buchanan-Jardine's black-and-tan Dumfriesshire were ineligible for registration. But Bathurst was shutting the kennel door after the hound had bolted. He couldn't eradicate Welsh blood that was already registered, and by the 1920s the Welsh cross was well established. In 1939, 115 of the 175 kennels in the FKSB had Welsh blood.[35]

CHAPTER TEN

War and Peace

'It may be unfashionable to show
yourself keen and enthusiastic, but if you
start bored with horses and hunting
you will end – on the floor!'

LADY DIANA SHEDDEN and
LADY APSLEY, *To Whom the Goddess*, 1932

The First World War broke out as cub hunting began in August 1914.

The Masters of Foxhounds Association decreed that no hunt should cease to exist. 'The hunting,' explained *Baily's*, 'was to be kept on so that the supply of foxes could be kept down, and so that everything might be kept in such a position that the ordinary routine could be resumed when happier times returned.'

This remained the policy throughout the war. But it became increasingly difficult to carry out. As fields shrank, subscriptions dried up. To *Baily's* the moral was clear. 'The extravagance which has surrounded hunting of recent years' – and which *Baily's* attributed to 'the participation of *nouveaux riches* from the towns' – must be abandoned. Hunting must retrench if it was to survive.[1]

By 1917 the Pytchley subscription had fallen from £2,600 to £1,300, forcing the hunt to cut down from six to two days a week, give up second horses and reduce its kennel to twenty-seven and a half couple. Willoughby de Broke was joint Master of the Warwickshire throughout the war. He found it a thankless task. 'To ride a horse half-fit and to ride that horse all day; to hunt Hounds that are poorly fed; to know that even if they were in good enough condition to tire their Fox he would almost surely find an open earth; to be short-handed both in the hunting-field and in the kennel; to have a diminishing number of walks for puppies; – and all these things have not made the management of hunting during the War a very pleasing occupation.'

What made the sacrifice bearable for Willoughby de Broke was the thought that he was doing his bit to ensure the survival of the foxhound. 'In the last resort this was the only thing that really mattered.'[2] The great governing kennels continued to breed and enter hounds.

Cosmopolitan Leicestershire was immediately affected by the war. The birds of passage on whom the Melton packs depended stopped coming. The Austrian Count Charles Kinsky, a well-known Leicestershire figure who won the Grand National in 1891, went back to fight in the Austrian cavalry. Kinsky's stud of first-class hunters was taken for the British army. It was rumoured that he'd given orders for his horses to be shot or poisoned. In fact the rumour was invented, allegedly by German agents. Kinsky had asked for his horses to be distributed among his friends in the British Army.[3]

The Cottesmore was left high and dry in 1915 when the rich American Master, Mr Strawbridge, resigned on account of the war. Hugh Lonsdale came to the rescue. It was a generous gesture, as Lonsdale had been badly treated by the 'old gang' at the Cottesmore, who forced him to resign the Mastership in 1911. He paid to keep the hunt going at full pre-1914 throttle. At the Belvoir, Tommy Bouch, the Master, paid for the hunt throughout the war, though he himself was at the front.[4]

Provincial packs survived on a shoestring. Not that sport suffered. On the contrary, at the East Kent, for instance, H. W. Selby Lowndes found the war years provided the best sport of his entire Mastership. 'There was no one out to head foxes, no indiscriminate halloaing, and hounds, not being over-ridden, did most of the work themselves.'[5]

At the South Berks Cecil Aldin, the sporting artist, combined the Mastership with the duties of remount officer. Ex-Masters came out of retirement for the war. The North Northumberland was kept going by Freddy Lambton, who had hunted the country in the 1880s. At the age of sixty-one he took hounds and hunted them himself, helped by one old whip. 'He used to say how hard it would be for the young men who were fighting, if they should find their hunting gone when they came back.'[6]

When men went to the war, women held the fort. During the war the number of female MFHs doubled, rising from six to twelve. One of the best known was Mrs Inge of the Atherstone (1914–20), affectionately drawn by Siegfried Sassoon in *Memoirs of a Fox-Hunting Man* as Mrs Oakfield of the Packlestone, 'in her tall hat and perfectly fitting black habit with a bunch of violets in her buttonhole'.[7]

Many more women took over unofficially. At the Pytchley, Lady Lowther was acting Master while her husband, Sir Charles, was at the war. Lady Dalmeny whipped in, and ladies made up the entire field. Cecil Aldin used women as grooms to look after his remounts. Will Ogilvie caught the spirit of wartime hunting in *The First Whip*, 1915.

As I wandered home
By Hedworth Combe
I heard a lone horse whinny,
And saw on the hill
Stand statue-still
At the top of the old oak spinney
A rough-haired hack
With a girl on his back –
And '*Hounds!*' I said – '*for a guinea!*'

The wind blew chill
Over Larchley Hill,
And it couldn't have blown much colder;
Her nose was blue,
And her pigtails two
Hung damply over her shoulder;
She might have been ten,

Or – guessing again –
She might have been twelve months older.

To a tight pink lip
She pressed her whip
By way of imposing quiet;
I bowed my head
To the word unsaid
Accepting the lady's fiat,
And noted the while
Her Belvoir style
As she rated a hound for riot.

Hounds didn't all stay at home. A few went out to France, summoned by cavalry officers who craved hunting as they waited behind the lines for the push. Hunting wasn't popular with French farmers, and in deference to them it was abandoned on the Western Front until the occupation of the Rhine. In the Middle East the sport was better. In Palestine officers hunted foxes and jackal around Jaffa and point-to-pointed near Gaza; there was hunting around Salonika and the Sultan of Turkey kept hounds to hunt jackal.[8]

In 1917–18 the going got rough on the home front. Food for hounds was in short supply. Hunting was under attack from outside. Racing was suspended in May 1917, when the government claimed it was against public opinion that it should continue. Racing was a 'sport', unacceptable in time of war.[9] The same was urged against fox hunting. Critics called for the mass destruction of hounds.

The ban on racing was lifted in July 1917. The Jockey Club convinced the government that racing must go on if the horse-breeding industry was to survive. Fox hunters urged that hunting was the vital link between horse breeding and the army. By providing peacetime demand for blood horses, hunting supplied the reserve of horses for the army to take in time of war.

A hundred and seventy thousand horses were mobilized in the first fortnight after war was declared. Most of them were hunters, listed by the Remount Department of the War Office in a census taken in 1912. 'It is not too much to say,' claimed Willoughby de Broke, 'that the Expeditionary Force [in 1914] could not have left

26 The ninth Duke of Beaufort hunted his own hounds but never jumped

27 Sylvia Portman at the meet, 1925

28 The Galway Blazers present Isaac Bell, their retiring Master, with a silver fox, 1908

England unless the nation could have drawn upon studs of well-bred hunters to bring the peace Establishment of the Army horses up to strength.' Harry Chaplin rammed the point home in a speech to the Masters of Foxhounds Association in 1918. 'In these days of motors, it is hunting, and hunting alone, which provides the constant supply in time of peace which is required by the Army in time of War.'[10]

Hunting escaped a ban. Food shortages nevertheless compelled hunts to put down a lot of hounds. Because of the craze for good looks, the choice of hounds to keep was often more influenced by looks than working qualities. Many hunts emerged from the war with packs short on nose and drive.[11]

After the carnage in the trenches came a revolution in landownership. Between 1918 and 1921 a quarter of the land of England and Wales was sold – about the same proportion that changed hands through the dissolution of the monasteries. Estates were broken up and sold to tenants. Though this pattern of sales began in 1910–14, it accelerated after the war. The proportion of owner-occupied land rose from 11 per cent in 1914 to 36 per cent in 1927.

Historians have seen this as the end of the road for the aristocracy. Books on the subject end with a bang with the post-war liquidation of the aristocracy, which is thereafter allegedly in eclipse, lingering on as curator of its heritage. This is probably jumping the gun. Historians have a habit of writing the aristocracy into premature decline. Since Tudor times at least, elderly pessimists have lamented the decline of old families and the rise of new wealth.

In 1921 Willoughby de Broke sold his beloved Compton Verney to Joe Watson, a soap boiler; Willoughby died soon after of a broken heart. 'The greatest blow to hunting in England,' declared Brigadier General Bruce, historian of the Essex Foxhounds, in 1926, 'was the break-up of the great landed estates.'

In fact few great estates were dismembered altogether. The historian of Lord Abergavenny's Eridge Hunt noted in 1936 that in the Eridge country (Kent) the big estates of 1880 were with one exception still intact.[12] Great estates also survived in the Heythrop. Here bits of Blenheim, Sezincote, Ditchley, Batsford and Sherborne were sold off after 1919, but only two estates were dismembered and sold up altogether. Big estates were still intact in the Tynedale in the 1950s. They survived too in the Northumbrian part of the Braes of Derwent; but on the Durham side of the country landowners were pushed out after the Great War by colliery development.[13]

Far more smaller gentry-owned estates were sold. In the 1930s Guy Paget toured the Belvoir country and noted how few pre-war landed gentry survived, and how few of those that did hunted. So many of their sons had been killed in the war. The Pytchley was the same. 'Take the Monday country – a desert, that's what it is now, just a desert.' The Fernie country was the same: the big houses had been pulled down, shut or turned into schools, nursing homes or asylums.[14]

Rural tensions blew up at the Whaddon Chase, which had been hunted by the Selby Lowndes family since the eighteenth century. Colonel William Selby Lowndes, brother of the East Kent MFH, went to the war and left his wife in charge. He returned to find the Rothschild foxhounds hunting his country, with Lord Dalmeny – heir to ex-Prime Minister Lord Rosebery and son of Hannah Rothschild – as their MFH.

The Rothschilds had always hunted carted stags in Buckinghamshire by permission of Selby Lowndes. But Selby Lowndes's rental income had been shrinking since the agricultural depression of the 1880s, and the Rothschilds thought he could no longer afford to hunt the country properly. In July 1917 the Rothschilds held an irregular meeting of Bucks landowners at Tattersall's, and appointed Dalmeny Master. The Masters of Foxhounds Association condemned the Rothschild faction as 'outlaws'. In 1919–20 both Selby Lowndes and Dalmeny tried to hunt the country. The Whaddon was always a small country, and there were clashes between the two packs. Once when they found themselves hunting the same fox, the Masters dismounted and fought each other with their whips.

In 1920 the dispute was referred to the Masters of Foxhounds

Association. They ruled that both Masters should stand down and agree to a new one, to be appointed by a hunt meeting. The meeting chose Lord Orkney, a member of the Rothschild camp; in 1923 he gave up in favour of Lord Dalmeny, later Rosebery, who remained Master until 1940.[15]

The row was widely reported. *The Times* carried leaders on it. It was a case of plutocracy versus the new poor. Rosebery, remembered as 'a fat pig of a chap', was an autocrat in the field. Dorian Williams's father, who was Master of the Grafton 1928–31, once went out with the Whaddon Chase and jumped a fence in front of Rosebery, who sent him home. As Williams was boxing up, the hunt came past, and Rosebery – who'd presumably been told that he shouldn't behave like that to a neighbouring Master – called out: 'You must come and have another day with us some time.' Williams replied, 'Thanks, I'd very much like to when you've got a gentleman as Master.' Dorian Williams himself became Master of the Whaddon Chase in 1954, and he found the country still divided. Farmers he visited often asked him whether he was a Dalmeny man or a Selby Lowndes man.[16]

Most of the land sold in 1918–21 was bought by tenant farmers. Farming enjoyed a frenetic post-war boom. Farmers bought hunters at inflated prices – horses were in short supply after the war – and went in for an orgy of sport. In Wiltshire, A. G. Street farmed four hundred acres, kept two hunters, shot twice a week in winter and played tennis all summer.

War-induced prosperity was a blip on a downward curve. In 1921 the government withdrew price guarantees for corn, and prices collapsed during the glut that followed. Farmers who had bought their farms at the high prices of 1918–21 now found themselves paying bank interest out of falling incomes on mortgages for land which was losing its value.[17]

Farming became a struggle for survival. The farmer who came out in tweed cap, gaiters and brown breeches after doing a morning's work on the farm was rarer than before the war. Most hunts didn't expect farmers to pay subscriptions; but farmers could now afford neither time nor horses to hunt.

Non-hunting farmers weren't so hospitable to the hunt as before. Owner-occupiers exposed to the price blizzard no longer had landlords' money at their backs. Gates and fences, formerly the responsibility of the estate, were neglected. More wire went up. Farmers who before the war had looked to the estate to make good hunt damage now appealed directly to the hunt. Claims for fences, crops and poultry shot up.

Motor cars created difficulties too. The old hands complained that they ruined scent, and exhaust fumes and tarmac surfaces certainly made the huntsman's job harder. But the real problem was that the motor car had superseded the horse. Riding was no longer essential to get about the countryside. Chauffeurs replaced grooms, and grooms turned into chauffeurs, hissing at their motors like horses and braking downhill in case they were run away with. Hunting could no longer be defended as training for war. The complete disappearance of the horse seemed only a question of time.

Meanwhile, motor cars encouraged an irresponsible attitude among the young. General Bruce snorted angrily at the young man or woman who danced in London until the small hours, breakfasted on a cup of coffee and 'the inevitable cigarette', and then drove down to the shires in a six-cylinder automobile. 'Does not that swift, smooth dart out of London at forty-five m.p.h. breed a distinct distaste for slow and methodical drawing for the fox?'[18]

The hardest blow was the war itself. Lady Apsley, redoubtable daughter-in-law of the hound-breeding Lord Bathurst, thought it touch and go whether hunting would survive the post-war period. 'Broken hearts, physical wrecks, and ruined county families did not appear promising material with which to rebuild Hunting.' Lady Apsley lived through the trauma of the war only to break her back falling from a horse in 1930, and spend the rest of her life in a wheelchair.[19]

In Ireland, breeding ground of good hunters, the outlook was even bleaker. Post-war Ireland was a country of 'burnt and derelict country houses, of empty stables that were once full of good horses, of blank fox coverts, silent kennels and poached rivers'.[20]

The lead came from what then seemed a surprising direction: the Royal Family.

In 1919 Edward, Prince of Wales started to hunt in the shires. He was the first royal to dedicate himself to fox hunting since George IV. His grandfather had hunted the Pytchley in 1863, stopping in the middle of a run to drink a flagon of ale and smoke a cigar the size of a sausage roll.

From 1923 until 1928 the Prince of Wales brought his horses to Craven Lodge, a hunting club in Melton Mowbray, where he took a suite for the season. His brothers, the Dukes of Gloucester and Kent, came too; the Duke of York, later George VI, hunted with the Pytchley.

Royalty was not an unmixed blessing. Once the Prince of Wales jumped into a field of roots on top of the Quorn hounds. Major Burnaby, who was Master through the 1920s, roared, '*Hold hard, you!* You double-dyed bounder!' Then, seeing who it was, weakly, with the field dissolving into laughter behind him: 'Oh I say, sir, ripping, ripping!'[21]

Melton became fashionable once more. Rich carpet-baggers descended for the season. Not all of them came for the hunting. There was a sizable road brigade of riders who turned up immaculate at the meet, followed the hunt along the roads, and went home for lunch. The hunting itself was organized as a social event. The Quorn stopped for lunch, when grooms came up with a change of horse and sandwiches. It was not done to carry a sandwich box or flask on your saddle yourself. The army of second horsemen formed a kind of shadow hunt, led by the hunt staffs' second horsemen in red, and followed by a cavalcade of grooms in bowlers and black coats, some of them leading side-saddle horses.

Many of the carpet-baggers were really there for the *après-chasse*. Evenings in Melton were a whirl of cocktails and fancy dress, poker and adultery. Millionaires like 'Banker' Lowenstein and Lord

Furness wined and dined equestrian socialites such as Miss Monica Sheriffe or the much-married Mrs Fred Cripps, one of the many Duchesses of Westminster.[22]

This was a far cry from high Victorian earnestness or the hearty horseplay of Lady Augusta Fane's day. What was 'vice' for the Victorians was 'fun' in the 1920s. Melton was England's answer to Kenya's Happy Valley. Those who wanted to forget the pain of war sought in hunting a mind-numbing narcotic. The generation who had expected to die in the trenches found Meltonian fun as good as any in a life they hadn't really bargained for anyway. Frivolous perhaps; but Melton did much less harm than dressing up in uniforms and playing at fascist politics like the displaced aristocracies of the Continent.

Meltonians had themselves and their horses painted by Alfred Munnings. Munnings's list of commissions in the 1920s and 1930s reads like a social column for the shires: the Duke of Marlborough and Lord Ivor Churchill changing horses near Melton, Mr Strawbridge, rich American friend of the Prince of Wales, Ronald Tree, American socialite Master of the Pytchley 1927–33. Another fashion-conscious sitter was the Duchess of Westminster, before she was Mrs Cripps. Climbing down from the wooden saddle horse she was sitting on, she pulled her jacket hard down in front. 'See,' she said to Munnings, pointing to her bosom, 'I want to be flat as a board.'

In 1921 Munnings painted the Prince of Wales. The Prince drove himself to Munnings's London studio each morning in breeches and boots, then donned a pink coat and top hat and sat on the saddle horse, occasionally adjusting his hat in the mirror – he always wore his top hat on the side of his head. Sir Theodore Cook, editor of the *Field*, who'd commissioned the picture, brought a basket containing vintage port and glasses, and read to the Prince from *Handley Cross* while he sat.[23]

The Prince was not a social fox hunter; he took his riding seriously. After the abdication he was rubbished as a horseman. His riding became a political issue: he had, after all, lost his seat. But Leicestershire stayed loyal to him. J. H. Marshall, who knew what he was talking about, thought the Prince went well in the best of company. He rode like a jockey, favouring short leathers and a snaffle bridle. He went like a bomb, falling off uncomfortably often.[24]

Leicestershire between the wars was a fox hunter's dream. Agricultural depression meant more grass than ever. Wire was taken down in winter, allowing fences to be jumped anywhere. There were no cars to get in the way, as very few roads were tarmaced.

For the first time ladies outnumbered men. Some of the younger ones rode astride. During the 1920s the cross-saddle became acceptable for ladies. Medical objections of an obscure and unlikely nature were waived in an era when women cropped their hair and wore trousers.

Riding astride was altogether cheaper and more convenient than side-saddle. A woman astride rode about one and a half stone lighter than side-saddle. She could use smaller, cheaper horses, dispensing with the cumbersome and expensive side-saddle which was so prone to give a horse a sore back. Clothes were cheaper too. At seven guineas apiece, well-cut breeches were far less expensive than riding habits.

Even so, most women in the shires still rode side-saddle. Apart from anything else, it looked so much nicer. Hefty thighs were elegantly concealed, and a woman on a side-saddle could ride a much bigger, better, galloping horse.

The ideal side-saddle hunter was a Thoroughbred or near-Thoroughbred 16.1 or 16.2 hands high. Ladies rode in a double bridle on a loose rein, and controlled their horses through horsemanship not brute strength. Ladies always wore spurs but the rowels were sawn off to avoid jabbing the horse by mistake. The horse was kidded and humoured into doing what the rider wanted it to do. 'Horses,' said Lady Apsley, 'are like husbands: they are the strong silent ones and dearly love to think they have their own way.'[25]

Making slashing, strong Thoroughbred horses into hunters for side-saddle ladies was an art, perfected by skilled nagsmen like J. H.

Marshall. The art of horsemanship was probably at its peak in the shires between the wars. The Caprilli revolution, which brought the forward seat and the snaffle bridle, made little impact in the shires. The forward seat was all right for show jumping but considered far too loose for the hunting field.

Balance and collection were the nagsman's aims, double bridles his instrument. 'A gentleman's hunter,' said Bert Drage, the Pytchley dealer, 'can be collected between his hands and his legs, and a lady's hunter is collected between her hand and the horse's hind leg.' You could tell a nagsman by his hands: his first fingers were bent in and the others bent out, the consequence of riding eight hours a day in a double bridle. 'A touch of the curb and a beautifully made horse would come back to you. A horse that pulled wasn't fit for a gentleman to ride.'

The Thoroughbred hunter probably realized its genetic potential between the wars. Analysis of classic flat race timings has shown that the performance of Thoroughbred racehorses peaked before 1914. Gains in race winning times are more significant between 1880 and 1910 than at any time before or since. The racehorse is the product of eighteenth-century breeding techniques, and it may have fulfilled its genetic potential between 1880 and 1910.[26] Hunter performance is much harder to measure and anyway unrecorded, but given the time it takes for classic racehorse blood to filter through to hunter breeding, it's likely that hunter performance peaked in the 1920s.

Horse dealers like Harry Beeby or William Young and Sons of Melton were at the height of their glory. They bought young horses bred in Ireland, the Borders or the West Country, made them, showed them off out hunting and sold them. J. H. Marshall was head nagsman to Harry Beeby in the 1920s, when there were a hundred horses in the yard, and two men who clipped horses full time.

Riding a big Thoroughbred horse across country was an art form. Lady Apsley waxed lyrical about the 'feeling of serene elation when one's horse responds to the lightest touch of hand and leg to our call for effort at the big black uncompromising place'. The riding ideal of hunting, which dates from Whyte-Melville, had come into its own.[27] Whyte-Melville's ideal of sympathetic horsemanship was reinforced after the war by Geoffrey Brooke's teaching about horse psychology, or what he called horse sense.

Hunting ladies gave a spur to the new sympathetic riding. Not that the ladies were saints. The shires were highly competitive. Knowing where you were or where the hounds were didn't matter in the least; but jumping the fence in front first and jumping it well mattered like hell. Unscrupulous ladies cut through the crowd at gates, and ruthlessly rode off competitors at fences.

There was nothing democratic about this kind of hunting. When Lady Apsley went to Tyneside during the slump and told out-of-work pitmen they ought to go hunting she wasn't well received. The hunting lady in Lady Diana Shedden and Lady Apsley's *To Whom the Goddess* (1932) is an old-fashioned lady bountiful. Even if she only takes a house for the season, she must do her bit. 'The time spent in a draughty hall lit by one smoky lamp, slowly discussing the arrangements for the Summer Flower Show on a winter's evening after a tiring day's hunting is not wasted.'

Black or navy blue habits must be cut by the best London tailors – Busvine or Roberts and Carroll. Top hats from Lock's must always be worn with a veil and bun (false if necessary). Boots from Maxwell or Peal gleamed with a velvety lustre never since equalled, the product of countless man-hours of boning (rubbing with a deer's femur). For cleaning dirty riding habits a good valet and brushing room were essential. The muddy habit must be soaked in cold water, vigorously scrubbed and marks removed with ammonia.

The stables were the province of the stud groom. The hunting lady who turned up for breakfast in boots and breeches, cardigan and 'gay silk handkerchief' knotted round her neck – for 'it is easier to put a tie on after one's hat is secured' – had no intention of getting her own horse ready. Men wore silk aprons to protect their spotless white leather breeches until they mounted their horse at the meet. Woe betide the child whose marmaladey fingers touched its father's immaculate boots.

Saddlery was taken as seriously as clothes. You had a saddle made to fit by Champion and Wilton or Whippy, and side-saddles were made to fit not just the rider and her preferred seat ('straight' or 'old fashioned') but the horse as well. Bits must always be stitched on to double bridles (buckles were unsightly). Through your good pair of gloves (Swaine and Adeney, and a spare pair tucked under the girth) you held reins soaped to a perfection of suppleness. Even the contents of your pocket were standardized: Mrs Le Coq's hunting chocolate, shillings and sixpences for people who opened gates, a ten-shilling note in case your horse had to be caught and a pocket-size hunting map from Map House of St James's.

The trouble about the new ideal of riding across country was that hunting wasn't essential to it. The exhilaration came from the horse not the hounds. Today's most skilled and dedicated cross-country riders are to be found at Badminton, not in Leicestershire.

CHAPTER ELEVEN

Gone To Ground

Refortified by exercise and air,
I, jogging home astride my chestnut mare,
Grow half-humane, and question the propriety,
Of *Foxes Torn to Bits in Smart Society*.

Spurts past me Fernie-Goldflake in his car . . .

I wonder if these Nimrods really are
Crassly unconscious that their Reynardism
Is (dare I say it) an anachronism.

SIEGFRIED SASSOON, 1922

The Prince of Wales sold his horses in 1928 and ceased hunting. In 1929 came yet another slump. James Baird, Master of the Cottesmore since 1921, was forced to give up in 1931. At the Grafton, 'Pudding' Williams, Dorian's father, gave up too. Pudding sold his house in 1932 and went abroad to follow the sun. The Quorn subscription fell from £11,462 in 1929 to £7,882 in 1932. Sir Harold Nutting, newly rich from bottling Guinness, was co-opted into the Mastership in 1930. 'We don't want your personality, we want your purse,' wisecracked his joint Master, Algie Burnaby. Sir Harold lavished around fifteen thousand pounds a year on the Quorn throughout the 1930s.[1]

Michael Berry, hunting correspondent to *The Times* 1932–9, drew attention to the provinces, writing for an era of shrinking private incomes and depressed farmers. Berry thought local enthusiasm was the key. It wasn't enough to throw a shilling at the labourer who opened the gate – you should talk to him too, at the very least say good morning. Hunting mustn't become an amusement imported into the country and tolerated for the money it brought.

Berry showed how far the MFH's job had changed. He believed much more was involved than wearing a velvet cap and shouting 'Hold hard!' The MFH must know each farmer – and there might be as many as two thousand – by name, and befriend all shooting tenants, gamekeepers and shepherds. Hunting days were the outward sign of a continuous process of organization and fox preservation; no MFH could expect foxes in the autumn if he went up to London for the summer season when hunting stopped. Point-to-point races in spring were primarily in aid of farmers – the local hunt gave them lunch and a day out.

More and more of the Master's work was being shared. Committees for wire, committees for earth-stopping or poultry relieved the MFH of some of the load. And joint Masterships were far more common than before the 1914–18 war.[2]

Farmers found it very difficult to make a living in the eastern corn countries. Their fields were wet and their hedges were like forests. By 1930 the East Anglian farmer had lived with decline for so long that he could neither move nor think. 'There he was, bogged down in the best corn area of England with ruin right up to his farmhouse door.' English farmers clung pathetically to outward signs of status, keeping their wives in the best room and employing maids in the kitchen. The Scots who had replaced them scoffed at 'feudalism', refused to ape the big house and had little time for the hunt.[3]

Some hunts in eastern England prospered during the 1930s. The Puckeridge killed a record fifty-seven and a half brace of foxes in 1937–8. It benefited from a rich and long-lived Master, Edward Barclay, a member of the Quaker banking clan. The Essex also benefited from an infusion of banking wealth: between the wars the Mastership was shared between Colonel S. F. Gosling, John Swire and Captain G. B. Hoare.

Not that foxes were easy to kill in the plough countries. When the hounds lost their fox on bare, poor-scenting plough, there was no point in the huntsman making a cast. Every field in sight was plough too, and there was no better-scenting ground the fox could have crossed. The huntsman had to learn to pit his wits against the fox and put his knowledge of the country to good use.[4]

In the north east the Braes of Derwent prospered. The seasonal average of foxes killed rose from eight and a half brace before 1914 (hunting two days a week) to forty brace between 1924 and 1939 (four days). Lewis Priestman, Master 1896–1945, was a rich coal-owner: between the wars he spent well over £4,000 a year on the hunt, and received a subscription of only £750. Priestman gave his many overcoats different names. 'Instead of having to tell his man that he would wear the second-best blue overcoat with the velvet collar and the big buttons, he would just say, "Give me Rufus."'[5]

Sport was good down in the West Country too. Ikey Bell used the Welsh cross to build a famous pack in the difficult South and West Wilts. Another Welsh enthusiast was Miss Guest, daughter of Merthyr and Lady Theodora, who hunted her own pack next to the Blackmore Vale from 1914 through to the 1950s.

The Rev. E. A. Milne gave up as Master of the Cattistock in 1931. Since 1900 he had hunted the hounds himself. He wore scarlet in the field and scarlet tails in the evening throughout the season. On Sundays in his remote village he always wore a black coat and tall hat. He never swore, but kept his followers in order by giving little homilies on the duties of the field.[6]

In his last season, Milne was joined in the Mastership by the American A. Henry Higginson. Higginson was generous with his dollars and in many ways a brilliant fox hunter. Some thought him the oracle and others thought him half cracked. Each day after hunting he sat down and typed his diary, charting the progress of his Welsh hounds. He eventually filled nine fat volumes, one for each season he was Master. Higginson also built up a distinguished collection of hunting books, and wrote well-researched biographies of his Cattistock predecessors, the great Peter Beckford and J. J. Farquharson.[7]

Hunting prospered in parts of Ireland. 'Snaffles' depicted the Irish sporting scene of about 1930: snaffle bridles – not a double bridle in sight – a smattering of Anglo-Irish in red coats, and Irish farmers on blood hunters. The Anglo-Irish who stayed after the Troubles went on hunting, but it was the Irish themselves who kept hunting going. 'What matter?' asked the Irish farmer. 'With horses unsaleable, overdrafts at the bank, and farming a dead loss' – why not hunt?[8]

Sassoon's *Memoirs of a Fox-Hunting Man* appeared in 1928. The sporting autobiography of young George Sherston (alias Sassoon), it is a pastoral elegy for the Elysian hunting fields – a book of long hot summers and village cricket that came to an end with the outbreak of the First World War in August 1914.

George Sherston is brought up in Kent, where he hunts with the unfashionable 'Dumborough'. The 'Dumborough' is recognizable as Lord Abergavenny's Eridge, and many of the characters in the *Memoirs* are drawn from life.[9] Sherston's friend and hero Denis Milden was in real life Norman Loder. In 1913 Loder has become Master of the Atherstone ('Packlestone' in the book), and Sassoon went with him for a season in the Midlands.

During the war when Sassoon was stationed in Liverpool he managed to snatch a few days with the Cheshire. After a day in 1917, his diary reads:

> A few hours in the pre-war surroundings – 'Loderism' and so on. Pleasant enough; but what a decayed society, hanging blindly on to the shreds of its traditions. The wet, watery-green meadows and straggling bare hedges and grey winding lanes; the cry of hounds, and thud of hoofs, and people galloping bravely along all round

> me; the ride home with hounds in the chilly dusk – these are *real* things. But comfort and respectable squiredom and the futile chatter of women, and their man-hunting glances, and the pomposity of port-wine-drinking buffers – what's all that but emptiness?[10]

After the war Sassoon still hunted a bit, but he did so half-heartedly. He bought a horse, which he kept with Norman Loder near Cirencester and hunted with the VWH. He was almost glad to give up in 1923 when he could no longer afford it. Hunting he found unsettled him and interfered with his writing.

Before the 1914–18 war Sassoon had zigzagged between his hunting cronies and his London literary friends, talking differently to each.[11] *Memoirs of a Fox-Hunting Man* makes no mention of Sassoon's literary friends or the poetry he wrote, but it does show hunting through an artist's eyes. Sassoon cherished the simple moments: riding home in the twilight of a March evening, with the 'creak of the saddle and the clop and clink of hoofs' – moments when he 'understood so little of the deepening sadness of life'. *Memoirs of a Fox-Hunting Man* is almost painterly in its acute awareness of light: half-lit stables on winter evenings, or day breaking from purple to gold on cub-hunting mornings. Or being called early on a hunting day: 'the quiet morning greyness, and the undefinable feeling produced by the yellow candle-light and the wintry smelling air from the misty garden'.

It is impressions like these that count for Sassoon; he's concerned with how hunting *feels*, rather than whether it's good for you or not. And he's honest about his feelings in a way few had been before the 1914–18 war. He admits that during a fast hunt he was flustered, uncomfortable and out of breath, and the hounds might as well not have been there, since they were two fields ahead throughout, and he wasn't following them but the Master. He shows how little the stylized entries in hunting diaries revealed about what the day was really like. 'Took a toss over a stile,' is what he wrote in his diary:

> What I ought to have written was – that I couldn't make up my mind whether to go at it or not, and the man behind me shouted 'go on if you're going', so I felt flustered and let Harkaway rush at it anyhow and then jerked his mouth just as he was taking off, and he didn't really fall, but only pecked badly and chucked me over his head and then stood quite still and waited for me to scramble up again, and altogether it was rather an inglorious exhibition.

Memoirs of a Fox-Hunting Man became a best-seller: it is one of the few hunting books that non-hunting readers can enjoy. It made hunting an aesthetic as well as an exciting experience. But though beautiful, hunting for Sassoon is also cruel. The tension between cruelty and beauty is expressed in the awful moment when the schoolboy George Sherston sees Denis Milden halloaing a fox and, to his everlasting shame, cries out: 'Don't do that; they'll catch him!'

In the 1930s Molly Keane dissected hunting more ruthlessly than Sassoon had done. Writing as M. J. Farrell, she tracked the decline of Anglo-Irish country-house life. Like Sassoon, she didn't want her hunting friends to know what she wrote. Hunting for the young Molly Keane was a way of life and a religion. In *The Rising Tide* (1937) she tries to analyse it. Cynthia the heroine goes out hunting the morning she hears that her husband has been killed in the war in France. Cynthia's hunting is a drug. It fills her with excitement, fear, or content: out hunting she is 'never, as it were, in slack water'.

Cynthia forces her frightened children to hunt. 'You had to feel ashamed and embarrassed if your children did not take keenly to blood sports, so they must be forced into them. It was only fair to them.' But the children hate it. They long for frost and feel distinctly queasy on hunting mornings, when being driven to the meet in too-tight white stocks tied by Mummy, looking out apprehensively at the fences in the fields and at their corned-up ponies, dreading the falls and knowing that Mummy is bound to find them out if they funk the jumps.

Lionel Edwards, Cecil Aldin, Snaffles (C. J. Payne) and G. D.

29 The Craven Hounds' Christmas meet at the Kingsclere workhouse, 1920s

30 Chauffeurs now followed the hunt as well as the traditional terrier men, 1920s

31 Beaufort point to point, 1927. The Duke of Beaufort MFH is second from right. Sylvia Portman centre. The Dowager Duchess second from left.

32 The Buccleuch moves off from Riddell, 1930s

Armour tried to paint hunting as it really was. Set pieces of meets and posed equestrian portraits were avoided. Lionel Edwards thought Munnings was the only contemporary artist who could get away with hunting in the sun. Grey skies, rain, dark fences and water are characteristic of Edwards's own work. Another artist who excelled at conveying the feel of winter – cold, mud, wet and sweating horses – was G. D. Armour.

Sporting clients valued factual accuracy more than 'art'. It was wrong to paint someone jumping a fence surrounded by the hounds, or to make riders follow each other too closely over a fence. Riders coming home mustn't be spotlessly clean. Nor must hounds run with their mouths shut, or foxes be made too big.

Snaffles's best-known picture, 'The Finest View in Europe' (1921), is a view of the Pytchley country with a horse's ears in the foreground. But the shires were no longer the centre of the sporting artists' world. Nineteenth-century painters like Ferneley, Alken and Francis Grant had lived and worked in Leicestershire; Lionel Edwards lived in the provinces and made a virtue of it, for he found the provinces far more picturesque than the shires.

His work is full of movement. Motion was the key to realism. The old rocking-horse convention – all four horse's legs off the ground, stretched out fore and aft – had been exploded by photography. Lionel Edwards knew that the horse has only one moment of suspension when all his legs are off the ground, and that's when they are flexed under him. He created the illusion of speed by losing a horse's foot in grass or snow, or making riders lean forward. Lots of horses' legs suggest galloping, but regular gaps between horsemen stop the picture. He painted galloping horses slightly strung out and overlapping each other. He made riders lean forward rising at the jump; putting the rider upright as the Victorians had ridden at their fences stops the horse pictorially.[12]

Henry Williamson, the writer, lived on Exmoor and sympathized with the red deer (though he did in fact hunt). Between 1921 and 1924 he wrote a series of stories, published as *The Old Stag*, describing the fear and pain of the hunted otter, badger and stag. The stories are strongly anthropomorphic. Williamson sometimes appears himself in his stories: the young officer physically and emotionally crippled by the Great War. In one story his pet otter is killed by the hounds.

Williamson's anti-blood-sports feeling grew out of his disgust at the carnage of 1914–18. After the war, he began to believe that the 'same attitude of mind which endowed glory and nobility to the acts which helped to make the World War was the very mental attitude that had made such a thing possible'. Sportsmen were like the generals of 1914–18, who'd calmly sent thousands and thousands to their deaths without a qualm. Williamson noted how stag hunters distanced themselves from the red deer, talking 'in a curious semi-scientific jargon about animals, as though they really were structurally and biologically without relationship to the human species'. Williamson thought he knew otherwise.[13]

Stag hunting on Exmoor was the target of the League Against Cruel Sports, which had been founded in 1924 by two former members of the RSPCA, Henry Amos and Ernest Bell, who were disillusioned by the RSPCA's inactivity over hunting. The fox-hunting Prince of Wales became president after the war, strengthening RSPCA links with the huntin', shootin' classes. The breakaway LACS filled the gap left by the Humanitarian League, which Henry Salt had disbanded in 1919. By 1927 the LACS had about 1,000 members.

The LACS's photographs of stags at bay made very good copy. In 1929 a poll of RSPCA members voted by 3,125 to 1,142 in favour of banning wild deer hunting by hounds. In 1930 the RSPCA sponsored a private member's bill banning deer hunting.[14]

What were hunters to do? Fred Beadle, a stag-hunting Devonshire farmer, thought stag hunting could only be effectively protected by a society which represented all field sports, and the British Field Sports Society was the result. Fox hunters, shooters and fishers must be made to understand that the attack on deer hunting was the first step of a campaign to outlaw all field sports.

In December 1930 Beadle enlisted two influential stag hunters: Lord Bayford, Master of the Devon and Somerset Staghounds (1895–1907), and Earl Fortescue, who was often to be seen following the hunt in an ancient open Ford, wearing an equally ancient mackintosh. Lord Fortescue's family had dominated the Devon and Somerset throughout the nineteenth century. The Duke of Beaufort became president of the new society. Membership rose from 3,450 in May 1931 to 8,548 in March 1932, stabilizing at around 10,000 in 1938.[15]

At the inaugural meeting of the BFSS Lord Winterton stressed that the society was in no sense political. Winterton himself was a Tory politician, and his disclaimer was somewhat disingenuous. Between the wars the BFSS was virtually an arm of the Conservative Party. The society's chairman, Lord Bayford, formerly Robert Sanders, was an ex-Tory MP and Minister of Agriculture, 1922–4. Maroon-faced, he was cleverer than he looked. Briefed by the society's researchers, he acted as BFSS spokesman in the Lords.[16]

Bayford accused the RSPCA of double standards. It took sportsmen's money, and campaigned against their field sports. The BFSS sent 777 copies of pro-hunting articles to the press in 1933, and another 1,136 copies in 1936.[17] At the same time, the BFSS told its members to avoid press publicity for hunting. Press reports of kills or 'incidents' merely fuelled popular misconceptions about 'blood sports', providing skilled LACS propagandists with ammunition to discredit hunting.

Few sportsmen took the opposition to hunting seriously in the 1930s, but fox hunters really couldn't ignore the outbreak of war in 1939. Hunting went to ground. *The Times* stopped reporting it and *Baily's* directory of hunts, hitherto published annually, suspended publication from 1939 until 1948.

The 1939–40 season is still remembered as an excellent one with the Quorn. The grass hadn't been ploughed up yet, and relatively few officers in uniform and a few locals came out. When Anthony Nutting escaped from France in May 1940 just before

Dunkirk, he tried to telephone his father, Sir Harold, Master of the Quorn. Sir Harold wasn't at home, he was at Badminton. Asked what he was doing, Sir Harold testily replied, 'What do you think I am doing at Badminton at this time of year? Judging Master's [the Duke of Beaufort's] young entry of course!'[18]

The war bit really hard after 1940–1. The Earl of Harrington dispersed his entire pack in 1940. A few hunts gave up altogether. Most packs struggled on, reducing their hounds to a nucleus for breeding and destroying the rest.

At the Glamorgan, the authorities asked for hounds to be reduced to one-sixth of the pre-war level (i.e. to seven and a half couple) and horses to one-twelfth. The War Agricultural Committee allocated only four hundredweight of food per month for the hounds. Captain Homfray, the Master, moved the hounds to his home and looked after them himself with his wife and daughter. He paid all hunt expenses and kept the hounds alive by scrounging meat; he hunted hounds himself, going out when former subscribers came home on leave. Keep for hunt horses was made available when Captain Homfray formed a mounted unit of the Home Guard, known as 'Homfray's Cossacks'.[19]

That hunting survived the war at all was ultimately due to farmers. They insisted that it should go on. They sent carcases unfit for human consumption to the kennels, and sometimes set up their own packs when hunts gave up. The Chiddingfold Farmers' was formed in 1943 to hunt country belonging to the dormant Surrey Union.

Hunts were no longer able to control the fox population efficiently, and foxes became a major pest to farmers. Organized fox shoots took place. Fox destruction societies were set up in the Welsh mountains and in the Pennines, offering a bounty of a pound for each fox killed. Some but not all of the fox destruction societies used hounds. In the mountainous Plas Machynlleth country the huntsman, Harry Roberts, was released from the army at the request of the local Agricultural Committee in order to keep down foxes for the farmers.[20]

Because hunting went on throughout the war, the LACS went

on too. The league attacked hunting in wartime as unpatriotic. J. Sharp, the secretary, campaigned almost single-handed, tirelessly writing letters to the press: 110 of his 556 letters were published in 1942. The LACS pointed out that War Agricultural Committees were packed with fox hunters and charged them with conniving at hunting in wartime. When Lord Halifax, wartime ambassador to America and ex-Master of the Middleton, was reported to have gone hunting, a letter appeared in the *New York Times*: 'Are we going to war for the sake of a lot of English fox hunters?' The LACS was jubilant.[21]

In 1940 John Wyndham went hunting from Petworth with his Uncle Charles, Lord Leconfield, Master and owner of the Leconfield Hounds. They were the only people out. They found a fox and lost it. Hearing a hullabaloo two miles away, Lord Leconfield shouted at his huntsman, 'Can't you hear a holler?', and they galloped off towards the noise. They arrived to find a village football match. Hounds, huntsman, and Lord Leconfield slithered to a stop; so did the footballers. 'There was silence, then Uncle Charles, who had turned red in the face, stood up in his stirrups and shouted: "Haven't you people got anything better to do in wartime than play *football*?"' He then went on hunting.[22]

CHAPTER TWELVE

Keep Politics Out of Country Sport

'On balance, I have come to the view that organized sport, disciplined by rules and sanctions, will in the end cause less suffering and cruelty than unlicensed, unsupervised private enterprise. I accept that it is the discipline, the rules, the uniform, the ritual and the buttons that to many are provocative. That is what they dislike about organized sport. They must judge whether, at root, they are seeking to promote the welfare of wild animals or to demote those who organize the pursuit of them for sport.'

W. F. DEEDES in the House of Commons,
14 May 1970

he tenth Duke of Beaufort started riding in a basket on a donkey at the age of two. His father gave him a pack of harriers for his eleventh birthday in 1911. Ever after he was known as 'Master', even by his wife. 'Obviously,' he wrote in his memoirs, 'the hunting of the fox is my chief concern.' As a young officer in the Blues, he got permission to hunt two days a week instead of taking the annual two months' leave. He succeeded his father as Duke, and Master and huntsman of the Beaufort Hounds in 1924.

A duodenal ulcer made Master unfit for military service in 1939. Queen Mary, his wife's aunt, occupied Badminton throughout the war. The Queen had never lived in the country before, and she developed a passion for 'improving' the estate. She lopped ivy from the house and precious shrubs off the outside of the stable walls. And Master once returned from hunting to find the stableyard full of agricultural implements brought in from the fields by order of Queen Mary, who was collecting scrap metal for the war effort.[1]

After the war, Master dedicated himself to the revival of hunting. He held the first three day event at Badminton in 1949. He was chairman of the Masters of Foxhounds Association, and for over forty years he reigned as king of hunting, his car number plates bearing the proud initials 'MFH 1'.

People loved him. He was a man of great charm, an old-fashioned paternalist. No nonsense about democracy for him. In 1964 it was revealed that there had been no election to the Badminton Parish Council for seventeen years. Seven candidates always stood for the seven seats – the Duke, the Duchess and five estate employees. 'We always consult his Grace first,' said one.[2] In 1962 Master started the Banwen Valley Hunt, a Welsh miners' pack. But this wasn't democracy; it was a unique kind of industrial feudalism.

His book, *Fox-hunting*, was a worthy successor to his grandfather's Badminton Library *Hunting*, published almost a century before. Master included a chapter of hints on how to reply to antis. Never, he advised, say the fox enjoys being hunted. Of course it doesn't. But make the point that the fox is not like us. Too many antis have a sentimental, Peter Rabbit view of nature. If an opponent of hunting identifies too closely with the fox, you should ask him if he'd like to live in a hole and eat nasty things like rats, mice, beetles and raw frogs' legs. That should shut him up.[3]

Master died in February 1983. On Boxing Day 1984 Britain woke to lurid news. Master's grave had been desecrated on Christmas night by a group of antis. After trying to dig up the body, they'd stolen the cross which stood over the grave, and they'd sprayed anti-hunt slogans round the graveyard. Fortunately, their plan of sending Master's head to Princess Anne in a parcel came to nothing. The Hunt Retribution Squad claimed responsibility, and the League Against Cruel Sports was quoted as saying that the Hunt Retribution Squad was nothing to do with them.[4]

The only other well-known fox hunter dug up by antis was John Peel. Three members of the extremist Animal Liberation Front had desecrated John Peel's grave at Caldbeck in Cumbria in 1977. Convinced that Peel's headstone was a shrine to which hunters paid homage, they broke off a corner. They dug a large hole in the grave, into which they put a stuffed fox's head, together with a note:

> John Peel, John Peel come blow on your horn
> Come blow till your cruel heart turns blue
> No rest for the thousands of foxes you've torn
> But at least this one's got the last laugh on you.[5]

Master had spent much of his life trying to make sure that the antis didn't have the last laugh. As president of the British Field Sports Society, he had been virtually in command of fox hunting's defence.

Hunting was particularly vulnerable in post-war austerity Britain. In 1947 a new pink coat required eighteen clothing coupons and new bowlers and top hats were unobtainable. Record-breaking snow and frost in the winter of 1947 stopped all hunting after January. In 1947 the Labour government requisitioned the park in front of Britain's biggest country house, Lord Fitzwilliam's Wentworth Woodhouse in Yorkshire, for open-cast coal mining. Landed society gasped. Chain-smoking cigarettes over congealed food in icy dining rooms, the aristocracy complained about the servant problem and waited for the nationalization of land. Meanwhile, high taxation and death duties forced sales of land and the desertion of country houses.[6]

Many people feared hunting would be next to go. The League Against Cruel Sports claimed thirteen million supported a ban, and *Baily's* noted a spirit of concern in every hunting home, 'be it a country mansion, a farm, or a house in a suburban street'.[7] Mr

Churchill hoisted his unfit frame on to an unfamiliar hunter in a demonstration of support.

Two anti-hunting bills were announced in 1949. Seymour Cocks's private members' bill banned hare coursing and deer, badger and otter hunting. A second bill outlawed fox hunting. Toby Fitzwilliam, secretary of the British Field Sports Society, likened hunting's situation to Dunkirk – sportsmen had waited until the enemy was almost upon them. The BFSS managed to collect a million signatures opposing the bills.[8]

Cocks's bill was debated in Parliament at the end of February 1949. Cocks and the bill's supporters claimed they were on the side of St Francis of Assisi against Attila the Hun(t). Civilization, said Cocks, is but 'a small island in the vast ocean of cruelty, selfishness and insanity inherited from millions of years of sub-human ancestry'. Opponents of the bill preferred St Hubert to Attila. Lord Winterton suggested that animal lovers were mentally unbalanced unfortunates who couldn't attract the opposite sex. Like Goering, who'd banned stag hunting in Nazi Germany, they thought nothing of torturing humans. Oscar Wilde and the Bloomsbury Boys had mocked huntin', shootin' and fishin', declared Winterton, because they were sickened by sportsmen's manliness.

The Labour Minister of Agriculture, Tom Williams, had supported an anti-hunting bill in 1925 but he opposed the 1949 bill because farmers really hated it, and because the National Farmers' Union officially supported the BFSS. Hunting, said Williams, was the recreation not of the idle rich, but of the farming community. In isolated areas it was the *only* winter recreation available to farm workers and shepherds. Farmers wanted the foxes on their land to be controlled by hunting, not by fox destruction societies. Government support for the anti-hunting bill would jeopardize the food production programme. To country people, argued Williams, the cruelty argument seemed a mere cloak. Country people read about townsmen using short supplies of fuel to drive to football matches or cinemas, and resented their only amusement being singled out as cruel. Anti-hunting was really a case of townsmen attacking the life of the countryside.[9]

Tom Williams's defence of hunting echoes the views of early-nineteenth-century Tories. They had defended hunting because it kept the gentry at home in the country and gave them something to do. Well over a century later, here was a Labour government making out a very similar case – only this time the beneficiaries of hunting were not squires but farmers.

Williams's support for hunting was decisive. The Seymour Cocks bill was defeated by 214 to 101. Hunting England celebrated. The Duke of Beaufort warned fox hunters not to become too complacent, however. In March 1949 the Labour government announced its decision to set up a Committee on Cruelty to Wild Animals, and the bill banning fox hunting was withdrawn.

Critics complained that the Scott Henderson Committee was being packed with field sports partisans. Miss Frances Pitt, nature writer, Master of the Wheatland Hunt since 1929 and vice-president of the British Field Sports Society, was unlikely to sign an anti-hunting report. Major Pugh, veterinary surgeon to the West Kent Foxhounds, and Mr Brown of the *Field* were hardly likely to call for the abolition of hunting. The only committee member whose credentials the antis approved was the zoologist Peter Medawar.

The Scott Henderson Report of 1951 takes a pragmatic line. It denies that 'it is ethically wrong to pursue or kill an animal for sport if the infliction of any degree of suffering is involved'. Killing for sport is not wrong in itself. Quite the contrary. Scott Henderson approved of traditional field sports which serve a useful purpose. Providing sport and recreation for country people is a useful purpose in itself. If hunting also contributes to the control of a wild animal, so much the better.

Cruel sports, according to Scott Henderson, are sports which cause animals more suffering than necessary. Does hunting cause more suffering than other forms of control? This is the Scott Henderson test, and fox hunting passes it easily. The committee was satisfied that other forms of control, such as shooting or snaring, caused far more suffering than hunting with hounds.

Scott Henderson condemned otter hunting as cruel. The committee called for an inquiry to consider whether otter control was necessary to protect fish supplies. Eventually in 1957 otters were acquitted of serious damage to fisheries by Marie Stephens. Though otter hunting wasn't actually banned, otters were made a protected species in 1978.

Scott Henderson called on the Masters of Foxhounds Association to tighten up its rules about digging. The practice of bolting a fox which runs to ground and then letting the hounds hunt it again is needlessly cruel and should be prohibited, the committee thought. If a fox which runs to ground *has* to be killed, death should be immediate, preferably by means of a humane killer.

The Scott Henderson Report was certainly a tonic to fox hunters. By 1951, however, hunting had already emerged from its wartime doldrums. An estimated twenty thousand people hunted each season after the war. Sustained agricultural prosperity after 1945 injected hunting with greater vitality than it had enjoyed in the 1920s and 1930s. Farmers who feared a repetition of the Great Betrayal of 1921, when wartime support was abruptly withdrawn, were reassured by Tom Williams's 1947 Agriculture Act guaranteeing continued government support. Far from reverting to the dog-and-stick farming of the 1930s, agriculture became ever more capital-intensive. Landowners benefited from the boom, too. Tax rebates and grants for agricultural improvement encouraged investment, and land prices started to climb.

More and more farmers were seen out hunting. Their contribution to the revival of hunting after the war, often applauded at hunt dinners, was probably crucial. At the Braes of Derwent, middle-aged farmers unable to afford to hunt before the war could now be seen riding as hard and straight as their sons, who took their hunting for granted.[10] In 1960 Wilson Stephens, editor of the *Field*, estimated that a season's hunting cost the farmer (who paid no subscription) less than smoking twenty cigarettes a day, which cost fifty-five pounds a year. In an average hunt, he reckoned farmers made up half the mounted field; in the West Country farmers were nine-tenths of the field.[11]

The Heythrop was the show hunt of the era. Fox-hunting backwoodsmen who'd sold up or moved out of houses requisitioned by the army migrated to the Cotswolds. In 1952 Ronnie Wallace began his twenty-five-year Mastership. A gifted organizer, Wallace was a far more important figure in the Cotswolds than the MP (my father). And the ladies loved him. Wallace's earth-stopper, Charlie Parker or 'Midnight Charlie', was a non-driving old Etonian who knew the whereabouts of every fox in the country. City men flocked to the Heythrop, attracted by good trains to London and, perhaps, by the smallness of the Heythrop stone walls (Leicestershire has always been scornful of Heythrop fences). Sir Cyril Kleinwort, a generous hunt chairman, bought fox coverts for the hunt. Though few farmers hunted, they didn't object to the hunt as Wallace's popularity pushed up the value of their land.

The antis must have seemed very remote to Heythrop followers in Wallace's day. But since the war, the morality of hunting had become a political issue. In 1957 a Gallup poll showed 53 per cent of respondents *approving* the prohibition of fox hunting and 24 per cent disapproving (23 per cent didn't know). But the press wasn't interested, and the Conservative governments of 1951–64 were unsympathetic – about one in three entries in *Who's Who* in 1949 listed field sports as their hobby.

Membership of anti pressure groups slumped. The National Society for the Abolition of Cruel Sports, whose members were dons or churchmen like Lord Soper or Harold Laski, dwindled from 1,500 in 1950 to 1,000 in 1960. Robert Churchward gave up as joint Master of the South Shropshire in 1953 and declared his conversion to anti-blood sports. He published a pamphlet called 'The Master of Hounds Speaks' describing his road to Damascus. In the *People* he made startling disclosures about what goes on behind the scenes in a hunt. The Duke of Beaufort came to hunting's defence in the *People*, and Churchward and his wife were ostracized by their hunting friends, allegedly receiving hate mail and abusive telephone calls. But Churchward's secession didn't do the antis much good, and his campaign for replacing fox hunting by drag hunting made little impact.[12]

In 1958 the League Against Cruel Sports produced their so-called secret weapon – laying an aniseed trail to confuse the hounds. In the 1960s, however, the secret weapon was dropped in favour of a strategy of penetrating vicarage tea parties and mayoral parlours. The aim was to convert the Conservative party, rather than mobilize Labour. But anti-coursing bills sponsored by the league in the 1960s and early 1970s were parliamentary flops, and the league sank into gloom.[13]

A group of young radicals split off from the League Against Cruel Sports to form the Hunt Saboteurs Association in 1964. Leaving political action to the league, the saboteurs attacked hunting in the field. Publicity drove their membership up to 3,000 in 1977, and there were 4,000–5,000 members in 1983.

Saboteurs plan their hunting days carefully. Diverting the hounds from the scent of the fox takes some skill. Laying false trails with aniseed or spraying with Anti-mate helps confuse the hounds. The saboteur should also know how to speak to hounds, as well as mastering the difficult art of blowing a hunting horn. Veterans tour Britain's universities, lecturing on hound work to student volunteers who are then bussed out to distant country meets. Saboteurs need to know in advance where the hunt will draw. They depend on secret informers. The British Field Sports Society engages in counter-espionage, employing consultants from MI5.

In 1979 Mike Huskisson, newly emerged from six months in prison for desecrating John Peel's grave, disguised himself in hunt supporters' uniform of Barbour coat and green gumboots. Armed with a camera, he set out to record atavistic savagery and brutality. Flaunting a British Field Sports Society badge, Huskisson befriended terrier men and hunt servants, and spent long, cold, foot-stamping hours outside foxes' earths waiting for the kill. Once, after a hunt servant had gone to fetch a spade, leaving Huskisson alone to guard the earth, Huskisson unblocked the holes and fled. Over four years he took about five thousand photographs of dead and dying stags, minks and foxes.[14]

Many saboteurs declare themselves non-violent, insisting that their only concern is to let the fox go free. In practice, non-violence is confined to foxes. Groups of five or six well-armed saboteurs in two cars with walkie-talkies immobilize hunts by letting down tyres and destroying tack. Fox hunters and hunt followers are provoked to retaliate. Incidents *do* happen. In Devon piano wire was stretched at neck height in woodland through which hunters were riding. In Warwickshire a fox hunter was scarred for life when a broken bottle was pushed in his face. The Hunt Retribution Squad is overtly pro-violence. 'We feel it is important to escalate slowly,' said a spokesman in 1985. 'At first we will just inflict injuries, which will increase in severity. When a hunter ends up in hospital with very severe injuries, the next stage then will be to actually take a hunter out completely.'[15]

Antis claim that hunting *desensitizes* the hunters. 'Someone who is willing to press a button that would blow away millions of innocent people is the same sort of person who would hunt a fox without any consideration for the morality of what he or she is doing.'[16] For them men like the tenth Duke of Beaufort were nukes in fancy dress.

A psychological survey of MFHs was made in the 1970s. The MFHs' replies to a questionnaire devised by Professor Eysenck came pretty close to the attitudes normally found in their peer group – middle-class, male and middle-aged. On issues like the death penalty they were slightly more authoritarian than their peers, tending to what Eysenck termed 'conservative tough-mindedness'. The question MFHs felt most strongly about was whether occupation by a foreign power was better than war. They showed a much stronger preference for war than their peers. Of course, a foreign occupation would interfere with their hunting. But their vehemence on the question maybe stems from hunting's historical association with manliness and patriotism.[17]

The psychological questionnaire was also circulated to hunt saboteurs. They diverge far more from their peer group than the MFHs do. Saboteurs are far more extreme – far odder – than many people of their age and class.[18] And a survey of MFHs is obviously not representative of the fifty thousand people who hunt.

Though most MFHs are men, most people who hunt today are women.

By the 1970s hunting was probably a more genuinely popular sport than ever before, as cars brought the hounds within reach of an ever-increasing following of hunt supporters. A handful of anti activists launched a new campaign for a ban. Their first target was the RSPCA. To the dismay of anti members, the RSPCA had supported the Scott Henderson Report. In 1958 the RSPCA hit upon a compromise acceptable both to antis and fox hunters. Yes, it was opposed to hunting with hounds for sport, but fox hunting it tolerated as the most effective and least painful form of *control*. Shooting, trapping and poisoning caused more suffering than hunting. So did gassing, as foxes moving from earth to earth risked being only partially gassed and dying slowly in agony. Anti activists within the RSPCA formed a reform group, and in 1976 they pushed through a policy statement pledging the RSPCA to oppose *all* hunting with hounds, fox hunting included. In 1977 Richard Ryder, an ex-saboteur, became RSPCA chairman.[19]

It was the same story at the League Against Cruel Sports. Elderly conservatives were pushed out of the leadership by radical antis. Richard Course, a member of the Hunt Saboteurs Association, became chairman of the league in 1979. The key to Course's campaign was media support – the BBC was particularly sympathetic. Publicity boosted funds. Like the proverbial cats' home, the league attracted a windfall of legacy income. Course bought up 'sanctuary' land for deer on Exmoor, where the Devon and Somerset Staghounds were banned. Whenever hounds crossed the sanctuaries, the league took the hunt to court for trespass. In 1985 the Devon and Somerset paid out seventy-five thousand pounds in legal costs and damages for trespassing on league sanctuaries.

Course lobbied institutional landowners. In 1982 the Co-op banned hunting on its fifty thousand acres, seriously affecting the Fernie which lost a day's hunting a week and a fifth of its country. By mid-1982 fifteen Labour-controlled councils had voted to ban hunting on their land. They included the London boroughs of Enfield and Haringey, which aren't exactly in prime hunting country. In 1985 the Warwickshire County Council banned hunting on forty-five thousand acres of farmland.[20] Course gave eighty thousand pounds to the Labour party, which pledged itself to outlaw all forms of hunting with dogs in 1983.

In 1988 the league failed in its attempt to ban hunting on the National Trust's six hundred thousand acres. Despite allegations of foul play by league sympathizers – many trust members received no ballot papers – the motion for a ban was defeated by a ballot of members. There are signs that in the conservation-conscious 1990s, the debate is going hunting's way. Hunting farmers don't plough out their hedges, landowners who hunt don't grub up ancient bits of woodland. By cloaking themselves in green, fox hunters may well have outwitted the antis – for now.

Notes

Introduction

1 Reverend W. B. Daniel, *Rural Sports* (1807 edn), vol. i, 213–14.
2 Ibid., 129–30.
3 Quoted in *Kings of the Hunting-Field* by Thormanby, 2.
4 Ibid., 3.
5 Earl of March, *Records of the Old Charlton Hunt*.
6 Nicholas Cox, *The Gentleman's Recreation* (1928 edn), 1–4, 22–3; Stephen Deuchar, *Sporting Art in Eighteenth-Century England*, 26–38.
7 Quoted from the *Roxburgh Ballads* in Lady Apsley, *Bridleways Through History* (1948 edn), 325.
8 W. A. Baillie-Grohman ed., *The Master of Game*, 231.
9 Thormanby, op. cit., 71–2.
10 Ibid., 204.
11 Ibid., 268–70.
12 Ibid., 4–5, 30–1.
13 March, op. cit., 61–7.
14 Ibid., 107–8.
15 Peter Beckford, *Thoughts on Hunting*, 126, 217.
16 Thormanby, op. cit., 34–43.
17 R. S. Surtees, *Handley Cross* (1854 edn), 263–4.
18 Thomas Smith, *Extracts from the Diary of a Huntsman*; Thormanby, op. cit., 187–8.
19 Charles Chevenix-Trench, *A History of Horsemanship*, 192; Thormanby, op. cit., 207.
20 Nicholas Russell, *Like Engend'ring Like*, 113–14.
21 Cox, op. cit., xv–xvi, 38.
22 Earl Bathurst, *The Charlton and Raby Hunts*, 1–3, 123.
23 Beckford, op. cit., 140; John Beresford ed., *Diary of a Country Parson*, e.g. vol. ii, 52, 59.
24 C. B. Andrews ed., *The Torrington Diaries*, vol. ii, 50–1; vol. iv, 66.
25 Thormanby, op. cit., 19.
26 C. J. Apperley, *Nimrod's Hunting Tours*, 144–5.
27 William Cobbett, *Rural Rides* (1912 edn), vol. i, 37–8.
28 *Recollections of the Early Days of the Vine Hunt* by A Sexagenarian [J. E. Austen-Leigh], 1–15.
29 Apperley, op. cit., 155–61.
30 Beckford, op. cit., 300–6; Apperley, op. cit., 57; Nimrod, *Life of John Mytton* (1903 edn), 40.
31 H. G. Lloyd, *The Red Fox*, 173–81.
32 *Sporting Magazine*, vol. i (1793), 319–20.
33 Thormanby, op. cit., 334–8.
34 P. J. W. Langley and D. W. Yalden, 'The Decline of the Rarer Carnivores in Great Britain during the Nineteenth Century', *Mammal Review*, vol. 7 (1977), 95–116.
35 G. F. Underhill, *The Master of Hounds*, 12, 16.

Chapter One

1 Colin Ellis, *Leicestershire and the Quorn Hunt*; John Hawkes, *The Meynellian Science*; Thormanby, *Kings of the Hunting-Field*, 57–68; Apperley, *Nimrod's Hunting Tours*, 1–8.
2 Apperley, op. cit., 43–61.
3 Earl Bathurst, *The Earl Spencer's and Mr John Warde's Hounds*, 157–202.
4 Beckford, *Thoughts on Hunting*, 9, 322–3
5 See Deuchar, *Sporting Art in Eighteenth-Century England*, 39–58.
6 Andrews ed., *The Torrington Diaries*, vol. iv, 48–50.
7 Lady Apsley, *Bridleways through History*, 343–4; Lord Willoughby de Broke, *Hunting the Fox*, 135–6; Duke of Beaufort, *Fox-Hunting*, 201.
8 Raymond Carr, *English Fox Hunting*, 136–7; R. S. Surtees, *Analysis of the Hunting Field*, 2–3, 55–6; *Handley Cross*, ch. 32.
9 Lord Ribblesdale, *The Queen's Hounds*, 48–58.
10 *Silk and Scarlet* by The Druid [H. H. Dixon], 58–9.
11 E. D. Cuming ed., *Squire Osbaldeston: His Autobiography*, 31.
12 The Druid, op. cit., 47.
13 Apperley, op. cit., 240; Thormanby, op. cit., 89–93.
14 Sir Charles Mordaunt Bart and the Hon. and Rev. W. R. Verney, *Annals of the Warwickshire Hunt 1795–1895*, vol. i, 165–6.
15 Surtees, *Analysis of the Hunting Field*, 120–1.
16 Thormanby, op. cit., 180–1.
17 Nimrod, *The Chase, the Turf and the Road*.
18 Thormanby, op. cit., 85–6, 164.
19 Apperley, op. cit., 226, 243, 253–4, 559–60.
20 Nimrod, *Memoirs of the Life of John Mytton*.
21 Bathurst, *Charlton and Raby Hunts*, 129–53; Frank H. Reynard, *The Bedale Hounds*, 18; Apperley, op. cit., 478–500.
22 Meriel Buxton, *Ladies of the Chase*, 38–41.
23 Harriette Wilson, *Memoirs* (1929 edn), 515–17.
24 F. P. Delmé Radcliffe, *The Noble Science*, 67–8, 133, 140.
25 Quoted in A. Henry Higginson, *Peter Beckford*, 187. See also P. B. Munsche, *Gentlemen and Poachers: the English Game Laws, 1671–1831*, 164–6.

Chapter Two

1 Rudyard Kipling, 'My Son's Wife', in *A Diversity of Creatures*. The best biography is John Welcome, *The Sporting World of R. S. Surtees*.
2 Chevenix-Trench, *A History of Horsemanship*, 193.
3 Hawkes, *Meynellian Science*, 23–4. The ideal of hunting as open to all is explored by David Itzkowitz, *Peculiar Privilege*, esp. 17–26. Stephen Deuchar has demonstrated that the idealization of hunting goes back at least to the seventeenth century; it doesn't begin, as Itzkowitz claims, with the emergence of hunting journalism in the 1780s (*Sporting Art in Eighteenth-Century England*, 39–58).
4 *Apperley, Nimrod's Hunting Tours*, op. cit., 543.
5 Delabere P. Blaine, *An Encyclopaedia of Rural Sports*, 491; H. O. Nethercote, *The Pytchley Hunt*, 112–16.

6 Harry Hieover, *Sporting Facts and Sporting Fancies*, 382.
7 Surtees, *Analysis of the Hunting Field*, 157, 227.
8 Itzkowitz, *Peculiar Privilege*, 78–9.
9 Robert Vyner, *Notitia Venatica* (1902 edn), 41–2.
10 T. F. Dale, *The Eighth Duke of Beaufort and the Badminton Hunt*.
11 Henry S. Davenport, *Memories at Random*, 11.
12 A. Henry Higginson, *The Meynell of the West*.
13 George Tancred of Weens, *Annals of a Border Club*.
14 Joseph Crawhall, 'Records of the Park House Club', MS at Alnwick Castle, Northumberland.
15 *A Century of Foxhunting with the Warwickshire Hounds* by Castor [Lord North], 8–18.
16 Apperley, op. cit., 166–7.
17 Grantley Berkeley, *Reminiscences of a Huntsman*, 90–117; Grantley Berkeley, *My Life and Recollections*, vol. i, 306–7.
18 Reynard, *Bedale Hounds*, 11–14; Apperley, op. cit., 388–9.
19 Ibid., 410–13.
20 R. E. Egerton Warburton, *Hunting Songs*.
21 Vyner, op. cit., 70.
22 Carr, *English Fox Hunting*, 114–16; Surtees, *Ask Mamma*, ch. 91.
23 Vyner, op. cit., 14–15; Anthony Trollope, *British Sports and Pastimes*, 83–4.
24 Lord Willoughby de Broke, *The Passing Years*, 57–8.
25 E. W. Bovill, *English Country Life, 1780–1830*, 214–32.
26 Berkeley, *Reminiscences of a Huntsman*, 388; Itzkowitz, op. cit., 67–73.
27 Lord Egremont, *Wyndham and Children First*, 43–52.
28 Vyner, op. cit., 70–2; A. Henry Higginson, *Two Centuries of Foxhunting*, 153–5.
29 Colonel John Cook, *Observations on Fox-Hunting*, 125–6; Apperley, op. cit., 21.
30 George E. Collins, *History of the Brocklesby Hounds*, 10; Thormanby, *Kings of the Hunting-Field*, 76–81.
31 Cook, op. cit., 120–1; Surtees, *Handley Cross*, ch. 32.
32 Surtees, *Analysis of the Hunting Field*, 171; *Ask Mamma*, ch. 44.
33 Berkeley, *Reminiscences of a Huntsman*, 61–3; *My Life and Recollections*, vol. i, 298–306.
34 Hieover, op. cit., 379–80.
35 Richard Clapham, *Foxhunting on the Lakeland Fells*; Thormanby, op. cit., 46–56.
36 J. Fairfax Blakeborough, *England's Oldest Hunt*.
37 A. E. Pease, *The Cleveland Hounds as a Trencher-Fed Pack*, 21–53.
38 Captain F. Chapman, *The Wensleydale Hounds*.
39 Higginson, *Two Centuries of Foxhunting*, 113–14.
40 E. W. Cuming ed., *A Hunting Diary* by Newton Wynne Apperley, 50–7, 130.
41 Scrutator, *Recollections of a Fox-Hunter*, 109–10. See Carr, op. cit., 58–61.
42 [Austen-Leigh], *Recollections of the Early Days of the Vine Hunt*, 3.
43 Cuming ed., op. cit., 35.

Chapter Three

1 Itzkowitz, *Peculiar Privilege*, 137–8; Sir John Eardley-Wilmot, *Reminiscences of the late Thomas Assheton Smith*; Thormanby, *Kings of the Hunting-Field*, 94–107.

2 Lord Charles Bentinck, *Lord Henry Bentinck's Foxhounds*; Duke of Portland, *Memories of Racing and Hunting*, 249–51; Mordaunt and Verney, *Annals of the Warwickshire Hunt*, vol. i, 154; J. Anstruther Thomson, *Eighty Years' Reminiscences*, vol. i, 265; Daphne Goodall, *Huntsman of a Golden Age*.

3 Trollope, *British Sports and Pastimes*, 101.

4 Thormanby, op. cit., 411–19; Carr, *English Fox Hunting*, 209; Moreton Frewen, *Melton Mowbray and Other Memories*, 75–6.

5 Ribblesdale, *The Queen's Hounds*, 181.

6 Lord Charles Beresford, *Memoirs*, vol. i, 139.

7 Anstruther Thomson, op. cit., vol. i, 354–5; Thormanby, op. cit., 280–8.

8 Davenport, *Memories at Random*, 137.

9 Mordaunt and Verney, op. cit., vol. i, 212.

10 Scrutator, *Recollections of a Fox-Hunter*, 107–9.

11 G. Whyte-Melville, *Riding Recollections*, 111.

12 *Charles Kingsley. His Letters and Memories of his Life*. Edited by his Wife, vol. ii, 27.

13 Anstruther Thomson, op. cit., vol. i, 407; Moreton Frewen, op. cit., 75.

14 Thormanby, op. cit., 166–74.

15 Guy Paget, *History of the Althorp and Pytchley Hunt*, 177–9; Thormanby, op. cit., 375–83.

16 [Austen-Leigh], *Recollections of the Early Days of the Vine Hunt*, 68; E. W. L. Davies, *Memoir of the Rev. John Russell*.

17 [Austen-Leigh], op. cit., 68; Surtees, *Town and Country Papers*, 214–15.

18 F. C. Loder-Symonds and E. Percy Crowdy, *A History of the Old Berks Hunt*, 207; Anthony Trollope, *Hunting Sketches* (1952 edn), 105.

19 F. P. De Costobadie, *Annals of the Billesdon Hunt*, 62–88.

20 Kingsley, op. cit., vol. i, 349.

21 Surtees, *Analysis of the Hunting Field*, 295.

22 Lady Augusta Fane, *Chit-Chat*, 136; Buxton, *Ladies of the Chase*, 42–7.

23 Surtees, *Analysis of the Hunting Field*, 295.

24 Blaine, *Encyclopaedia of Rural Sports*, 497–8.

25 Whyte-Melville, op. cit., 77, 125; Chevenix-Trench, *A History of Horsemanship*, 272–88.

26 John Welcome denies that Lucy Glitters is based on Skittles, pointing out that when Lucy Glitters first appeared in *Mr Sponge's Sporting Tour* (1852) Skittles was only thirteen (*Surtees*, 131). But Lucy reappears in *Mr Facey Romford's Hounds* (1865), and her adventures in this novel are very similar to Skittles's recent experiences with the Quorn.

27 De Costobadie, op. cit., 24–5, 123; Carr, op. cit., 172–5.

28 Scrutator, *Practical Lessons on Hunting and Sporting*, 29–32; Hippolyte Taine, *Notes on England* (1957 edn), 98.

29 Trollope, *Hunting Sketches*, 69–70.

30 Berkeley, *Life and Recollections*, vol. ii, 185–8.

31 Itzkowitz, op. cit., 89–90.

Chapter Four

1 Deuchar, *Sporting Art in Eighteenth-Century England*, 93–113.
2 John Bright and J. E. Thorold Rogers ed., *Speeches by Richard Cobden*, 145; J. E. Thorold Rogers ed., *Speeches by the Right Hon. John Bright*, 416.
3 Cook, *Observations on Fox-Hunting*, 125–6.
4 B. Disraeli, *Lord George Bentinck: A Political Biography* (1852 edn), 38, 299–300.
5 Mordaunt and Verney, *Annals of the Warwickshire Hunt*, vol. i, 208–9.
6 Anstruther Thomson, *Eighty Years' Reminiscences*, vol. i, 153–5.
7 Delmé Radcliffe, *The Noble Science*, 129–31.
8 Ibid., 278; Surtees, *Town and Country Papers*, 193; Willoughby de Broke, *The Passing Years*, 14–16.
9 Hieover, *Sporting Facts and Sporting Fancies*, 378.
10 Duke of Beaufort and Mowbray Morris, *Hunting*, 273–85; Itzkowitz, *Peculiar Privilege*, 52.
11 Anstruther Thomson, op. cit., vol. i, 122; Scrutator, *Practical Lessons on Hunting and Sporting*, 123–36.
12 Cecil, *Hunting Tours*, 205; 336–9.
13 Surtees, *Town and Country Papers*, 172–3.
14 Taine, *Notes on England*, 203–4.
15 Trollope, *British Sports and Pastimes*, 72–3; *Hunting Sketches*, 79–80.
16 John Morley, *Life of Richard Cobden* (1906 edn), 430–1, quoting Cobden's diary, 12 February 1847; Michael MacEwan, 'After the High Roman Fashion', *The Field* (November 1987), 65–6. See Higginson, *Two Centuries of Foxhunting*, 13–42, for early American fox hunting.
17 Anthony Trollope, *An Autobiography*, 54–5, 147–8.
18 Trollope, *British Sports and Pastimes*, 74–7.
19 Morley, op. cit., 518, quoting Cobden to Bright, 4 November 1849.
20 T. F. Dale, *History of the Belvoir Hunt*, 39–40.
21 C. J. Blagg, *History of the North Staffordshire Hounds and Country*, 189, 279.
22 Cecil, op. cit., 1–2.
23 Willoughby de Broke, op. cit., 167; Thormanby, *Kings of the Hunting-Field*, op. cit., 393.
24 J. L. Randall, *History of the Meynell Hounds and Country*, vol. i, 62.
25 Egerton-Warburton, *Hunting Songs*; David McLellan, *Engels*, 20–1.

Chapter Five

1 Keith Thomas, *Man and the Natural World*, 115, 176.
2 Itzkowitz, *Peculiar Privilege*, 139–40.
3 *Speech of Lord Erskine in the House of Peers on . . . Cruelty to Animals.*
4 Vyner, *Notitia Venatica*, 1–2.
5 Robert W. Malcolmson, *Popular Recreations in English Society 1700–1850*, 153.
6 Ibid., 154.
7 Harriet Ritvo, *The Animal Estate*, 129–57; Brian Harrison, 'Animals and the State in Nineteenth-Century England', *English Historical Review*, vol. 88 (1973).
8 Beckford, *Thoughts on Hunting*, 178–9, 286, 293–4; Cook, *Observations on Fox-Hunting*,

170–1; Apperley, *Nimrod's Hunting Tours*, 536.
9 Hieover, *Sporting Facts and Sporting Fancies*, 357–8.
10 Blaine, *Encyclopaedia of Rural Sports*, 503–4; Anthony Trollope, 'Mr Freeman on the Morality of Hunting', *Fortnightly Review*, vol. 12 (1869), 620.
11 Berkeley, *Life and Recollections*, vol. i, 290; Itzkowitz, op. cit., 142.
12 E. A. Freeman, 'The Morality of Field Sports', *Fortnightly Review*, vol. 12 (1869), 353–85.
13 Trollope, *Fortnightly Review*, vol. 12 (1869), 625.
14 W. R. W. Stephens, *Life and Letters of Edward A. Freeman*, vol. i, 166, 220, 374; E. A. Freeman, 'The Controversy on Field Sports', *Fortnightly Review*, vol. 14 (1870), 684.
15 T. B. Macaulay, *History of England*, vol. i, ch. 3.
16 'The Progress of Sport', *Baily's Magazine*, vol. 43 (1885), 75–84.
17 'The Defence of Field Sports', *Baily's*, vol. 44 (1885), 317–27; Itzkowitz, op. cit., 145–6.
18 Captain Pennell-Elmhirst ('Brooksby'), *The Cream of Leicestershire*, 155–9, 'A Protest Against Butchery'.
19 Peter Brent, *Charles Darwin* (1983 edn), 488; Ritvo, op. cit., 157–67; Beaufort and Morris, *Hunting*, 68–70.
20 Henry S. Salt, *Seventy Years Among Savages*, 13, 70, 133–4, 151, 154, 175; *Animals' Rights* (1900 edn), 8–14, 46–7.
21 Salt, op. cit., 153, 157; Lord Ribblesdale, *Impressions and Memories*, 179–81; Ribblesdale, *The Queen's Hounds*, 82–91; Thormanby, *Kings of the Hunting-Field*, op. cit., 217–18; E. S. Turner, *All Heaven in a Rage*, 238–42.
22 *Rum'uns to Follow* by a Melton Roughrider [Guy Paget], 21; Salt, *Seventy Years*, 159–60; Buxton, *Ladies of the Chase*, 91–2.
23 'The Defence of Field Sports', *Baily's*, vol. 44 (1885), 317–27.
24 W. Bromley-Davenport, *Sport* (1933 edn), 70–1.
25 J. A. Bridges, *Reminiscences of a Country Politician*, 127.
26 Pennell-Elmhirst ('Brooksby'), *Fox-Hound, Forest and Prairie*, 153; Beaufort and Morris, op. cit., 74.
27 Willoughby de Broke, *The Passing Years*, 167–8.
28 'A Peasant Proprietary and Game Preservation', *Baily's*, vol. 44 (1885), 397–405.
29 J. W. Mackail and Guy Wyndham, *Life and Letters of George Wyndham*, vol. ii, 531, 715.
30 Shaw's preface to Henry S. Salt ed., *Killing for Sport*; Matthew Arnold, *Culture and Anarchy*.
31 Marchioness of Londonderry, *Henry Chaplin. A Memoir*, 128, 191–251; Portland, *Memories of Racing and Hunting*, 251.
32 T. F. Dale, *Eighth Duke of Beaufort and the Badminton Hunt*.
33 Report of the Royal Commission on the University of Oxford (1852), 22–4; Nethercote, op. cit., Viscount Long of Wraxall, *Memories*, 40–9, Loder-Symonds and Crowdy, *History of the Old Berks Hunt*, 273; Willoughby de Broke, op. cit., 151.
34 Beaufort and Morris, op. cit., 100; C. Anstruther Thomson, *Art and Man*, 9.

35 Fane, *Chit-Chat*, 145–6, 164–5.
36 Portland, op. cit., 221; A Melton Roughrider [Paget], op. cit., 16.
37 Portland, op. cit., 212.
38 Fane, op. cit., 136, 170; Ellis, *Leicestershire and the Quorn Hunt*, 110–13; Pennell-Elmhirst, *Foxhound, Forest and Prairie*, 173–4.
39 Collins, *History of the Brocklesby Hounds*, 13; Buxton, op. cit., 65–6, 91; Frances, Countess of Warwick, *Life's Ebb and Flow*, 182.
40 Mrs Nannie Power O'Donoghue, *Ladies on Horseback*, 279.
41 Timothy Eden, *The Tribulations of a Baronet*, 28.
42 Osbert Sitwell, *The Scarlet Tree*, 184–5.
43 Lord Berners, *First Childhood and Far From the Madding War* (1983 edn), 43.

Chapter Six

1 Trollope, *Hunting Sketches*, 82.
2 John Cornwell, *Earth to Earth* (1984 edn), 85–93.
3 Bridges, *Reminiscences of a Country Politician*, 11–12.
4 Itzkowitz, *Peculiar Privilege*, 123–5; Ellis, *Leicestershire and the Quorn Hunt*, 102–3; Cecil, *Hunting Tours*, 268–9.
5 Anstruther Thomson, *Eighty Years' Reminiscences*, vol. i, 340–2.
6 Itzkowitz, op. cit., 109–112; Ellis, op. cit., 104–5.
7 Willoughby de Broke, *The Passing Years*, 44–7.
8 Celia Miller ed., *Rain and Ruin. The Diary of an Oxfordshire Farmer John Simpson Calvertt 1875–1900*.
9 Eardley-Wilmot, *Reminiscences of the late Thomas Assheton Smith*, 79; W. Scarth Dixon, *History of the York and Ainsty Hunt*.
10 John Welcome, *The Sporting Empress*.
11 Paget, *History of the Althorp and Pytchley Hunt*, 207, 214.
12 Dale, *History of the Belvoir Hunt*, 312, 332.
13 A Melton Roughrider [Paget], *Rum'uns to Follow*, op. cit., 19–20; Ellis, op. cit., 93–101, 117–20; Fane, *Chit-Chat*, 15; Mordaunt and Verney, *Annals of the Warwickshire Hunt*, vol. ii, 144.
14 Ellis, op. cit., 133–45; A Melton Roughrider [Paget], op. cit., 83–4; Itzkowitz, op. cit., 169–72.
15 Carr, *English Fox Hunting*, 182–3.
16 G. T. Hutchinson, *The Heythrop Hunt*, 88; Paget, op. cit., 207.
17 Blagg, *History of the North Staffordshire Hounds*, 78; Itzkowitz, op. cit., 168.
18 A. G. Street, *Farmer's Glory* (1983 edn), 78.
19 H. S. Davenport, *Memories at Random*, 168.
20 C. D. Bruce, *The Essex Foxhounds 1895–1926*, 184–5.
21 E. Pennell-Elmhirst, *The Best Season on Record*, 30.
22 Beaufort and Morris, *Hunting*, 165; Itzkowitz, op. cit., 156; Blagg, op. cit., 81.
23 Mordaunt and Verney, op. cit., vol. ii, 124.
24 Randall, *History of the Meynell*, vol. ii, 146–9, 234–41, 247–8, 357–9.
25 Seasonal totals of foxes killed and run to ground together with the number of days out are given in Mordaunt and Verney, op. cit.; Blagg, op. cit.; and Collins, *History of the Brocklesby Hounds*. Michael Harrison's unpublished paper 'Fox Numbers in the Nineteenth Century – Trends

and Causes' (1988) is a valuable source.

26 'The Ground Game Act and Fox-Hunting', *Baily's*, vol. 37 (1881), 341–4; Mordaunt and Verney, op. cit., vol. ii, 66.

27 Earl Bathurst, *History of the V.W.H. Country*, 152–74; Itzkowitz, op. cit., 172–3.

28 Michael F. Berry, *History of the Puckeridge Hunt*, 103–21.

29 Itzkowitz, op. cit., 236.

30 Mordaunt and Verney, op. cit., vol. ii, 187.

31 Ellis, op. cit., 130; Itzkowitz, op. cit., 167; H. Rider Haggard, *Rural England* (1906 edn), vol. ii, 275.

32 Guy Paget ed., *Bad 'Uns to Beat*, 125; Itzkowitz, op. cit., 164.

33 Ibid., 174.

34 Mordaunt and Verney, op. cit., vol. ii, 164; Itzkowitz, op. cit., 174.

35 Mordaunt and Verney, op. cit., vol. ii, 194.

Chapter Seven

1 Eardley-Wilmot, *Reminiscences of the late Thomas Assheton Smith*, 78; Delmé Radcliffe, *The Noble Science*, 39–41; Max Hastings ed., *The Oxford Book of Military Anecdotes*, 209, 219.

2 Delmé Radcliffe, op. cit., 5; *Dictionary of National Biography*.

3 Cook, *Observations on Fox-Hunting*, 146; Blaine, *Encyclopaedia of Rural Sports*, 445; Surtees, *Mr Sponge's Sporting Tour*, chs 21, 22.

4 Elizabeth Longford, *Wellington. The Years of the Sword*, 303; Eardley-Wilmot, op. cit., 78; Welcome, *Surtees*, 38; Fiona Campbell book catalogue, undated press cutting.

5 Earl Stanhope, *Notes of Conversations with the Duke of Wellington* (1888 edn), 87.

6 Michael Howard, *Studies in War and Peace*, 51–2; John Raymond ed., *Reminiscences and Recollections of Captain Gronow*, 74–5; *The Words of Wellington*, 51; Stanhope, op. cit., 220–1.

7 John Keegan, *The Face of Battle* (1978 edn), 194.

8 Berkeley, *Reminiscences of a Huntsman*, 385.

9 Lord George Paget, *The Light Cavalry Brigade in the Crimea*, 170, 183–4; Alexander Kinglake, *The Invasion of the Crimea*, vol. iv, 299, 312–13; Anstruther Thomson, *Eighty Years' Reminiscences*, vol. i, 418–19.

10 G. Whyte-Melville, Obituary of Cardigan, *Baily's*, vol. 15 (1868), 58.

11 Donald Thomas, *Charge! Hurrah! Hurrah! A Life of Cardigan of Balaclava* (1976 edn), 17–18, 176.

12 Anstruther Thomson, op. cit., vol. i, 76–7, 89–90, 113; Thormanby, *Kings of the Hunting-Field*, 280–8.

13 Major General M. F. Rimington, *Our Cavalry*, 156; Colonel R. S. Liddell, *Memoirs of the 10th Royal Hussars*, 566.

14 Ibid., 337, 375; Marquess of Anglesey, *A History of the British Cavalry 1816–1919*, vol. ii, 368, vol. iii, 143.

15 Sir Evelyn Wood, *From Midshipman to Field Marshal*, vol. i, 104.

16 Anglesey, op. cit., vol. ii, 395; Brian Bond, 'Doctrine and Training in the British Cavalry 1870–1914' in Michael Howard ed., *The Theory and Practice of War*, 100–1.

17 Sir Evelyn Wood, 'British Cavalry 1853–1903', *Cavalry Journal*, vol. 1 (1906), 150; Anglesey, op. cit., vol. iv, 468–70.
18 L. E. Nolan, *Cavalry; Its History and Tactics*, 141–2, 148–9; Chevenix-Trench, *A History of Horsemanship*, 166–7.
19 Valentine Baker, *The British Cavalry*, 29; C. S. March Phillipps, *Horse and Man*, vii–viii.
20 E. A. H. Alderson, *Pink and Scarlet*, 8–9.
21 Rimington, op. cit., 196; Chevenix-Trench, op. cit., 171.
22 Anglesey, op. cit., vol. i, 106–7.
23 Ibid., vol. ii, 421; Baker, op. cit., 17; Thormanby, op. cit., 285; Michael Howard, *The Franco-Prussian War*, 8.
24 Anglesey, op. cit., vol. iv, 287, 349–65; Rimington, op. cit., 23.
25 Colonel F. V. Wing, 'Foxhunting and Soldiering', *Cavalry Journal*, vol. 1 (1906), 497–8. Compare Anglesey, op. cit., vol. iv, 252–3.
26 A. R. Godwin-Austen, *The Staff and the Staff College*, 134, 171–7; Evelyn Wood, *From Midshipman to Field Marshal*, vol. ii, 260.
27 Anglesey, op. cit., vol. iv, 388–423; Alderson, op. cit., 215–16.
28 Captain B. H. Liddell Hart, *The Remaking of Modern Armies*, 52; Robert Blake ed., *The Private Papers of Douglas Haig*, 90, 147.
29 Robert Hartman, *The Remainder Biscuit*, 99–100, 134–6.
30 Jay Luvaas, *The Education of an Army*, 355.
31 C. S. Forester, *The General*, ch. 14.
32 Lord Carrington, *Reflect on Things Past* (1988), 24.

Chapter Eight

1 *Memoir of the Kilkenny Hunt*, Compiled by One of its Members, 15, 38–9; Roger Longrigg, *History of Foxhunting*, 156–67; Muriel Bowen, *Irish Hunting*, 92–5.
2 Bernard Fitzpatrick, *Irish Sport and Sportsmen*, 105, 129; Bowen, op. cit., 39–40, 69–70.
3 Fitzpatrick, op. cit., 127–8.
4 Ibid., 18.
5 E.OE. Somerville and Martin Ross, *Wheel-Tracks*, 26.
6 Colin A. Lewis, *Hunting in Ireland*, 69–80, 119.
7 Quoted in J. S. Donnelly, *The Land and People of Nineteenth-Century Cork*, 10–11.
8 See Gifford Lewis, *Somerville and Ross*, 112–13.
9 Karl Marx, *Selected Works* (1942), vol. ii, 642; E.OE. Somerville and Martin Ross, *Irish Memories*, 15–17.
10 See Donnelly, op. cit., 111–315.
11 Whyte-Melville, *Riding Recollections*, 144–62.
12 Fitzpatrick, op. cit., 27–41.
13 Ibid., 46–54.
14 Isaac Bell, *A Huntsman's Log Book*, 154–7.
15 Fitzpatrick, op. cit., 159; Bowen, op. cit., 7.
16 Fitzpatrick, op. cit., 172, 186, 205–8, 239.
17 *Memoir of the Kilkenny Hunt*, 68–83; Fitzpatrick, op. cit., 257.
18 W. E. Vaughan, 'An Assessment of the Economic Performance of Irish Landlords, 1851–81' in F. S. L. Lyons and R. A. J. Hawkins eds, *Ireland under the Union*.
19 Elizabeth, Countess of Fingall, *Seventy Years Young*, 200.

20 Somerville and Ross, *Irish Memories*, 24.
21 Ibid., 34.
22 'The Future of Sport in Disturbed Ireland', *Baily's*, vol. 36 (1881), 336–40; 'The Fate of Fox-Hunting in Ireland', *Baily's*, vol. 37 (1882), 270–4; Bowen, op. cit., 51, 104, 125, 138, 165, 190, 210.
23 Fingall, op. cit., 72; Bell, op. cit., 133–4; Thormanby, *Kings of the Hunting-Field*, 402–10.
24 'The Hunting Season in Ireland', *Baily's*, vol. 41 (1889), 93–8.
25 Fingall, op. cit., 200.
26 Ibid., 98.
27 Ibid., 119, 198–9; Bell, op. cit., 136–44; Lord Dunsany, *My Ireland*, 123–8.
28 Bell, op. cit., 144–6.
29 Mark Bence-Jones, *Twilight of the Ascendancy*, 97–8.
30 Fingall, op. cit., 282.
31 'The Finger of Mrs Knox' in E.OE. Somerville and Martin Ross, *In Mr Knox's Country*.
32 'Great-Uncle McCarthy', and 'The Policy of the Closed Door', in E.OE. Somerville and Martin Ross, *Some Experiences of an Irish R.M.*
33 Somerville and Ross, *Wheel-Tracks*, 121–2.
34 Somerville and Ross, *Irish Memories*, 83, 138, 290. See Gifford Lewis, *Somerville and Ross*.

Chapter Nine

1 Douglas Sutherland, *The Yellow Earl*; Ellis, *Leicestershire and the Quorn Hunt*, 129–31.
2 Paget ed., *Bad 'Uns to Beat*, 25, 76–7, 128.
3 George Millar ed., *Horseman. Memoirs of Captain J. H. Marshall*, 24–35, 71–2.
4 'Masters of Hounds on the Etiquette of Hunting Dress', *Baily's*, vol. 90 (1908), 445–9; 'Masters of Hounds on Motors', ibid., 3–6.
5 J. Fairfax-Blakeborough ed., *Hunting and Sporting Reminiscences of H. W. Selby Lowndes MFH*, 39; Paget, *History of the Althorp and Pytchley Hunt*, 233.
6 T. F. Dale, *Fox-Hunting in the Shires*, 11.
7 Sutherland, op. cit., 240–6; A. H. Higginson, *Try Back*, 99–100; Guy Paget, *Life of Frank Freeman Huntsman*, 59; Bell, *A Huntsman's Log Book*, 55–7.
8 Fane, *Chit-Chat*, 172–3; Paget ed., *Bad 'Uns to Beat*, 93.
9 Paget, *Life of Frank Freeman Huntsman*, 49–50.
10 Bell, op. cit., 70.
11 Cuthbert Bradley, *Reminiscences of Frank Gillard*; Paget ed., *Bad 'Uns to Beat*, 25–31.
12 Bell, op. cit., 19–28, 66–76, 204–5; Paget, *History of the Althorp and Pytchley Hunt*, 233; Paget, *Life of Frank Freeman Huntsman*, 34–42, 58–61.
13 Randall, *History of the Meynell*, vol. ii, 18–19.
14 'Is Foxhunting Doomed?', *Baily's*, vol. 85 (1906), 41; Dale, op. cit., 310–11.
15 *Country Gentleman and Land and Water*, 14 October 1911; 10 February 1912; 2 March 1912; 9 March 1912. T. F. Dale, 'Foxhunters, Farmers and Damage', *Baily's*, vol. 97 (1912), 163–7; Dale, 'Farmers in the Hunting Field', ibid., 276–80.
16 Collins, *History of the Brocklesby*

Hounds, 14; Itzkowitz, *Peculiar Privilege*, 156–9.

17 Willoughby de Broke, *The Passing Years*, 109.

18 Lionel Edwards, *Famous Foxhunters*, 52–5; Simon Blow, *Fields Elysian*, 37, 40.

19 Paget, *Life of Frank Freeman Huntsman*, 8–9; Leslie Field, *Bendor*, 117.

20 Fairfax-Blakeborough ed., op. cit., 36.

21 W. Phillpotts Williams, 'The Position of Provincial Countries', *Baily's*, vol. 73 (1900), 171–2; 'Foxhunting. Why so Many Resignations?' by One over Sixty, *Baily's*, vol. 91 (1909), 184–7.

22 Richard Beaumont, 'The 2nd Lord Ripon's Sporting Life', *Country Life*, 26 July 1984; 'Foxhunting. Where are We?' by 'Venator', *Baily's*, vol. 84 (1905), 487; Richard Mabey, *The Common Ground* (1981 edn), 186–7; Charles Richardson, *The Complete Foxhunter*, 26–51.

23 Fairfax-Blakeborough ed., op. cit., 71, 174.

24 Carr, *English Fox Hunting*, op. cit., 166.

25 Cuming ed., *A Hunting Diary* by N. W. Apperley, 52–3; Lionel Edwards, *Reminiscences of a Sporting Artist*, 6–8.

26 Higginson, *Two Centuries of Foxhunting*, 121–2.

27 Phillpotts Williams, 'The Position of Provincial Countries', *Baily's*, vol. 73 (1900), 172; Will Ogilvie, *Galloping Shoes*, 28.

28 Higginson, op. cit., 230–1.

29 Davenport, *Memories at Random*, 25.

30 Quoted in Jane Ridley, Oxford D. Phil. thesis, 1984, 162.

31 Quoted in Avner Offer, *Property and Politics 1870–1914*, 371.

32 Sir Alfred Munnings, *The Second Burst*, 230.

33 Earl Bathurst, *The Breeding of Foxhounds*, 3–6, 123.

34 Paget, *Life of Frank Freeman Huntsman*, 43–4; Higginson, op. cit., 157–8.

35 Bell, op. cit., 81–97, 207–12; Blow, op. cit., 73–7.

Chapter Ten

1 'The Future of Foxhunting', *Baily's*, vol. 104 (1915), 107–8; Blow, *Fields Elysian*, 50–60.

2 Paget, *History of the Althorp and Pytchley Hunt*, op. cit., 248; Willoughby de Broke, *Hunting the Fox*, 2–3.

3 George Lambton, *Men and Horses I Have Known*, 66–7.

4 Paget ed., *Bad 'Uns to Beat*, 31, 135–7.

5 Fairfax-Blakeborough ed., *Hunting and Sporting Reminiscences of H. W. Selby Lowndes MFH*, 174.

6 Lambton, op. cit., 15; Cecil Aldin, *Time I Was Dead*, 165 ff.

7 Buxton, *Ladies of the Chase*, 118–23.

8 Apsley, *Bridleways through History*, 356.

9 Lambton, op. cit., 308–13.

10 Higginson, *Two Centuries of Foxhunting*, 228; Willoughby de Broke, op. cit., 2.

11 Higginson, op. cit., 229.

12 Brigadier-General C. D. Bruce, *The Essex Foxhounds 1895–1926*, 31; Harry S. Eeles, *The Eridge Hunt*, 34–5.

13 G. A. Cowen, *The Braes of Derwent Hunt*, 66; Hutchinson, *Heythrop Hunt*, 117. See Madeleine Beard, *English Landed Society in the Twentieth Century*, ch. 3.

14 Paget ed., *Bad 'Uns to Beat*, 32, 168, 235–40.
15 Carr, *English Fox Hunting*, 235–6; Blow, *Fields Elysian*, 68–70; *The Times*, 5 January 1920.
16 Dorian Williams, *Between the Lines*, 30, 70–1.
17 Street, *Farmer's Glory*, 205–15.
18 Bruce, op. cit., 24–5.
19 Apsley, op. cit., 357; Buxton, op. cit., 131–2.
20 Molly Keane and Snaffles, *Red Letter Days* (1987 edn), 72.
21 *Memoirs of J. H. Marshall*, 225.
22 Blow, op. cit., 98–128; Ulrica Murray Smith, *Magic of the Quorn*, 1–11.
23 Munnings, *The Second Burst*, 149, 153–4.
24 *Memoirs of J. H. Marshall*, 242; Paget ed., *Bad 'Uns to Beat*, 148.
25 Lady Diana Shedden and Lady Apsley, *To Whom the Goddess*.
26 Nicholas Russell, 'Well-Groomed or Well-Bred?', *History Today*, vol. 39 (January 1989), 10–12.
27 Apsley, op. cit., 355.

Chapter Eleven

1 Blow, *Fields Elysian*, 107, 136; Paget ed., *Bad 'Uns to Beat*, 138; Williams, *Between the Lines*, 28–32.
2 Michael Berry, *Fox Hunting from The Times*.
3 Ronald Blythe, *Akenfield* (1972 edn), 316–17.
4 Michael Berry, *History of the Puckeridge Hunt*, 124; *Fox Hunting from The Times*, 16–17.
5 Cowen, *Braes of Derwent Hunt*, 83–5.
6 Mrs Stuart Menzies, *Sporting Parsons in Peace and War*, 33–4.
7 *Memoirs of J. H. Marshall*, 308. Higginson's diaries are in the London Library, to which he left his collection of books.
8 Keane and Snaffles, *Red Letter Days*, 71–81.
9 Eeles, *The Eridge Hunt*, 157.
10 Rupert Hart-Davies ed., *Siegfried Sassoon Diaries 1915–1918*, 118–19.
11 Siegfried Sassoon, *The Weald of Youth*, 214.
12 Edwards, *Reminiscences of a Sporting Artist*, 34, 38, 149–61; John Welcome and Rupert Collins, *Snaffles. Life and Work of Charlie Johnson Payne*.
13 Henry Williamson, *The Wild Red Deer of Exmoor*, 12–13.
14 Richard H. Thomas, *The Politics of Hunting*, 65–8, 85–7.
15 Suzanne Beadle, *The Beginning*; Thomas, op. cit., 129–31.
16 *The Times*, 5 December 1930; Thomas, op. cit., 208; John Ramsden ed., *Real Old Tory Politics*, 250–1.
17 *The Times*, 17 July 1931; Thomas, op. cit., 140.
18 Murray Smith, *Magic of the Quorn*, op. cit., 25–6.
19 L. H. W. Williams, *A History of the Glamorgan Hunt*, 17–18.
20 *Baily's Hunting Directory 1939–49*, 35–7.
21 Thomas, op. cit., 88–9.
22 Egremont, *Wyndham and Children First*, 62–3.

Chapter Twelve

1 *The Times*, 6 February 1984; James Pope-Hennessy, *Queen Mary* (1959), 597–609.
2 Caroline Blackwood, *In the Pink*, 13–24; Thomas, *The Politics of Hunting*, 94.

3 Beaufort, *Fox-Hunting*, 181–90.
4 *The Times*, 27, 28 December 1984.
5 Mike Huskisson, *Outfoxed*, 37–8.
6 Beard, *English Landed Society in the Twentieth Century*, 85–97.
7 *Baily's Hunting Directory 1939–49*, 38.
8 Ibid., 45; *Baily's Hunting Directory 1949–50*, 35–6.
9 *Hansard*, 5th series, vol. 461 (1949), cols 2179–80; 2236–7; 2227–34.
10 Cowen, *Braes of Derwent*, op. cit., 248–9.
11 Colin Willock ed., *The Farmer's Book of Field Sports*, 230–1.
12 Thomas, op. cit., 114–22, 190; Blackwood, op. cit., 142–54; Robert Churchward, 'Fox-hunting' in *Against Hunting*, ed. Patrick Moore; *Baily's Hunting Directory 1960–61*, 297.
13 Thomas, op. cit., 89–90; Peter Singer ed., *In Defence of Animals*, 187.
14 Huskisson, op. cit.
15 *Country Sports*, October 1985; Bernard Levin, 'The Animal Lovers Lusting for Blood', *The Times*, 3 July 1986.
16 Richard Course quoted in Singer ed., op. cit., 188.
17 Thomas, op. cit., 157–76.
18 Ibid., 168–9.
19 Ibid., 68–75.
20 Ibid., 96–103; *The Times*, 23 December 1985.

Bibliography

My selection of hunts has been governed by the availability of printed sources. These tend to be more abundant for the more fashionable packs than for those in the provinces.

Place of publication is London unless otherwise indicated.

Alderson, E. A. H., *Pink and Scarlet*. William Heinemann, 1900.

Aldin, Cecil, *Time I Was Dead*. Eyre and Spottiswoode, 1934.

Marquess of Anglesey, *A History of the British Cavalry 1816–1919*. Leo Cooper, 1973–86.

Anstruther Thomson, J., *Eighty Years' Reminiscences*. Longmans & Co., 1904.

Apperley, C. J., *see* Nimrod.

Lady Apsley, *Bridleways Through History*. Hutchinson & Co., 1948 edn.

Lady Apsley and Lady Diana Shedden, *To Whom the Goddess*. Hutchinson & Co., 1932.

Arnold, Matthew, *Culture and Anarchy*. Smith, Elder & Co., 1869.

[Austen-Leigh, J. E.], *Recollections of the Early Days of the Vine Hunt* by A Sexagenarian. Spottiswoode & Co., 1865.

Baillie-Grohman, W. A., ed., *The Master of Game*. Chatto & Windus, 1909.

Baily's Hunting Directory. Vinton & Co., 1897.

Baily's Magazine, 1860–1926.

Baker, Valentine, *The British Cavalry*. Longman & Co., 1858.

Earl Bathurst, *The Breeding of Foxhounds*, Constable & Co., 1926.

——— *The Earl Spencer's and Mr John Warde's Hounds*. Cirencester Newspaper Co., Cirencester, 1932.

——— *History of the V.W.H. Country*. Constable & Co., 1936.

——— *The Charlton and Raby Hunts*. Constable & Co., 1938.

Beadle, Suzanne, *The Beginning*. British Field Sports Society, 1971.

Beard, Madeleine, *English Landed Society in the Twentieth Century*. Routledge, 1989.

Duke of Beaufort, *Fox-Hunting*. David & Charles, Newton Abbot, 1980.
Duke of Beaufort and Mowbray Morris, *Hunting*. Longmans, Green & Co., 1889.
Beckford, Peter, *Thoughts on Hunting*. Sarum, 1781.
Bell, Isaac, *A Huntsman's Log Book*. Eyre & Spottiswoode, 1947.
Bence-Jones, Mark, *Twilight of the Ascendancy*. Constable & Co. Ltd, 1987.
Bentinck, Lord Charles, *Lord Henry Bentinck's Foxhounds*. Hutchinson & Co., 1930.
Beresford, Lord Charles, *Memoirs*. Methuen, 1914.
Berkeley, Grantley, *Reminiscences of a Huntsman*. Longman & Co., 1854.
——— *My Life and Recollections*. Hurst & Blackett, 1865.
Lord Berners, *First Childhood*. Constable & Co. Ltd, 1934.
Berry, Michael F., *Fox Hunting from The Times*. 1933.
——— *History of the Puckeridge Hunt*. Country Life, 1950.
Blackwood, Caroline, *In the Pink*. Bloomsbury Publishing Ltd, 1987.
Blagg, C. J., *History of the North Staffordshire Hounds and Country*. Sampson Low & Co., 1902.
Blaine, Delabere P., *An Encyclopaedia of Rural Sports*. Longman & Co., 1840.
Blew, W. C. A., *The Quorn Hunt and Its Masters*. John C. Nimmo, 1899.
Blome, Richard, *The Gentleman's Recreation*. S. Roycroft, 1686.
Blow, Simon, *Fields Elysian*. J. M. Dent & Sons Ltd, 1983.
Blythe, Ronald, *Akenfield*. Allen Lane, Harmondsworth, 1969.
Bond, Brian, 'Doctrine and Training in the British Cavalry 1870–1914' in Michael Howard ed., *The Theory and Practice of War*. Cassell, 1965.
Bovill, E. W., *The England of Nimrod and Surtees 1815-54*. Oxford University Press, 1959.
——— *English Country Life, 1780-1830*. Oxford University Press, 1962.
Bowen, Muriel, *Irish Hunting*. The Kerryman, Tralee, 1955.
Bowers, Georgina, *Notes from a Hunting Box not in the Shires*. Bradbury, Agnew & Co., 1873.
——— *Leaves from a Hunting Journal*. Chatto & Windus, 1880.
——— *Hunting in Hard Times*. Chapman & Hall, 1889.
Bradley, Cuthbert, *Reminiscences of Frank Gillard*. E. Arnold, 1898.
Brent, Peter, *Charles Darwin*. William Heinemann Ltd, 1981.
Bridges, J. A., *Reminiscences of a Country Politician*. T. Werner Laurie, 1906.
Bright, John, and Thorold Rogers, J. E., eds., *Speeches by Richard Cobden*. Macmillan & Co., 1870.
Bromley Davenport, W., *Sport*. Chapman & Hall, 1885.
Brooksby [E. Pennell-Elmhirst], *The Cream of Leicestershire*. Routledge & Sons, 1883.

——— *The Best Season on Record*. Routledge & Sons, 1884.
——— *Fox-Hound, Forest and Prairie*. Routledge & Sons, 1892.
Bruce, C. D., *The Essex Foxhounds 1895–1926*. 1926.
Buxton, Meriel, *Ladies of the Chase*. 1987.
Byng, John, *The Torrington Diaries* ed. C. B. Andrews. Eyre & Spottiswoode, 1934–38.

Carr, Raymond, *English Fox Hunting*. Weidenfeld & Nicolson, 1976.
Cavalry Journal, 1906.
Cecil [Cornelius Tongue], *Hunting Tours*. Otley & Co., 1864.
Chapman, Captain F., *The Wensleydale Hounds*. V. T. Sumfield, Eastbourne, 1908.
Chevenix-Trench, Charles, *A History of Horsemanship*. Longman, Harlow, 1970.
Clapham, Richard, *Foxhunting on the Lakeland Fells*. Longmans & Co., 1920.
Cobbett, William, *Rural Rides*. J. M. Dent & Sons, 1912 edn.
Collins, George E., *History of the Brocklesby Hounds*. Sampson Low & Co., 1902.
Cook, Colonel John, *Observations on Fox-Hunting*. The Author, 1826.
Cornwell, John, *Earth to Earth*. Allen Lane, 1982.
Country Gentleman and Land and Water, 1911–12.
Cowen, G. A., *The Braes of Derwent Hunt*. Northumberland Press, Gateshead, 1955.
Cox, Nicholas, *The Gentleman's Recreation*. E. Flesher, 1674.
Crawhall, Joseph, Records of the Park House Club. MS at Alnwick Castle, Northumberland.
Cuming, E. D., *Robert Smith Surtees*. W. Blackwood & Sons, Edinburgh & London, 1924.
——— (ed.), *Squire Osbaldeston: His Autobiography*. John Lane, 1926.
——— (ed.), *A Hunting Diary* by Newton Wynne Apperley.Nisbet & Co., 1926.

Dale, T. F., *History of the Belvoir Hunt*. Archibald Constable & Co., 1899.
——— *Eighth Duke of Beaufort and the Badminton Hunt*. Archibald Constable & Co., 1901.
——— *Fox-Hunting in the Shires*. Grant Richards, 1903.
Daniel, Reverend W. B., *Rural Sports*. Bunny & Gold, 1801.
Davenport, Henry S., *Memories at Random*. Heath Cranton, 1926.
Davies, E. W. L., *Memoir of the Rev. John Russell*. R. Bentley & Son, 1878.

De Costobadie, F. P., *Annals of the Billesdon Hunt*. Chapman & Hall, 1914.
Delmé Radcliffe, F. P., *The Noble Science*. 1839.
Deuchar, Stephen, *Sporting Art in Eighteenth-Century England*. Yale, 1988.
Disraeli, B., *Lord George Bentinck: A Political Biography*. Colburn & Co., 1852.
Dixon, W. W., *see* Thormanby.
Donnelly, J. S., *The Land and People of Nineteenth-Century Cork*. Routledge & Kegan Paul, 1975.
The Druid [H. H. Dixon], *Silk and Scarlet*. Rogerson & Tuxford, 1859.
Lord Dunsany, *My Ireland*. Jarrolds, 1937.

Eardley-Wilmot, Sir John, *Reminiscences of the late Thomas Assheton Smith*. John Murray, 1860.
Eden, Timothy, *The Tribulations of a Baronet*. Macmillan & Co., 1933.
Edwards, Lionel, *Famous Foxhunters*. Eyre & Spottiswoode, 1932.
——— *Reminiscences of a Sporting Artist*. Putnam & Co., 1947.
Eeles, Harry S., *The Eridge Hunt*. Courier Printing & Publishing Co., Tunbridge Wells, 1936.
Egerton Warburton, R. E., *Hunting Songs*. Henry Young & Sons, Liverpool, 1912.
Lord Egremont, *Wyndham and Children First*. Macmillan, 1968.
Ellis, Colin, *Leicestershire and the Quorn Hunt*. Edgar Backus, Leicester, 1951.
Speech of Lord Erskine in the House of Peers on Cruelty to Animals. 1809.

Fairfax-Blakeborough, J., *England's Oldest Hunt*. Northallerton, 1907.
——— *Hunting and Sporting Reminiscences of H. W. Selby Lowndes MFH*. P. Allan & Co., 1926.
Fane, Lady Augusta, *Chit-Chat*. Thornton Butterworth, 1926.
Fingall, Elizabeth, Countess of, *Seventy Years Young*. Collins, 1937.
Fitzpatrick, Bernard, *Irish Sport and Sportsmen*. Dublin, 1878.
Forester, C. S., *The General*. Michael Joseph, 1936.
Frederick, Sir Charles Bart, *Fox-Hunting*. Seeley, Service & Co., 1930.
Freeman, E. A., 'The Morality of Field Sports', *Fortnightly Review*, vol. 12. 1869.
——— 'The Controversy on Field Sports', *Fortnightly Review*, vol. 14. 1870.
Frewen, Moreton, *Melton Mowbray and Other Memories*. Herbert Jenkins, 1924.

Godwin-Austen, A. R., *The Staff and the Staff College*. Constable & Co., 1927.
Goodall, Daphne M., *Huntsmen of a Golden Age*, H. F. & G. Witherby, 1956.

Harrison, Brian, 'Animals and the State in Nineteenth-Century England', *English Historical Review*, vol. 88. 1973.
Hart-Davies, Rupert, ed., *Siegfried Sassoon Diaries 1915–1918*. 1983.
Hartman, Robert, *The Remainder Biscuit*. André Deutsch, 1964.
Hastings, Max, ed., *The Oxford Book of Military Anecdotes*. Oxford University Press, Oxford, 1985.
Hawkes, John, *The Meynellian Science* [1808]. Edgar Backus, Leicester, 1932 edn.
Hieover, Harry [Charles Bindley], *The Hunting-Field*. 1850.
——— *Sporting Facts and Sporting Fancies*. 1853.
Higginson, A. H., *Try Back*. Collins, 1932.
——— *The Meynell of the West*. Collins, 1936.
——— *Peter Beckford*. Collins, 1937.
——— *Two Centuries of Foxhunting*. Collins, 1946.
Horlock, K. W., *see* Scrutator.
Howard, Michael, *Studies in War and Peace*. Maurice Temple Smith, 1970.
Huskisson, Mike, *Outfoxed*. Michael Huskisson Associates, 1983.
Hutchinson, G. T., *The Heythrop Hunt*. John Murray, 1935.

Itzkowitz, David, *Peculiar Privilege*. Harvester Press, Hassocks, 1977.

Keane, Molly, *The Rising Tide*. Collins, 1937.
Keane, Molly, and Snaffles, *Red Letter Days*. Collins, 1933.
Keegan, John, *The Face of Battle*. Jonathan Cape, 1976.
Memoir of the Kilkenny Hunt. Compiled by One of its Members. Hodges, Figgis & Co., Dublin, 1897.
Kinglake, Alexander, *The Invasion of the Crimea*. Edinburgh & London, 1863–87.
Charles Kingsley. His Letters and Memories of his Life, Edited by his Wife. H. S. King & Co., 1877.
Kipling, Rudyard, 'My Son's Wife', in *A Diversity of Creatures*. Macmillan & Co., 1917.

Lambton, George, *Men and Horses I Have Known*. Thornton Butterworth, 1924.

Langley, P. J. W., and Yalden, D. W., 'The Decline of the Rarer Carnivores in Great Britain during the Nineteenth Century', *Mammal Review*, vol. 7. 1977.
Lever, Charles, *Charles O'Malley*. Dublin, 1841.
Lewis, Colin A., *Hunting in Ireland*. J. A. Allen, 1975.
Lewis, Gifford, *Somerville and Ross*. 1985.
Liddell, Colonel R. S., *Memoirs of the 10th Royal Hussars*. Longmans & Co., 1891.
Liddell Hart, B. H., *The Remaking of Modern Armies*. John Murray, 1927.
Lloyd, H. G., *The Red Fox*. Batsford, 1980.
Loder-Symonds, F. C., and Crowdy, E. Percy, *A History of the Old Berks Hunt*. Vinton & Co., 1905.
Marchioness of Londonderry, *Henry Chaplin. A Memoir*. Macmillan & Co., 1926.
Viscount Long of Wraxall, *Memories*. Hutchinson & Co., 1923.
Longford, Elizabeth, *Wellington. The Years of the Sword*. Weidenfeld & Nicolson, 1969.
Longrigg, Roger, *History of Foxhunting*. Macmillan, 1975.
Luvaas, Jay, *The Education of an Army*. 1965.

Mabey, Richard, *The Common Ground*. Hutchinson, 1980.
Mackail, J. W., and Wyndham, Guy, *Life and Letters of George Wyndham*. Hutchinson & Co., 1925.
Malcolmson, Robert W., *Popular Recreations in English Society 1700–1850*. Cambridge University Press, Cambridge, 1973.
Earl of March, *Records of the Old Charlton Hunt*. Elkin Mathews, 1910.
March Phillipps, C. S., *Horse and Man*. 1869.
Masefield, John, *Reynard the Fox*. William Heinemann, 1919.
Menzies, Mrs Stuart, *Sporting Parsons in Peace and War*. Hutchinson & Co., 1917.
Millar, George, ed., *Horseman. Memoirs of Captain J. H. Marshall*. Bodley Head, 1970.
Miller, Celia, ed., *Rain and Ruin. The Diary of an Oxfordshire Farmer John Simpson Calvertt 1875-1900*. Allan Sutton, Gloucester, 1983.
Moore, Patrick, ed., *Against Hunting*. Victor Gollancz, 1965.
Mordaunt, Sir Charles, Bart, and Verney, the Hon. and Rev. W. R., *Annals of the Warwickshire Hunt 1795–1895*. Sampson Low & Co., 1896.
Morley, John, *Life of Richard Cobden*. Chapman & Hall, 1881.

Munnings, Alfred, *An Artist's Life*. Museum Press, 1950–2.
Munsche, P. B., *Gentlemen and Poachers: the English Game Laws, 1671–1831*. Cambridge University Press, Cambridge, 1981.
Murray Smith, Ulrica, *Magic of the Quorn*. J. A. Allen, 1980.

Nethercote, H. O., *The Pytchley Hunt*. Sampson Low & Co., 1888.
Nimrod [C. J. Apperley], *Nimrod's Hunting Tours*. 1835.
——— *The Chase, the Turf and the Road*. John Murray, 1837.
——— *Life of John Mytton*. Rudolph Ackermann, 1835.
Nolan, L. E., *Cavalry; Its History and Tactics*. 1953.
[Lord North] *A Century of Foxhunting with the Warwickshire Hounds* by Castor. John Potts, Banbury, 1891.

Ogilvie, Will H., *Galloping Shoes*. Constable & Co., 1923.

Paget, Lord George, *The Light Cavalry Brigade in the Crimea*. John Murray, 1881.
Paget, Guy, *Rum'uns to Follow* by a Melton Roughrider. Country Life, 1934.
——— *Bad 'Uns to Beat*. Collins, 1936.
——— *History of the Althorp and Pytchley Hunt*. Collins, 1937.
——— *Life of Frank Freeman Huntsman*. Edgar Backus, Leicester, 1948.
Pease, A. E., *The Cleveland Hounds as a Trencher-Fed Pack*. Longmans & Co., 1887.
Pennell-Elmhirst, E., *see* Brooksby.
Duke of Portland, *Memories of Racing and Hunting*. Faber & Faber, 1935.
Powell, Anthony, *From a View to a Death*. Heinemann, 1933.
Power O'Donoghue, Mrs Nannie, *Ladies on Horseback*. W. H. Allen & Co., 1881.

Randall, J. L., *History of the Meynell Hounds and Country*. Sampson Low & Co., 1901.
Raymond, John, ed., *Reminiscences and Recollections of Captain Gronow*. Bodley Head, 1964.
Reynard, Frank H., *The Bedale Hounds*. Darlington, 1908.
Lord Ribblesdale, *The Queen's Hounds*. Longmans & Co., 1897.
——— *Impressions and Memories*. Cassell & Co., 1927.
Richardson, Charles, *The Complete Foxhunter*. Methuen & Co., 1908.
Rider Haggard, H., *Rural England*. Longmans & Co., 1902.

Rimington, Major-General M. F., *Our Cavalry*. Macmillan & Co., 1912.
Ritvo, Harriet, *The Animal Estate*. Harvard University Press, 1987.
Rose, R. N., *The Field*. Michael Joseph, 1953.
Russell, Nicholas, *Like Engend'ring Like*. Cambridge University Press, Cambridge, 1986.

Salt, Henry S., *Animals' Rights*. G. Bell & Sons, 1892.
——— *Killing for Sport*. G. Bell & Sons, 1915.
——— *Seventy Years Among Savages*. G. Allen & Unwin, 1921.
Sassoon, Siegfried, *Memoirs of a Fox-Hunting Man*. Faber & Faber, 1928.
——— *The Weald of Youth*. Faber & Faber, 1942.
Scarth Dixon, W., *History of the York and Ainsty Hunt*. R. Jackson, Leeds, 1899.
[Scott Henderson Report] *Report of the Committee on Cruelty to Wild Animals*. 1951.
Scrutator [K. W. Horlock], *Recollections of a Fox-Hunter*. 1861.
——— *Practical Lessons on Hunting and Sporting*. 1865.
Singer, Peter, ed., *In Defence of Animals*. Blackwell, Oxford, 1985.
Sitwell, Osbert, *The Scarlet Tree*. Macmillan & Co., 1946.
Smith, Thomas, *Extracts from the Diary of a Huntsman*. 1838.
Somerville, E.OE., and Ross, Martin [Violet Martin], *The Silver Fox*. Lawrence & Bullen, 1898.
——— *Some Experiences of an Irish R.M.* Longmans & Co., 1899.
——— *Further Experiences of an Irish R.M.* Longmans & Co., 1908.
——— *In Mr Knox's Country*. Longmans & Co., 1915.
——— *Irish Memories*. Longmans & Co., 1917.
——— *Wheel-Tracks*. Longmans & Co., 1923.
Somerville, William, *The Chase*. 1735.
Sporting Magazine, vol. i. 1793.
Earl Stanhope, *Notes of Conversations with the Duke of Wellington*. John Murray, 1888.
Steele, Richard, and Addison, Joseph, *The Spectator*. 1711–12.
Stephens, W. R. W., *Life and Letters of Edward A. Freeman*. Macmillan & Co., 1895.
Street, A. G., *Farmer's Glory*. Faber & Faber, 1932.
Surtees, R. S., *Jorrocks' Jaunts and Jollities*. Walter Spiers, 1839.
——— *Handley Cross*. 1843.
——— *Hillingdon Hall*. 1845.

——— *The Analysis of the Hunting Field*. R. Ackermann, 1846.
——— *Hawbuck Grange*. Longmans & Co., 1847.
——— *Mr Sponge's Sporting Tour*. Bradbury & Evans, 1852.
——— *Ask Mamma*. Bradbury & Evans, 1858.
——— *Plain or Ringlets*. Bradbury & Evans, 1860.
——— *Mr Facey Romford's Hounds*. Bradbury & Evans, 1865.
——— *Young Tom Hall* ed. E. D. Cuming. W. Blackwood & Sons, Edinburgh & London, 1926.
Surtees, *The Hunting Tours of Surtees* ed. E. D. Cuming. W. Blackwood & Sons, Edinburgh & London, 1927.
——— *Town and Country Papers* ed. E. D. Cuming. W. Blackwood & Sons, Edinburgh & London, 1929.
Sutherland, Douglas, *The Yellow Earl*. Cassell & Co., 1965.

Taine, Hippolyte, *Notes on England*. 1872.
Tancred of Weens, *George, Annals of a Border Club*. T. S. Smail, Jedburgh, 1899.
Thomas, Donald, *Charge! Hurrah! Hurrah! A Life of Cardigan of Balaclava*. Routledge & Kegan Paul, 1974.
Thomas, Keith, *Man and the Natural World*. Allen Lane, 1983.
Thomas, Richard H., *The Politics of Hunting*. Gower Publishing Co. Ltd., Aldershot, 1983.
Thompson, F. M. L., *English Landed Society in the Nineteenth Century*. Routledge & Kegan Paul, 1963.
Thormanby [W. W. Dixon], *Kings of the Hunting-Field*. Hutchinson & Co., 1899.
Thorold Rogers, J. E., ed., *Speeches by the Right Hon. John Bright*. Macmillan & Co., 1868.
Tozer, E. J. F., *The South Devon Hunt*. The Author, Teignmouth, 1916.
Trollope, Anthony, *The Kellys and the O'Kellys*. Henry Colburn, 1848.
——— *Hunting Sketches*. 1865.
——— *British Sports and Pastimes*. 1868.
——— 'Mr Freeman on the Morality of Hunting', *Fortnightly Review*, vol. 12. 1869.
——— *The Eustace Diamonds*. 1873.
——— *Phineas Redux*. 1874.
——— *The American Senator*. 1877.
——— *The Land-Leaguers*. Chatto & Windus, 1883.
——— *An Autobiography*. W. Blackwood & Sons, Edinburgh & London, 1883.
Turner, E. S., *All Heaven in a Rage*. Michael Joseph, 1964.

Underhill, G. F., *The Master of Hounds*. Grant Richards, 1903.

Vaughan, W. E., 'An Assessment of the Economic Performance of Irish Landlords, 1851–81', in F. S. L. Lyons and R. A. J. Hawkins eds, *Ireland under the Union*. Clarendon, Oxford, 1980.
Vyner, Robert, *Notitia Venatica*. 1841.

Warwick, Frances, Countess of, *Life's Ebb and Flow*. Hutchinson & Co., 1929.
Welcome, John, *The Sporting Empress*. Michael Joseph, 1975.
——— *The Sporting World of R. S. Surtees*. Oxford University Press, Oxford, 1982.
Welcome, John, and Collins, Rupert, *Snaffles. Life and Work of Charlie Johnson Payne*. 1987.
The Words of Wellington. 1869.
White, T. H., *England Have My Bones*. Collins, 1936.
Whyte-Melville, George, *Market Harborough*. 1861.
——— *Riding Recollections*. Chapman & Hall, 1875.
Williams, Dorian, *Between the Lines*. Methuen, 1984.
Williams, L. H. W., *A History of the Glamorgan Hunt*. Cowbridge, 1973.
Williams, Raymond, *The Country and the City*. Chatto & Windus, 1973.
Williamson, Henry, *The Old Stag*. G. P. Putnam's & Sons, London & New York, 1926.
——— *The Wild Red Deer of Exmoor*. Faber & Faber, 1931.
Willock, Colin, ed., *The Farmer's Book of Field Sports*. Vista Books, 1961.
Lord Willoughby de Broke, *Hunting the Fox*. Constable & Co., 1920.
——— *The Passing Years*. Constable & Co., 1924.
Wood, Sir Evelyn, *From Midshipman to Field Marshal*. Methuen & Co., 1906.
——— 'British Cavalry 1853-1903', *Cavalry Journal*, vol. 1. 1906.
Woodforde, Rev. James, *Diary of a Country Parson* ed. J. Beresford. Humphrey Milford, 1924–31.

Index